Clear and well-organized, this textbook is an introduction to Spanish syntax, which assumes no prior knowledge of current theory. Beginning with a descriptive overview of the major characteristics of the grammar, it goes on to describe facts about Spanish, such as its word order, notions of "subject," "direct object," "auxiliary verb" and so on. The book combines traditional grammatical description with perspectives gained from recent research in the Principles and Parameters framework. It also presents useful theoretical notions such as semantic roles, Case and Predication.

Accessibly written, the book gives just enough background so as to allow the reader to understand the lines of investigation that have been pursued in accounting for such issues as clause structure and constituent order. It will be of use to students who are interested in grammar, Spanish, or in some of the basic results of modern, formal linguistic theory.

KAREN ZAGONA is Associate Professor of Linguistics and adjunct Associate Professor of Spanish at the University of Washington. She is author of *Verb Phrase Syntax: A Parametric Study of English and Spanish* (1988), editor of *Grammatical Theory and Romance Languages* (1995), and co-editor, with Ivonne Bordelois and Heles Contreras, of *Generative Studies in Spanish Syntax* (1986).

D1628117

CAMBRIDGE SYNTAX GUIDES
General editors:
J. Bresnan, D. Lightfoot, I. Robertson, N. V. Smith, N. Vincent

Responding to the increasing interest in comparative syntax, the goal of the Cambridge Syntax Guides is to make available to all linguists major findings, both descriptive and theoretical, which have emerged from the study of particular languages. The series is not committed to working in any particular framework, but rather seeks to make language-specific research available to theoreticians and practitioners of all persuasions.

Written by leading figures in the field, these guides will each include an overview of the grammatical structures of the language concerned. For the descriptivist, the books will provide an accessible introduction to the methods and results of the theoretical literature; for the theoretician, they will show how constructions that have achieved theoretical notoriety fit into the structure of the language as a whole; for everyone, they will promote cross-theoretical and cross-linguistic comparison with respect to a well-defined body of data.

The Syntax of Spanish

KAREN ZAGONA

CAMBRIDGE
UNIVERSITY PRESS

CAMBRIDGE UNIVERSITY PRESS
Cambridge, New York, Melbourne, Madrid, Cape Town, Singapore, São Paulo

Cambridge University Press
The Edinburgh Building, Cambridge CB2 2RU, UK

Published in the United States of America by Cambridge University Press, New York

www.cambridge.org
Information on this title: www.cambridge.org/9780521571777

First published 2002

A catalogue record for this publication is available from the British Library

Library of Congress Cataloguing in Publication data

Zagona, Karen T., 1951–
The syntax of Spanish / Karen Zagona.
    p.   cm. – (Cambridge syntax guides)
Includes bibliographical references and index.
ISBN 0 521 57177 4 (hardback)
ISBN 0 521 57684 9 (paperback)
1. Spanish language – Syntax.   I. Title.   II. Series.
PC4361.Z34   2001
465 – dc21   2001035092

ISBN-13 978-0-521-57177-7 hardback
ISBN-10 0-521-57177-4 hardback

ISBN-13 978-0-521-57684-0 paperback
ISBN-10 0-521-57684-9 paperback

Transferred to digital printing 2005

For Heles

Contents

Preface

This textbook is intended to present a broad view of Spanish syntax, one which takes into account the results of recent research, but which does not focus on theoretical discussion, nor assume familiarity with current theory. In order to describe insights based on recent research, it is of course necessary to introduce enough theoretical machinery so that the approaches that have been explored are understandable. Earlier discussions, especially Chapters 2 and 3, are framed within the assumptions of the Principles and Parameters framework as developed in Chomsky (1981, 1986). Chapters 4 and 5 introduce some basic elements of the Minimalist framework of Chomsky (1993, 1995). That discussion is largely informal, and rather than providing a comprehensive introduction to the theory, it is intended to give just enough background to allow the reader to understand the lines of investigation that have been pursued in accounting for such issues as clause structure and constituent order.

Chapter 1 presents a descriptive overview of the grammar, combining many generalizations of a traditional nature with some generalizations that arise within generative grammar. This description is intended to include both those generalizations that would be of particular interest to students of Spanish linguistics, and information of a broader nature for readers who are not Spanish specialists. Chapter 2 focuses on the Noun Phrase (NP). In the course of the discussion, basic theoretical mechanisms of the Principles and Parameters framework, such as Theta-role assignment, Case assignment and Predication are introduced, in order to account for the external distribution of NP. In examining the internal structure of NP, we introduce the "DP-hypothesis," an important development which has a role in accounting for determiners, and for NP-internal constituent order. Chapter 3 discusses the Verb Phrase (VP) from a Principles and Parameters perspective. We begin with the external distribution of the phrase, focusing on Predication and the relationship between the Verb Phrase and Tense. In considering phrase-internal constituent relations, we return to Theta-role assignment, and introduce the distinction between "external" arguments and "internal" arguments, which, together with

Case features, determines the mapping of the grammatical subject and complements. The properties of these constituents are summarized, including how they differ from adjuncts.

Chapters 4 and 5 are concerned with the functional categories associated with VP. In Chapter 4, we examine the distribution of VP- and IP-adverbs, auxiliary verbs, clitics and negation. In each of these areas, we introduce certain empirical generalizations, then consider how the postulation of functional categories may account for them. Chapter 5 is devoted to the issue of the position of the clausal subject in declaratives, and, more generally, to the "flexible" order of constituents that is possible in Spanish declaratives. We will see how the idea that movement is not optional has affected the analysis of constituent order in a "flexible" constituent order language such as Spanish. We will also consider the hypothesis, developed in many recent studies, that the "information content" of constituents (reflected in such notions as "Topic" and "Focus") is central to the analysis of declarative constituent order. We will summarize recent analyses, and finish with an overview of the "null subject parameter." Finally, Chapter 6 discusses a variety of constructions whose standard analysis involves the uppermost part of the clause – the Complementizer Phrase – and whose derivation involves movement to a non-argument position such as the Specifier of the Complementizer Phrase. This chapter is primarily descriptive, as it discusses the constructions in Spanish which seem to have the properties of this type of movement.

Symbols and abbreviations

*	ungrammatical sequence
?	not fully grammatical
*()	ungrammatical in the absence of the parenthesized material
(*)	ungrammatical in the presence of the parenthesized material
V°	verb
P°	preposition
A°	adjective
N°	noun
D°	determiner
C°	complementizer (subordinating conjunction)
VP	Verb Phrase
PP	Prepositional Phrase
AP	Adjective Phrase
NP	Noun Phrase
DP	Determiner Phrase (a Noun Phrase introduced by a determiner, e.g., [the red car] is a DP)
CP	Complementizer Phrase (subordinate clause)
¿	an orthographic symbol which accompanies "?" to mark interrogatives
±	plus/minus: either value for a given feature
#	intonational juncture (pause)
m.	masculine
f.	feminine
neu.	neuter
1st.	first person
2nd.	second person
3rd.	third person
sg.	singular
pl.	plural
Refl.	Reflexive
CL	clitic (unstressed pronoun form)

Det	determiner
IO	indirect object
DO	direct object
inc.	inchoative
Nom.	Nominative
Gen.	Genitive
Dat.	Dative
Acc.	Accusative
Obl.	Oblique
PA	"Personal" (accusative) *a*
inf.	infinitive
fut.	future
cond.	conditional
pr.	present tense
pa.	past tense
imp.	past imperfect indicative
I	imperative
pret.	past preterite indicative
ind.	indicative mood
subj.	subjunctive mood
pas.	passive voice
prt.	present participle
pprt.	past participle

1

Overview of the grammar

1.1   Introduction

1.1.1   The extent of Modern Spanish

Modern Spanish is spoken by just under 300 million people world-wide, and is thus one of the three or four most widely spoken languages, after Mandarin Chinese, English and possibly Hindi.[1] Spanish is the primary or official language in numerous countries, including Spain and its dependencies, Equatorial Guinea, eighteen countries of Central and South America, and the US protectorate of Puerto Rico.[2] Spanish is robust as a first or second language in many areas of the southwestern United States, as well as in other agricultural areas of the US, and urban areas such as Miami and New York. According to the 1990 census, about 17.3 million people over the age of five speak Spanish at home in the US.

Many countries in which Spanish is the official or primary language are linguistically diverse, with bilingualism a common, but not universal, phenomenon. In the north of Spain, primary languages include Basque, Catalan and Galician.[3] In Latin America, many indigenous languages are used alongside Spanish. In Bolivia, for example, at least half the population speaks either Aymara or Quechua natively, and it is estimated that 40% of these speakers

[1] Mandarin has well over 700 million speakers, English over 400 million. Estimates for Spanish speakers range from 266 million (Bright 1992) to 290 million (Green 1992), and estimates for Hindi range from 182 million (Bright 1992) to 290 million (Décsy 1986).

[2] Spanish is the official language of most countries of Latin America. In Peru, both Spanish and Quechua are official languages. In Bolivia, Spanish, Quechua and Aymara are all official languages.

Although Spanish is the official language of Equatorial Guinea, it is estimated that only 4–5% of the population speaks Spanish (Kurian 1992:600).

[3] Galician or Gallego is considered more closely related to Portuguese than to Spanish. Catalan is more closely related to Occitan than to Spanish. Basque is a linguistic isolate.

do not speak Spanish (Grimes 1988:85–87; Kurian 1992:184). In Paraguay, Guaraní is spoken by over 3 million speakers, with a majority of rural speakers being monolingual (Grimes 1988:125). Relatively large populations of speakers of indigenous languages are also found in Peru (Ayacucho Quechua and Cuzco Quechua), Guatemala (Mayan languages) and Ecuador (Quichua). Many other indigenous languages are spoken, by populations numbering from dozens of speakers to tens of thousands. Relatively small populations speak Creole languages in Honduras, Nicaragua, Costa Rica, the Dominican Republic and Panama.[4] English is growing as a second language in some parts of the Caribbean, such as the Dominican Republic and Puerto Rico, in northern Mexico, and in urban areas elsewhere in Latin America.

Dialects of Modern Spanish on the Iberian peninsula include Castilian, the northern dialect families of Navarro-Aragonese, Leonese and Asturian, and the southern, Andaluz dialects.[5,6] *Ladino* or *Judeo-español* is a dialect of Spanish spoken by Sephardic Jews expelled from Spain at the end of the fifteenth century. It is a "fossil" dialect in that it retains characteristics of the pronunciation of that time. In Latin America, the problem of defining dialect boundaries is a complex one.[7] The grammar is differentiated along phonological, morphological, syntactic and lexical lines, but the degree of variation makes classifying "discrete" dialect boundaries extremely difficult. Latin America is more conveniently described in terms of dialect "areas" which are associated loosely with general linguistic patterns. These include such areas as the River Plate region of Uruguay and Argentina, the Andean highlands, and the Caribbean. Section 1.7 below summarizes general patterns of syntactic variation in these areas.

1.1.2   The spread of the Castilian dialect

Although Spanish is spoken over an extremely broad geographical expanse, it is nevertheless relatively uniform syntactically. This is due in part

---

[4] In Belize, 25–40% of the population is Spanish-speaking, and most of the population speaks an English-based Creole (Kriol). The official language of Belize is English. Statistics on the occurrence of Creoles are based on Grimes (1988) and Kurian (1992).

[5] For detailed discussion of Iberian dialects see Alvar (1996), Otero (1971).

[6] Among Andaluz dialects, which are characterized by weakening of word-final -*s*, there are areas in which final -*s* appears to be disappearing. This (eventually) may have syntactic consequences with respect to the "richness" of features for number and person, since -*s* distinguishes plurality in nominals and distinguishes 2nd person in verbal paradigms.

[7] For detailed discussion of the problem of classification of Latin American dialects see Lipski (1994).

to the early political unification of Spain, and to the spread of the Castilian dialect throughout the unified area. This unification was a consequence of the drive to re-conquer the peninsula after its occupation by the Moors in the early eighth century. The area from which the reconquest was launched was Castilla la Vieja (Old Castille). In the course of the centuries-long battle against the Moors, the Castilian dialect spread throughout much of modern Spain. Castilian thereby coexisted with other Spanish dialects that had evolved in various areas, and largely replaced them over the course of time.

Most of Iberia had been Romanized during the period of the expansion of spoken Latin.[8] With the decline of Rome, the peninsula was invaded by successive waves of Germanic tribes, and eventually came under the control of Visigothic kingdoms during the fifth to eighth centuries. This period marks a transition during which spoken Latin was initially similar enough to the written form of Classical Latin to remain viable for administrative purposes.[9] Meanwhile the increasing political weakness of the Visigothic kingdoms and the beginnings of feudalism accelerated the growth of local Romance varieties. This was especially characteristic of northern and northwestern Iberia, where Romanization was never extensive, urbanization was minimal, and Romance coexisted with Basque, and perhaps other indigenous languages.

With the Moorish conquest, Iberia was for a time severed from the rest of Europe, where emerging monasteries provided a linguistic and cultural counterweight to feudal isolation. Throughout much of Iberia, Mozárabe[10] became the standard form of Romance. The mountainous north, however, which the Moors never successfully settled, retained its dialect diversity (Alatorre 1989:108). As Moorish control of the peninsula receded, the north and northwest became Christian strongholds with renewed ties to the rest of Europe. Santiago de Compostela was an important destination for Christians from throughout Europe, and monasteries and cathedrals emerged. At the

---

[8] Although spoken Latin was in use and undergoing evolution from much earlier times, the period of its great geographic expansion might be taken to begin around 100 BC, when Latin replaced Oscan as the official language of central Italy, to AD 200, when the empire reached its broadest expanse. Although Romanization of the Hispanic peninsula began earlier with the Second Punic War, the legionnaires (and colonizers) of this period were perhaps not predominantly Latin speakers. Lapesa (1981:94–101) notes that significant numbers may have been speakers of the Oscan–Umbrian subfamily of Italic, which was spoken in southern regions of Italy.

[9] The question of whether speakers considered their spoken and written languages to be one and the same has been debated in recent studies. For discussion and references see Wright (1991).

[10] The term "Mozárabe" refers either to Christians who lived in Moorish-controlled Spain, or to the variety of Spanish spoken by Christians (and non-Christians). See Galmés de Fuentes (1996).

southern periphery of Asturias (the then kingdom of Oviedo), a relatively unpopulated area known previously as Bardulia (Alvar 1994:81) had been newly settled and fortified with *castiellas* against Moslem raids. By the ninth century the area was known as "the place of the castles," or Castille. According to Lloyd (1987:177), Castille was populated by settlers from different areas, who abandoned peculiar features of pronunciation associated with their origins. Castille was also an area where Basque was spoken, and some features of Spanish, such as initial *f>h* have been attributed to Basque influence.

Over the subsequent centuries, Castille became a dominant power in the north, and was the center from which the reconquest of the peninsula was launched. Although Castilian was not a prestige dialect, it gradually spread southward and became dominant as Spain was politically unified and Christianized.[11] The religious zealotry which followed the reconquest included linguistic "purification," as Arabic books were burned in Granada, and the use of Arabic (and even Arabic borrowings) was increasingly condemned throughout the sixteenth century. Between 1609 and 1614, as many as 300,000 *moriscos* (non-assimilated or partially assimilated Moors and their descendants) were expelled from Spain.

The form of the language that took root in Latin America was affected by a number of unifying influences. One of these was the social climate of conformity – including linguistic conformity – which held sway in Spain at the time of colonization. This tendency was made concrete policy with respect to colonization, as the monarchs prohibited emigration of Jews and Moors to the new world (Sánchez-Albornoz 1984:15). Another factor that minimized diversity during the era of colonization was the relatively short time frame during which much of the settlement occurred. Immigration was most extensive before 1650, and dropped off sharply by the 1700s.[12] Colonization also coincided with the introduction of the printing press, the first of which was brought to Mexico City by the 1530s (Alatorre 1989:138). Subsequent influences, such as ongoing commerce with Spain, the independence movements, bilingualism and the growth of mass media, have resulted in a rich range of

[11] Lloyd (1987:179–180) suggests that "reverse prestige" may have enhanced the spread of Castilian, given the role of Castille in the liberation of the peninsula from the Moors. An additional factor in the spread of Castilian was migration. An economic breakdown in the north triggered significant migration from northern Castille to the south during the sixteenth century, which reinforced the spread of Castilian.

[12] Sánchez-Albornoz (1984:15–16) estimates that from 200,000 to 243,000 people immigrated during the sixteenth century, and an almost equal number during the first half of the seventeenth century. The extent of immigration is small overall, compared with immigration to the United States from other countries.

phonological and morphological variations in the grammar, but less variation in the syntax.

1.1.3 The evolution of Spanish syntax

The evolution of spoken Latin into proto-Romance was characterized from early on by simplification of inflectional paradigms for nouns, adjectives and verbs, and emergence or broader use of periphrastic constructions which fulfilled some of the same grammatical functions. The nominal case paradigms were reduced to a Nominative/Accusative distinction, and prepositions emerged as markers of other cases. Definite and indefinite articles evolved (from Latin demonstrative *ille* "that" and the cardinal *unum* "one," respectively). Periphrastic comparative forms of adjectives replaced synthetic forms. In the verbal paradigms, simplification of Classical inflections included the loss of the future tense, of synthetic passives, and of diverse non-finite forms. Many of these changes were incipient or well underway in spoken Latin, and some were accelerated as a result of phonological changes such as loss of many word-final consonants and loss of distinctive vowel quantity. The most stable inflectional features were person, number and masculine/feminine gender markers, and the [±PAST] inflection for verbs.

The "break-up" of proto-Romance into the early differentiated Romance languages is generally dated from the point at which written Latin was no longer comprehensible to the Romance speaker, roughly between the fifth and ninth centuries.[13] Characteristics of early Spanish are deduced from documents dating from the eleventh century. Grammatical changes during this period continued those trends described above: inflectional simplification and grammaticalization of functional and quasi-functional morphemes; in many instances these changes were common across languages. For example, nouns lost their Nominative/Accusative distinction. In western varieties of Romance, accusative plural -*s* was reanalyzed as a plural marker. Object pronouns were de-stressed and became clitics. Verbal auxiliaries evolved in passives, compound perfect, future and conditional tenses. The clitic *se* (Latin 3rd.sg./pl. Refl.) was grammaticalized, first as a detransitive (anti-causative) morpheme, then as a marker of middles, and (in Spanish) as a marker of passive voice (Hanssen 1945:230–231).

---

[13] Because classical Latin was used as a written form under the Visigothic administrations, it is more difficult to date the transition from proto-Romance to Romance in the Iberian peninsula than elsewhere. In France, by contrast, "translations" began to occur in 813 (cf. note 8; see also Palmer 1954:178–179). Only in the eleventh century did Carolingian writing replace the Visigothic system (Lapesa 1981:169).

One syntactic innovation from this period is the emergence in Spanish of the "personal a," a marker of specific, human direct objects. Personal a occurred most consistently at first with proper names and pronouns, less consistently with common nouns (Lapesa 1981:213). Torrego (1998:42; citing Lapesa 1968) mentions an additional factor which governed the distribution of personal a around the thirteenth and fourteenth centuries. A appeared with the complements of verbs that denote an action that affects an individual physically or psychologically. Only later did it occur with non-affected animate direct objects.

The constituent order of Old Spanish differs from that of Modern Spanish in several respects. In Old Spanish, only phrases headed by closed class items (such as articles, complementizers and prepositions) were clearly head-initial. Lexical, or "open class," heads of phrases (nouns, adjectives and verbs) allowed both complement–head and head–complement order. The basic order of the verb and its objects is analyzed as having switched from OV to VO order (Otero 1975; Saltarelli 1994). It is interesting to note that auxiliary–main verb complexes gradually evolved from verb–auxiliary to auxiliary–verb (Rivero 1993; Lapesa 1981:217; Hanssen 1945:249, 251). The constituents of clauses also patterned differently in Old Spanish. Fontana (1993) argues that Old Spanish is a V2 (verb second) language, not of the German type (which exhibits second-position verbs in main clauses only), but of the Icelandic type: with verbs occupying second position in subordinate clauses also. Fontana terms this "symmetric V2."

Another difference between Old Spanish and Modern Spanish concerns the behavior and the placement of pronominal clitics. Modern Spanish clitics attach only to verbs, and either precede or follow the verb according to whether the verb is finite or non-finite. Old Spanish pronominal clitics occupied second position in the clause, and were phonologically dependent on the preceding constituent – whether that constituent was a verb or not. This is shown by the fact that they could not occur clause-initially following a pause.[14] In this respect, the pronominal clitics behaved like other atonic elements, including non "not," conjunctions and some auxiliaries. Auxiliaries mostly lost this restriction during the period of Old Spanish (cf. Hanssen 1945:251–252).

Old Spanish displayed auxiliary switch, similar to that of Modern French and Italian (Vincent 1982). Auxiliary ser "to be" alternated with $aver$ "to have" in the compound perfect tenses. In these tenses, ser was generally used with unaccusatives and "reflexive" (anticausative) intransitives, and $aver$ with

---

[14] For detailed discussion of the syntax of Old Spanish clitics see Rivero (1986, 1991), Wanner (1987), Fontana (1993).

transitives (Lapesa 1981:212; Hanssen 1945:230–233). The compound perfect tense also displayed past participle agreement with the object. However, both auxiliary switch and past participle agreement were inconsistent.[15]

1.2   General characteristics of the syntax

Many characteristics of Spanish syntax are typical of the Indo-European family, including the relative richness of verbal morphology compared with nominal morphology, and the overt movement of interrogative phrases and of noun phrases (e.g., in passives). Other characteristics are prevalent within the Romance family. These include head-initial constituent order, pronominal clitics, negative concord, rich agreement morphology and null subject phenomena. Two characteristics of Spanish which are relatively isolated within Romance include the so-called "personal a" which precedes animate direct objects under certain conditions,[16] and clitic "doubling" of indirect objects (and dialectally, direct objects). This section summarizes features of Spanish syntax which place the language typologically, and which provide an introduction for subsequent discussion.

1.2.1   Constituent order

Modern Spanish is a head-initial language. As shown in (1), the construction of a phrasal head, or X° with a complement, gives the order: head-complement. Thus, nouns, adjectives, verbs and prepositions precede their complements. Examples are in (2):

(1)

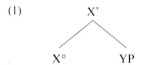

(2)   a. construyeron un puente $[V^{\circ} - NP]$
           built   a   bridge
           "(they) built a bridge"

---

[15] Lapesa (1981:212) notes the inconsistent usage of *ser* and of past participle agreement, and notes that "contradictory uses" due to foreign influences were not uncommon.

[16] Lapesa (1981:94–101) observes that the use of "personal a" is one of several grammatical features which Iberian dialects share with Sicilian and other southern Italian varieties.

b. con un martillo $[P^\circ - NP]$
   with a   hammer
c. estudiante de física $[N^\circ - PP]$
   student   of physics
d. leal   a los ideales $[A^\circ - PP]$
   loyal to the ideals

Functional categories also precede the lexical categories which they govern, for example determiners precede noun phrases, and complementizers precede clauses. Auxiliary verbs, which might be considered functional or quasi-functional items, also precede the main verb of the clause:

(3)   a. Habíamos hablado del   problema.
            had   spoken of+the problem
            "(We) had spoken about the problem."
         b. *Hablado habíamos del problema.

The order of adjuncts, or optional modifying phrases, relative to the head varies according to several factors. All of the positions in (4) are possible with normal (unbroken) intonation:

(4)   [(adjunct) head (adjunct) complement (adjunct)]

Structurally complex adjuncts typically follow the head and its complements. Several factors condition the availability of pre-head adjuncts, including structural and lexical properties of the adjunct as well as the category of the head. Adjunct order is discussed in relation to the Noun Phrase (Chapter 2), the Verb Phrase (Chapter 4) and the clause (Chapter 5). The order of subjects is addressed below (1.3.) and in Chapter 5.

1.2.2   Case

Spanish has a Nominative/Accusative case system. Case is not manifested morphologically on lexical nouns or determiners; only personal pronouns and some relative pronouns retain vestiges of Latin case distinctions. The strong (i.e., tonic, or stressed) personal pronouns display morphologically distinct forms to the extent shown in (5), illustrated with the 1st person singular form:

(5)   a. Nominative: yo   "I"
         b. Objective: mí   "me"
         c. Genitive: mí(o/ a (s))   "my"[17]
                           (m./f.(pl.))

[17] The strong forms of possessive pronouns agree in number and gender with the modified noun.

Objective Case in (5) is the form common to objects of prepositions. The weak pronouns (Section 1.2.4) may have different form and distribution depending on whether the object is direct or indirect. These differences lead to subclasses of Objective: (a) Accusative (direct object of V^o), (b) Dative (indirect object of V^o) and (c) Oblique (object of P^o). The following discussion will briefly summarize the contexts for Nominative, Genitive and the three subcases of Objective case.

Nominative is the case of subjects of finite clauses, both indicative and subjunctive; of predicative NPs linked to the clausal subject; and of subjects of participial and infinitival adjunct clauses. The example in (6) illustrates that pronominal subjects of both indicative and subjunctive clauses appear in Nominative form:

(6)   Insisto   **yo** en que lo hagas   **tú**.
        Insist-pr.ind.1st.sg. I on that it do-pr.subj.2nd.sg. you
        "I insist that you do it."

Predicative NPs with Nominative form are shown in (7):

(7)   a. El campeón eres **tú**.
           "The champion is you(Nom.)."
        b. Lo que encontraron era **yo**.
           "What (they) found was I(Nom.)."

In (7), the verb agrees in person and number with the predicative pronoun (cf. English "It *is/*am* I").

Adjunct clauses with Nominative subjects are shown in (8):

(8)   a. [Llegada **ella**]   empezó la   fiesta.
           arrived-f. she(Nom.) began   the party
           "(With) her arrived, the party began."
        b. [Habiendo llegado   **ella**],   empezó   la   fiesta.
           have-prt. arrive-pprt. she(Nom.) begin-pret. the party
           "With her having arrived, the party began."
        c. [Al   cantarlo   **tú**],   empezó la   fiesta
           upon+the sing-inf+it you(Nom.) began   the party
           "Upon your singing it, the party began."
        d. [De ganar   **ellos**]   los   felicitaremos.
           of   win-inf. they (Nom.) CL(DO) congratulate-fut.1st.pl.
           "If they win, we will congratulate them."

In the above constructions, the participle or infinitive must precede the subject, but some dialect variation occurs (see 1.7). The participial clause in (8a) shows number and gender agreement with the subject; the participial clause (8b) and infinitives (8c), (8d) are non-agreeing forms.[18]

---

[18] Rigau (1992) shows that constructions like (8c), which appear to be nominalized, are in fact clausal.

Genitive is the case assumed by the subject of a noun phrase, and is marked either by the preposition *de* with a non-pronominal, as in (9), or by the Genitive form of a pronominal, as in (10). Genitive pronominals have both weak (pre-nominal) and strong (post-nominal) forms, illustrated in (10a) and (10b) respectively:

(9)   el   retrato de Josefina
         the portrait of J.
         "Josefina's portrait"

(10)   a. mis   libros
            my-pl. book-m.pl.
            "my books"
         b. los   libros   míos
            the-m.pl. book-m.pl. my-m.pl.
            "my books"

In (9), the *de*-phrase is ambiguous between possessor, agent, and subject of the portrait. This illustrates that Genitives are not necessarily possessors, and also that *de* is not exclusively Genitive. The examples in (10) illustrate that Genitive pronominals agree in number (and gender) with the possessed noun. In contrast with Italian, determiners do not co-occur with a pre-nominal possessive (*los míos libros* "the my books") in most dialects of Spanish. In contrast with English, "double genitives" of the form "a book of his" (*un libro de suyo*) do not occur. Post-nominal genitives show either *de*, as in (9), or genitive morphology, as in (10b).

Relative pronouns display a distinguishable Genitive form, although interrogatives do not. This is illustrated by the contrast between the relative pronoun in (11a) and the interrogatives in (11b, c):[19]

---

[19] Interrogative forms do not show case distinctions in general. *Qué* "what," and *quién* "who," for example, serve as both Nominative and Accusative arguments:

(i)   a. ¿Qué   pesa   7 kilos?
            What(Nom.) weigh-pr.3rd.sg. 7 kilos
            "What weighs 7 kilos?"
         b. ¿Qué   dijo Susana?
            what(Acc.) said Susana?
            "What did Susana say?"
(ii)   a. ¿Quién trabaja aquí?
            "Who works here?"
         b. ¿(A) quién   buscan?
            PA who(Acc.) look-for
            "Who are they looking for?"

The case of non-Nominative interrogatives is marked by prepositions, including personal *a*, as in (iib).

(11)   a. la persona **cuyo** coche se   venderá
         the person whose car CL(pas.) sell-fut.
         "the person whose car will be sold"
    b. *¿**Cuyo** coche se   venderá?
         Whose car CL(pas.) sell-fut.
         "Whose car will be sold?"
    c. ¿Se venderá el coche **de quién**?
         pas. sell-fut. the car   of who
         (Lit.) Will be sold [the car of who]?
         "Whose car will be sold?"

As shown in (11b), the genitive pronoun *cuyo* is not possible as an interrogative form. In (11c), the interrogative phrase *de quién*, which remains "in-situ" – not moved to the beginning of the clause – is marked as Genitive by *de* rather than by the form of the pronoun.

Genitives do not occur as the subject of nominalized clauses corresponding to English gerunds. Nominative subjects are possible instead:

(12)   a. [El hacer eso **tú**]   sería   buena idea.
         the do-inf. that you(Nom.) be-cond.3rd.sg. good idea
         "For you to do that would be a good idea."
    b. *[**Su**   hacer eso] sería   buena idea.
         your(Gen.) do-inf. that be-cond.3rd.sg. good idea
         "Your doing that would be a good idea."

The three types of Objective case are distinguished on the basis of whether or not they co-occur with clitic pronouns, and, if so, the form which the clitic takes. Oblique case occurs as the complement of most prepositions,[20] both in prepositional phrases which are adjuncts and those which are prepositional

---

[20] The prepositions *hasta* "even," *como* "like/as" and *entre* "between" govern Nominative:

(i)   a. Todos bailaron   en la fiesta, hasta yo/*mí.
         all   dance-pa.3rd.pl. at the party, even I/*me
         "Everyone danced at the party, even I (did)."
    b. Nadie baila   como yo/*mí.
         nobody dance-pr.3rd.sg. like I/*me
         "Nobody dances like I (do)."
    c. Entre tú y   yo/* mí, ...
         between you and I/*me

Depending on its environment, the preposition *a* can mark Accusative, Dative or Oblique (*al mediodia* "at noon"). Likewise, *de* can mark Genitive or Oblique: *un amigo de Madrid* "a friend from Madrid."

complements of verbs.[21] Oblique complements of a verb do not admit weak (clitic) forms of pronouns, as shown in (13):[22]

(13)   a. Hablaron   [de Juan/él].
           spoke-3rd.pl. of Juan/him
           "They talked about Juan/him."
        b. *Le   hablaron.
           CL(3rd.sg.) spoke-3rd.pl.
           Lit.: (They) him-spoke
           "They talked about him."

Non-oblique objects of verbs do accept (or require) clitic forms. Accusatives require a clitic when the object is anaphoric or pronominal. For example, compare the reflexive objects in (14a), (14b):

(14)   a. *(Me)   vi   a   mí misma.
           CL(1st.sg.Acc.) saw-1st.sg. PA my self
           "I saw *(CL) myself."
        b. (*Me)   hablé de   mí misma.
           CL(1st.sg.Acc.) spoke about my self
           "I talked *(CL) about myself."

As shown in (14a), a reflexive direct object requires a clitic double. Oblique reflexives, as in (14b), disallow a clitic double.

An additional characteristic of Accusative case is that Accusative phrases

---

[21] As noted above, Oblique, Accusative and Dative strong pronouns all have the same morphological form. One exception is the forms occurring with the preposition *con* "with": *conmigo*, "with me"; *contigo*, "with you"; *consigo* "with him/her/you (formal)." These forms consist of *con*+pronoun+*go*; *-go* is the residue of Latin *cum* "with."

[22] A possible instance of oblique clitic-doubling with certain motion verbs is shown in (ic):

(i)   a. María fue   al   parque.
          M.   went to+the park.
          "Maria went to the park."
       b. María se   fue.
          M.   CL(3rd.sg.) went
          "Maria went away."
       c. María se   fue al   parque.
          M.   CL(3rd.sg.) went to+the park
          "Maria went off to the park."

Both PPs and clitics can express the Goal of the verb. In (ic), both are present. Other verbs which behave similarly are *escaparse* "to escape" and *fugarse* "to flee" (which allow both Goal and Source PPs). Unlike standard cases of clitic doubling, the clitic in (ic) agrees in person and number with the subject of the clause, not with the NP in the prepositional phrase.

are, under certain conditions, "marked" by a particular morpheme, often referred to as "Personal a" (PA). "Personal a" is, superficially, a preposition, identical to the preposition a which marks Dative case.[23] Personal a occurs primarily when the direct object is [+HUMAN] and [+SPECIFIC], as illustrated in (15) and (16). Compare (15a), with a [+HUMAN] object, with (15b), with an inanimate object. The contrast between specific and non-specific objects is shown in (16):

(15) a. En el   mercado vi   *(a) los vecinos.
         at the market   saw-1st.sg. PA the neighbors
         "At the market (I) saw the neighbors."
      b. En el   escritorio vi   (*a) los papeles
         on the desk   saw-1st.sg. PA   the papers
         "On the desk (I) saw the papers."

(16) a. (Yo) busco   a   una secretaria.
         (I)   look for PA a   secretary
         "I am looking for a (specific) secretary."
      b. (Yo) busco   una secretaria.
         (I)   look for a   secretary
         "I am looking for a (non-specific) secretary."

The contrast between (16a) and (16b) concerns whether a specific individual is sought (16a), or whether anyone who happens to be a secretary is sought (16b). Personal a may be used also with non-human animate direct objects, if the object is interpreted as specific and individual (as with pets, for example), or is in some manner personified.[24] Personal a also occurs with inanimate direct objects (from Hanssen 1945:296):

(17) a. El adjetivo modifica al (=a+el) sustantivo.
         the adjective modifies PA the   noun
         "The adjective modifies the noun."
      b. ¿Y   a   eso llamaban   libertad?
         and PA that call-pa.3rd.pl. liberty
         "And they called that liberty?"

In (17a), both subject and object are inanimate; in (17b) the verb *llamar* "call" selects a nominal small clause complement – in effect a double Accusative,

---

[23] Torrego (1998) argues that the choice of morpheme is not arbitrary. She observes that languages as diverse as Spanish and Hindi mark Accusatives using a morpheme that otherwise marks Dative Case.

[24] Hanssen (1945:296) gives the examples *Llamó a la muerte* and *Llamó la muerte* "S/He called out to death," which differ only in the presence or absence of personal *a*. The difference in interpretation might be described in terms of whether one calls out to an abstraction (perhaps an event), or personifies the abstraction.

where both subject and predicate nominal of the small clause are inanimate.[25] Zubizarreta (1994) notes that the distribution of personal *a* in cases such as these suggests that *a* is not so much a marker of [+HUMAN] as it is a direct object marker in constructions in which two arguments are animate or two arguments are inanimate. That is, when animacy differences do not independently do so, *a* identifies a unique Accusative argument. It is otherwise difficult to account for examples such as (17).

Turning now to Datives, these indirect objects of verbs occur in the context of the preposition *a*, and may co-occur with a clitic double, even if the argument is non-pronominal, non-anaphoric.

(18)   Juan le   mandó un paquete a   José.
        Juan CL(Dat.) sent   a package to(Dat.) José
        "Juan sent a package to José."

The preposition *a* in (18) marks Dative case; its presence is not contingent on any particular features of the argument, such as animacy (cf.: *Le mandé el formulario al departamento* "I sent the form to the department"). The dative clitic (*le*) in (18) is often characterized as required. However, Demonte (1995) observes that there are conditions which favor omission of the clitic. In particular, the clitic is, for many speakers, omissible if the transfer expressed by the verb is not asserted to have been completed.[26]

1.2.3   Inflectional morphology

The major types of affixal inflections in Spanish, and the types of elements which can exhibit them are summarized in (19):

(19)   a. NUMBER, GENDER:
        amigo   amiga   amigos   amigas
        friend(m.sg.) friend(f.sg.) friend(m.pl.) friend(f.pl)
        (nouns, demonstratives, definite and indefinite determiners,
        quantifiers, personal pronouns [strong and clitic], interrogative and
        relative pronouns, reflexive/reciprocals, adjectives, passive participles,
        absolute past participles)

[25] Personal *a* is optional for some speakers in cases like (17a). This may be due to aspectual characteristics of the verb *modificar* "modify." Torrego (1998:17 ff.) notes that predicates may differ in whether or not they require personal *a* on the basis of their aspectual properties.

[26] The contrast in interpretation associated with the presence versus absence of the Dative clitic is similar to the contrast between the English Dative shifted construction, *I sent him the package*, versus the non-shifted construction, *I sent the package to him*. The former sentence disfavors a reading in which the transfer is not completed, while the latter is compatible with this reading.

b. PERSON:
   yo   tú   él/ella
   I(1st.sg.)   you(2nd.sg.)   he/she(3rd.sg.)
   (personal pronouns [strong and weak], reflexive/reciprocals, finite verbs)
c. CONJUGATION CLASS:
   I   II   III
   cantar   temer   escribir
   sing-inf.   fear-inf.   write-inf.
   (finite and non-finite verbs)
d. PAST, PRESENT, FUTURE:
   canto   canté   cantaré
   sing(pr.1st.sg.) sing(pa.1st.sg.)   sing(fut.1st.sg.)
   (finite verbs)
e. PRETERITE/IMPERFECT TENSE:
   canté   cantaba
   sing(pret.1st.sg.) sing(imp.1st.sg.)
   (finite verbs)
f. PERFECTIVE AND PROGRESSIVE ASPECT:
   ha cantado   está cantando
   has(pr.) sing(pprt.)   is(pr.) sing(prt.)
   "has sung"   "is singing"
   (non-finite verbs)
g. MOOD:
   cantas   cantes
   sing(pr.ind.2nd.sg.)   sing(pr.subj.2nd.sg)
   (finite verbs)
h. VOICE:
   fue cantado
   be(pret.3rd.sg.) sing(pas.)
   "was sung"
   (participles)

As (19) suggests, many elements display number and gender agreement. Verbs display the broadest array of inflections. Other quasi-inflectional affixes include a diminutive suffix and an intensifier for adjectives (residue of Latin superlative suffixes). Neither adverbs, prepositions nor conjunctions display affixal inflection or contextually induced allomorphs.

1.2.4 Clitics

The term "clitic" refers to elements which are syntactically independent words or phrasal constituents, but which are phonologically dependent. Phonological dependence typically implies that the clitic undergoes phonological word-formation so that it joins a constituent which bears stress. For example, English contracted auxiliaries cliticize to a preceding constituent (e.g., *She'll leave*). Phonological and syntactic conditions of cliticization vary from language to language, as do the inventories and properties of particular clitics.[27] Spanish, and Romance in general, developed a robust system of clitics, derived from Latin demonstrative *ille* and from strong pronouns and reflexives. The inventory of Spanish clitics is shown in (20)–(22), organized according to their form when they correspond to subject, object and indirect object arguments:

(20)   Nominative:
        se   3rd. sg.   "one"

(21)   Accusative:
        me   1st.sg.   nos   1st.pl.
        te   2nd.sg   (os)   2nd.pl.[28]
        lo   3rd.sg m.   los   3rd.pl.m.
        la   3rd.sg.f.   las   3rd.pl.f.
        se   3rd. sg./pl. refl.

(22)   Dative:
        me   1st.sg.   nos   1st.pl.
        te   2nd.sg.   (os)   2nd.pl.
        le   3rd.sg.   les   3rd.pl.
        se   3rd.sg./pl.[29]

Spanish clitics are sometimes referred to as pronominal clitics. However, they are neither uniformly pronominal or anaphoric, nor necessarily related to verbal arguments. These same clitics may represent non-arguments (e.g., benefactives), and have other grammatical functions, including formation of middles and passives, and marking lexical aspect.

A simplified summary of the clitic "template" is given in (23), based on Perlmutter (1971):

(23)   [se] – [2nd.] – [1st.] – [3rd.(dat.)] – [3rd.(Acc.)]
        a. For sequences of non-reflexive 3rd person clitics, Dative precedes
           Accusative;
        b. Non-3rd person clitics precede 3rd person;
           second person precedes first person; i.e.: II – I – III;
        c. Se precedes other clitics;
        d. Sequences of phonetically identical clitics are excluded.

The first position clitic *se* may be the subject clitic, a reflexive 3rd person direct or indirect object, or an "inherent" clitic (not corresponding to an argument).[30]

---

[27] See Zwicky (1977) for an overview of clitic types. For detailed analysis of English auxiliary clitics see Kaisse (1983).

[28] Second person plural inflections and clitics are restricted to peninsular dialects.

[29] Dative *se* is both a reflexive/reciprocal clitic and an allomorph of (pronominal) *le*. *Se* replaces *le* if a third person Accusative clitic follows (e.g., *le+lo* → *selo*).

[30] A thorough description of clitic sequences and functions is found in Strozer (1976). See also Bonet (1991, 1995).

The only true subject clitic in Spanish is "impersonal" *se* "one."[31] Impersonal *se* clauses show 3rd person singular verb forms. Subject *se* does not "double" an overt subject:

(24)　　a. *Uno/él, se　　　　trabaja　　　demasiado allí.
　　　　　　one/he,　CL(Nom.)　work-3rd.sg.　too much　there
　　　　　　"One, one works a lot there."
　　　　b. *El hombre, se　　　　piensa　　　demasiado.
　　　　　　the man,　　CL(Nom.)　think-3rd.sg.　too much
　　　　　　"Man, one thinks too much."

Turning to Accusative and Dative clitics, 1st and 2nd person forms are identical in the two cases.[32] In some dialects, forms from one case encroach partially or wholly on the functions of the other.[33] Elsewhere, the syntactic conditions governing the appearance of direct and indirect object clitics remain distinct. As was shown in the previous section, a clitic is required for a pronominal or anaphoric direct object; clitics co-occur with indirect objects even when the object is non-pronominal, non-anaphoric.

Spanish does not have clitics corresponding to Oblique (prepositional) arguments, including locatives. Expressions corresponding to French locative/directional *y* are *allí, ahí, allá* "there," which are strong, non-clitic forms.

Modern Spanish clitics are always immediately adjacent to a verb, and never occur in construction with other grammatical categories. Clitics follow positive imperatives, infinitives and gerunds, as shown in (25)–(26). Notice that the orthographic conventions show enclitics as part of the verb, while proclitics (those preceding the verb) are orthographically separated:

(25)　　a. Haz**lo**　　　　　　ahora.
　　　　　　Do-I.+CL(Acc.)　now
　　　　　　"Do it now!"
　　　　b. Intentó　　　　mandár**melo**.
　　　　　　try-pa.3rd.sg.　send-inf.+CL(Dat.)+CL(Acc.)
　　　　　　"(S/he) tried to send it to me."
　　　　c. Estaba　　　　cantándo**lo**.
　　　　　　be(imp.3rd.sg.)　sing-prt.+CL(Acc.)
　　　　　　"(S/he) was singing it."

[31] The overt forms of personal pronouns are strong (stressed) forms (see 1.7 on Dominican Spanish).

[32] The 1st and 2nd person clitics derive from Latin pronouns, with normal phonological changes producing merger of Accusative and Dative forms. Non-reflexive 3rd person forms derive from demonstrative *ille*, which had the *-ol-a* inflectional ending in the Accusative and *-e* in the Dative.

[33] These are known as "Leísmo" (dative *le/les* are used also for masculine human Accusatives), "Laísmo," "Loísmo" (replacement of 3rd person Datives by Accusative forms).

(26)   a. *Lo haz ahora. (=25a)
         b. *Intentó me lo mandar. (=25b)
         c. *Estaba lo cantando. (=25c)

Clitics precede negated imperatives (27) and other finite verbs (28):

(27)   No lo   escriba   ahora.
         not CL(Acc.) write-I. now
         "Don't write it now!"

(28)   a. María lo   escribió   ayer.
            M.   CL(Acc.) write-pa.3rd.sg. yesterday
            "Maria wrote it yesterday."
         b. *María escribiólo ayer.

In progressives, clitics may either precede the auxiliary or follow the participle, as shown in (29); clitics cannot follow past or passive participles, as shown in (30b), (31b):

(29)   a. Juan lo   estaba preparando.
            J.   CL(Acc.) was   prepare-prt.
            "Juan was preparing it."
         b. Juan estaba preparándolo. (=29a)

(30)   a. María ya   lo   había   preparado.
            M.   already CL(Acc.) have-pa.3rd.sg. prepare-pprt.
            "Maria had already prepared it."
         b. *María ya había preparádolo. (=30a)

(31)   a. La carta ya   te   fue mandada.
            the letter already CL(Dat.) was send-pprt.
            "The letter was already sent to you."
         b. *La carta ya fue mandádate. (=31a)

Spanish shares with Italian the phenomenon of "Restructuring," or "clitic climbing," in which clitics related to a subordinate infinitive appear in construction with a "semi-auxiliary" matrix verb. Both (32a) and (32b) are grammatical:

(32)   a. Susana quiere   verte.
            S.   want-pr.3rd.sg. see-inf.+CL(Acc.)
            "Susana wants to see you."
         b. Susana te quiere ver. (=32a)

In addition, Spanish restructuring also includes verb-participle sequences:

(33)   a. María seguía   cantándolo.
            M.   continue-pa.3rd.sg. sing-prt.+CL(Acc.)
            "Maria kept on singing it."
         b. María lo seguía cantando. (=33a)

Clitics are an ongoing topic of investigation in Spanish syntax. Among the issues debated are such fundamental matters as the position in which clitics are generated, the manner in which they are grammatically linked to an argument position, and their syntactic features. General issues and proposals are introduced in Chapter 4. The phenomenon of restructuring has also been controversial with respect to the structure of the infinitive or participle. These issues will be considered in Chapter 6.

1.2.5   WH- and NP-movement

Interrogative phrases appear in clause-initial position in both direct and indirect questions. Compare the position of the direct object in the declarative in (34a), and the corresponding interrogative in (34b), (34c):

(34)   a. Juan leyó **ese libro**.
          J.   read that book
       b. ¿**Qué libro** leyó Juan?
          which book read J.
          "Which book did Juan read?"
       c. María no sabe [**qué libro** leyó Juan].
          M.   not knows which book read J.
          "Maria doesn't know which book Juan read."

Multiple interrogatives are possible, and require one interrogative constituent to appear in clause-initial position, while the rest remain *in situ*:[34]

(35)   a. ¿**A   quién** le   mandó **qué   libro**?
          to(dat.) whom CL(Dat.) sent   which book
          "To whom did (s/he) send which book?"
       b. ¿**Qué libro** le   mandó **a   quién**?
          what book CL(Dat.) sent   to(dat.) whom
          "What book did (s/he) send to whom?"

Processes such as passivization and subject-to-subject raising also show derived positions for NPs. However, since subjects have a degree of freedom of order relative to other elements, the effects of these processes are not always transparent. For example, consider the passives in (36):

[34] More than one interrogative constituent may move if a second clause-initial "landing-site" is available:

(i)   ¿Qué libro no sabe Juan [quién compró]?
       what book not know J.   who   bought
       "What book doesn't Juan know who bought?"

The grammaticality of this type of extraction out of an indirect question depends on the grammatical function of the constituents extracted. See Torrego (1984) for detailed discussion.

(36)   a. **El artículo** fue publicado.
        the article   was published
        b. Fue publicado **el artículo**
        was published **the article**

The order in (36a) shows that an object may move to pre-verbal subject position. In (36b), it appears that no movement has taken place. However, the phrase *el artículo* may occupy a structurally higher position than direct object – a position available for subjects even when a direct object is present, as in (37):

(37)   Analiza las preposiciones **el artículo**.
        analyzes the prepositions   the article
        "The article analyzes prepositions."

Example (37) shows that post-verbal subjects can occupy a position other than direct object position, since the latter is occupied by the phrase *las preposiciones* "the prepositions." Whatever position is available for the subject *el artículo* "the article" in (37) should therefore be available in principle also in (36b). In Chapter 3 (Section 3.3) and in Chapter 5 this issue is examined further.

1.2.6   Determiners

Determiners and demonstratives agree in number and gender (masculine or feminine) with nouns. Forms of the indefinite and definite determiners are shown in (38) and (39):[35]

(38)   un(o) m.sg.[36]   unos m.pl.
        una f.sg.   unas f.pl.

(39)   el m.sg.   los, m.pl.
        la f.sg.[37]   las, f.pl.

[35] Demonstratives, which also agree in number and gender with a noun, distinguish three degrees of proximity to the speaker: *este libro* "this book"; *ese libro* "that book"; *aquel libro* "that (distant) book."

[36] The final vowel in *uno* is elided before an overt noun. Compare (i) and (ii):

(i)   Dame   **un**   lápiz.
        give-I.2nd.sg.+CL(Dat.) a(m.sg.) pencil(m.sg.)
        "Give me a pencil."
(ii)   Dame   **uno**.
        give-I.2nd.sg.+CL(Dat.) a(m.sg.)
        "Give me one."

[37] For feminine nouns beginning with stressed *a*, such as *agua* "water", *la* is replaced by *el*: *el agua*, "the water," *las aguas* "the waters." Feminine *el* and *la* both derive from *ela* (*<illa*).

The neuter determiner *lo* occurs in DPs with no overt head noun; *lo* is followed by an adjective or relative clause:[38]

(40)   a. Lo   importante de esa película es el   diálogo.
            the(neu.) important of that film   is the dialogue
            "What is important in that film is the dialogue."
        b. Lo   que me   interesa es el diálogo.
            the(neu.) that CL(Dat.) interests is the dialogue
            "What interests me is the dialogue."

Non-overt nouns or noun phrases also occur with other determiners and demonstratives. The pronoun corresponding to English "one" is always silent (e.g., *el otro* "the other one").

DPs may lack an overt determiner under several circumstances. Predicative DPs normally lack an overt determiner unless the DP is modified:

(41)   a. Susana es doctora.
          S.   is doctor
          "Susana is a doctor."
        b. Susana es una doctora   excelente.
          S.   is a   doctor-f. excellent
          "Susana is an excellent doctor."

Referential DPs also occur without overt determiners under certain conditions. Bosque (1980) notes that singular DPs occur without determiners in negative contexts:

(42)   a. Ernesto no lee   libro sin   ilustraciones.
          E.   not read book without illustrations
          "Ernesto doesn't read (any) book without illustrations."
        b. *Ernesto lee   libro sin   ilustraciones.
          E.   read book without illustrations
          "Ernesto reads any book without illustrations."

"Negative contexts" include both the presence of negative *no* "not," and other negative elements which allow negative polarity items (see 1.4.).

Bare (determinerless) plural DPs are generally impossible before the verb, and generally possible in post-verbal positions. This is illustrated by the contrast between (43a) and (43b):

---

[38] *Lo* also replaces exclamative *qué* "how." Compare (i) and (ii):

(i)   ¡Qué bien escribe Caterina!
       how well writes C.
       "How well Caterina writes!"
(ii)   ¡Lo   bien que escribe Caterina!
       the(neu.) well that writes C. (=(i))

(43)   a. Llegaron estudiantes.   (Suñer 1982)
        arrived   students
        "(Some) students arrived."
        b. *Estudiantes llegaron.
        students   arrived (=43a)

However, pre-verbal bare plurals are possible if the DP is conjoined, contrastively focused, or a topic (left dislocated):

(44)   Viejos y   niños   escuchaban con atención sus   palabras.
                                              (Bello (1847) 1971:231)
        old-pl. and children listened   with attention 3rd.pl.(Gen.) words
        "Old people and children listened attentively to his/her words."
(45)   Estudiantes llegaron (y   no profesores).
        students   arrived (and not teachers)
(46)   Estudiantes, no creo que falten.
        Students   not think that lack
        "Students, (I) don't think are lacking."

Example (45) is grammatical with main sentential stress on *estudiantes*, indicating that it is contrastively focused (see Chapter 6, Section 6.2). In (46), *estudiantes* is not strongly stressed, and is separated from the following constituent by pause intonation.

Post-verbal bare plurals occur in complement positions, including as direct object of transitive verbs and as subjects of unaccusative verbs (e.g., *llegar* "arrive" in (43a)). Post-verbal subjects of ordinary intransitive verbs ("unergative" verbs) cannot normally be bare plurals. However, as noted in Torrego (1989), they become grammatical if locative inversion occurs:

(47)   a. *Juegan   niños.
        play-pr.3rd.pl. children
        "Children are playing."
        b. En este parque juegan   niños.
        in this park   play-pr.3rd.pl children
        "In this park children play."

Lois (1986) observes that bare plurals may generally appear as subjects in nonfinite clauses, except in the case of agreeing participles:

(48)   De llegar   estudiantes, habrá que dar clase.
        of arrive-inf. students   have that give class
        "If students arrive, one has to have class."

(49)   *Comprado   café, nos   fuimos a casa.
        bought-pprt.m.sg. coffee CL(1st.pl.) went   to home
        "With coffee bought, we went home."

In all the preceding ungrammatical examples with bare plural and bare mass nouns, the sentences become grammatical with the addition of an overt determiner, either definite or indefinite.

Items which are traditionally analyzed as determiners include quantifying elements such as *todos* "all," *pocos* "few," *muchos* "many." Some recent studies have proposed that such items should be differentiated from determiners, both on the basis of their logical form and on the basis of core syntactic properties such as coocurrence with determiners (but not with each other), modification and movement possibilities. This area of investigation is complicated by the fact that quantifying elements do not behave uniformly as a class in many respects. Some syntactic generalizations concerning quantifiers will be reviewed in Chapter 2.

1.2.7   Negative concord

Sentences in (50a) and (50b) are synonymous:

(50)   a. Nadie   salió.
       nobody left
       "Nobody left."
       b. No salió nadie.
       not left   anybody (=50a)

The pattern in (50) generalizes to other negated constituents: either a negated constituent or *no* precedes the verb:

(51)   a. María **no**   canta nunca.
       M.   not sings ever
       "Maria never sings."
       b. María **nunca** canta.
       M.   never sings (=61a)

(52)   a. *****Nadie no**   canta nunca.
       nobody not sings ever
       "Nobody ever sings."
       b. *****Nunca no**   canta nadie.
       never   not sings anybody

The phenomenon illustrated above has been termed "Negative Concord," which conveys that, in (51a) for example, there is only one negation, rather than two independent negative elements. The superficial appearance of two negative elements is analyzed as resulting from concord, or agreement.[39]

---

[39] A basic issue in the analysis of Negative Concord is whether *no* or *nadie* is the true negative element. Both positions have been adopted. See Bosque (1980), Zanuttini (1990).

Romance languages are generally Negative Concord languages. Characteristic of Negative Concord is the absence of lexical alternations between such pairs as *nobody/anybody*, both of which are *nadie* in Spanish.

There is a broader class of items which, although not intrinsically negative in meaning, nevertheless require a negative context to be grammatical. These include adverbs like *en absoluto* "at all," *todavía* "yet," as well as various other categories of items and many idioms. These items are referred to as Negative Polarity Items (NPIs), and are illustrated below:

(53)   Juan *(no) ha llegado **todavía**.
        J.   not has arrived yet
        "Juan hasn't arrived yet."

(54)   Ese niño *(no) come **en absoluto**.
        that child not eats   at all
        "That child doesn't eat at all."

(55)   Susana *(no) ha **movido un dedo** por él.
        S.   not has lifted   a finger for him
        "Susana hasn't lifted a finger for him."

Negative *no* is not the only element which can trigger the occurrence of NPIs. Others include certain interrogative contexts and certain classes of verbs (of lacking, absence, doubt, opposition), prepositions, conjunctions, comparatives and quantifiers.[40] The items discussed above with respect to Negative Concord (*nadie, nunca*, etc.) can also cooccur with some of these triggers, but not all.

1.2.8   Null subjects

The subject pronouns are displayed in (56). As shown in (57), pronominal subjects may be overt or covert:

(56)   Singular: Plural:
        1st: yo   nosotros(m.)
                  "I"   nosotras(f.)
                                     "we"
        2nd: tú (vos)   vosotros(m.)
                                     vosotras(f.)
                  "you"   "you all"
        3rd: él(m.)   ellos(m.)
                  "he"   "they"
                  ella(f.)   ellas(f.)
                  "she"   "they"
                  Usted (Ud.)   Ustedes (Uds.)
                  "you(formal)"   "you(formal)"

---

[40] A comprehensive summary of NPIs and NPI triggers is given in Bosque (1980).

(57)   a. Cantaron   ellos.
             sing-pa.3rd.pl. they(Nom.)
             "They sang."
         b. Cantaron.
             sing-pa.3rd.pl.

The overt subject pronouns in (56) are always strongly stressed. It is generally assumed that the richness of morphological agreement allows the content of the pronoun to be recovered, making the overt pronoun unnecessary. Under some conditions, subject pronouns cannot be overt. One instance is sentences whose subjects are non-referring:

(58)   (*Ello) es obvio que (*ello) llovió.
         "(It) is obvious that (it) rained."

Pronouns corresponding to pleonastic (non-referring) *it* and to the quasi-pleonastic subject of atmospheric verbs are always covert. Existential sentences have no overt form corresponding to *there*:

(59)   (*Allí) hay un unicornio en el   jardín.
         "(There) is   a   unicorn   in the garden."

    Personal subject pronouns are not strictly optional. For example, in a discourse in which *Juan* is the topic, subsequent references to *Juan* use the covert pronoun, not overt *él*, except for contrastive focus. In the following sequence, where a contrastive focus interpretation (shown by "HE" in the gloss) is impossible, *él*, is ungrammatical:

(60)   Vi a Juan en el mercado. (*Él) me saludó, y (*él) dijo que (él) pensaba que
         iba a llover.
         "I saw Juan at the market. *HE greeted me and *HE said that HE thought
         that it was going to rain."

Subject pronouns are overt only in contexts of contrastive focus or switching of reference. Consequently, (57a) and (57b) above are not strictly synonymous. The question arises as to whether the distinction between the two interpretations is represented in sentence-grammar or only in discourse-grammar.

    Following work by Jaeggli (1982) and Rizzi (1982), it has been argued that the option of null subjects is one of a cluster of phenomena which, although superficially unconnected, can be explained in terms of a single feature of the grammar. Properties observed in null-subject languages are summarized in (61):[41]

---

[41] Null-subject languages allow the use of null resumptive pronouns, which may be taken as a subcase of (61a).

(61)   a. Phonetically null pronominal subjects
         b. Non-overt pleonastic pronouns
         c. Free "postposing" of subjects
         d. Absence of "COMP–trace" effects
         e. Long extraction of subjects

(61a) and (61b) have been illustrated above. (61c) refers to the grammaticality of predicate–subject order in declaratives (*Juan cantó / Cantó Juan* "Juan sang"). The absence of "COMP–trace" effects is illustrated by (62):

(62)   ¿Quién crees   que vendrá?
         who   think-2nd.sg. that come-fut.
         "Who do you believe that will come?"

In (62), the interrogative subject of the subordinate clause is compatible with an overt complementizer *que*. The corresponding sentence in English is impossible with the complementizer (hence the name "COMP–trace" effects: the trace of a moved subject cannot cooccur with an overt complementizer).[42]

    "Long" extraction of the subject is shown in (63):

(63)   ¿Quién no sabes qué escribió?
         who   not know what write-pa.3rd.sg.
         "Who don't you know what (they) wrote?"

In (63), the complement of *saber* "know" is an interrogative clause which has two interrogative constituents: *qué*, which is in initial position in the subordinate clause, and *quién*, which is interpreted as the subject of the subordinate clause. *Quién* has been "long" extracted to clause-initial position of the main clause. The ungrammaticality of the corresponding English sentence shows that non-null-subject languages disallow long extraction of the subject.

    Analyses of the null-subject parameter have accounted for the clustering of these properties in terms of the "richness" of verbal inflection for subject features, which (stated informally) provides a "stronger" governor for the subject of finite clauses than is otherwise possible. Government of the subject by a "strong" governor makes possible phonetically null subjects, including null pronominals and traces of moved subjects.

1.3   The subject constituent

    The preceding discussion summarized the characteristics of null subjects. We turn our attention now to a description of overt subjects: their order relative to other constituents, their occurrence in non-finite clauses, and

---

[42] Perlmutter (1971) first observed the correlation between COMP–trace effects and null subjects.

subject–verb agreement. As the discussion in 1.3.1 and 1.3.2 will show, the position of the subject is relatively "free" in finite declarative clauses, while in non-declaratives and in non-finite clauses, the subject is more restricted in its distribution. Section 1.5.1 below will discuss constituent order in declaratives from the perspective of "information structure."

1.3.1   Order

In finite declarative sentences, the subject may either precede or follow the predicate, as shown in (64a) and (64b). V-S-O order is also possible, as in (64c):[43]

(64)   a. Escribió la   carta **mi   hermana**.
              wrote   the letter my sister
              "My sister wrote the letter."
         b. **Mi hermana** escribió la carta. (=64a)
         c. ?Escribió **mi hermana** la carta. (=64a)

V-S-O sequences in finite declaratives may be less natural than S-V-O and V-O-S orders. The naturalness of V-S-O sentences may vary from speaker to speaker, and may depend also on lexical properties of the sentence. For example, (66) is more natural than (65); both are V-S-O:

(65)   ?Pintó   el   artista retratos terribles.
         painted the artist   portraits terrible
         "The artist painted terrible portraits."

(66)   Sufrió   el   paciente dolores terribles.
         suffered the patient   pains   terrible
         "The patient suffered terrible pains."

The mixed results for V-S-O sentences differ from both pre-verbal and post-predicate subjects, which are uniformly grammatical in finite declaratives.

Another type of clause that has freedom of subject–predicate order is the *small clause*. These constituents contain a predicative phrase and a constituent that is the semantic subject of the predicate. Unlike full clauses, small clauses may lack a verb. In the examples in (67) and (68), the small clause consists of the bracketed sequence. The subjects of small clauses may precede or follow their predicate:

(67)   a. Eligieron   [presidente a   Juan].
              elected-3rd.pl. president PA J.
              "(They) elected Juan president."
         b Eligieron [a Juan presidente].   (=67a)

---

[43] Judgments seem to vary as to whether V-S-O order is fully acceptable in declaratives.

(68) a. Consideran   [válida la   prueba].
         consider-pr.3rd.pl. valid the proof
         "(They) consider the proof valid."
      b. Consideran [la prueba válida].   (=68a)

Non-finite clauses typically allow only post-verbal subjects, as is illustrated in (69)–(72). (See 1.7.5 for discussion of dialectal variation.)

(69) a. [Llegada   ella]   empezó la fiesta.
         arrive-pprt.f.sg. she(Nom.) began   the party
      b. *[ella   llegada]   empezó la fiesta.
          she(Nom.) arrive-pprt.f.sg. began   the party
         "(With) her arrived, the party began."

(70) a. [Habiendo llegado   ella],   empezó la fiesta.
         have-prt. arrive-pprt. she(Nom.) began   the party
      b. *[Ella   habiendo llegado], empezó la fiesta.
          she(Nom.) have-prt. arrive-pprt. began the party.

(71) a. [Al   cantarlo   tú]   empezó la fiesta.
         upon+the sing-inf.+CL(Acc.) you(Nom.) began the party
         "Upon your singing it, the party began."
      b. *[Al   tú   cantarlo]   empezó la fiesta.
          upon+the you(Nom.) sing-inf.+CL(Acc.) began the party

(72) a. [De ganar   ellos]   los   felicitaremos.
         of win-inf. they(Nom.) CL(Acc.) congratulate-fut.1st.pl.
         "If they win, we will congratulate them."
      b. *[De ellos   ganar] los   felicitaremos.
          of they(Nom.) win-inf. CL(Acc.) congratulate-fut.1st.pl.

Non-declarative finite clauses generally require a post-verbal subject. This is illustrated below for imperatives (73), constituent questions (74) and exclamatives (75). (See 1.7.5 for discussion of dialectal variation.)

(73) a. Hazlo   tú.
         do(I)+CL(Acc.) you(nom.)
         "You do it!"
      b. *Tú hazlo.[44]

(74) a. ¿Qué leyó Juan?
         what read J.
         "What did Juan read?"
      b. *¿Qué Juan leyó?

[44] Although imperatives do not freely allow pre-verbal subjects, as in (73b), it is possible to add a topicalized subject to an imperative:

(i)   ¡Tú, hazlo!
      "You, do it!"

In (i), the overt subject is separated intonationally from the imperative.

(75)   a. ¡Qué alto está **Julio!**
           how tall is   J.
           "How tall Julio is!"
        b. *¡Qué alto **Julio** está!

Relative clauses pattern with declaratives, rather than interrogatives: their subjects may be pre-verbal:

(76)   a. el   libro [que **Juan** leyó]
           the book that J.   read
        b. el libro [que leyó **Juan**]   (=76a)

In some cases, a post-verbal subject is required if a non-subject constituent is preposed. This will be illustrated in Chapter 6. Finite subordinate clauses pattern with main clauses with respect to subject position: the subject may be pre-verbal or post-verbal, except in embedded interrogatives and exclamatives, and clauses with preposed constituents.

1.3.2   Distribution in non-finite clauses

Nominative subjects are possible in non-finite adjunct clauses, as illustrated above in (69)–(72). Nominative NPs also occur as arguments of the prepositions *hasta* "even" and *entre* "between" (see note 20). With the exception of causative and perception constructions discussed below, non-finite argument clauses do not allow non-Nominative subjects. For example, gerunds do not admit Genitive subjects (*su partiendo* "your leaving"); there is no prepositional complementizer corresponding to English *for* (e.g., *for Mary to leave*); and "exceptional" case in complements of *believe* predicates is excluded:[45]

(77)   *Juan cree   María ser   inteligente.
         J.   believes M.   be-inf. intelligent
         "Juan believes María to be intelligent."

In infinitival causative constructions under *hacer* "make" or *dejar* "let," the infinitival subject is an Accusative or Dative object of the causative verb:

(78)   a. Susana le   hizo   leer la carta a   José.
           S.   CL(Dat.) made read the letter Dat. J.
           "Susana made José read the letter."
        b. Susana hará   caminar a la oficina a   José.
           S.   make-fut. walk   to the office PA J.
           "Susana will make José walk to the office."

[45] Unlike French, an interrogative is also excluded as the subject of a complement of *creer* "believe":

    (i)   *¿Quién cree   Juan ser   inteligente?
            who   believes J.   be-inf. intelligent
            "Who does Juan believe to be intelligent?"

In (78a), the infinitival subject (*José*) is Dative, and the object of the infinitive is Accusative. In (78b), the subject of the infinitive (*José*) is Accusative. Two factors determine the Case of the infinitival subject. The transitivity of the infinitive is one factor. If the infinitive has an Accusative object, the subject is necessarily Dative. That is, the causative "complex" cannot contain two Accusative arguments. A second factor is concerned with the contrast between direct and indirect causation. Intransitives such as (78b) allow the infinitival subject to be either Accusative (direct causation) or Dative (indirect causation).

Infinitival complements of perception verbs pattern with causative complements in the respects mentioned above. Gerundive and finite clause complements of perception predicates also have subjects that are grammatical objects of the perception verb:

(79)   a. Juan la   vio cruzando la   calle.
           J.   CL(f.sg.Acc.) saw cross-prt. the street
           "Juan saw her crossing the street."
        b. Juan vio a   María que cruzaba   la   calle.
           J.   saw PA M.   that cross-pa.3rd.sg. the street
           "Juan saw that Maria crossed the street."

The subjects of small clauses in argument positions take objective case:

(80)   a. La   nombraron   presidenta.
           CL(f.sg.Acc.) name-pa.3rd.pl. president
           "They named her president."
        b. Los   consideran   inteligentes.
           CL(m.pl.Acc.) consider-pr.3rd.pl. intelligent
           "They consider them intelligent."

In these examples, the subject of the small clause takes the case appropriate to the complement of the verb.

Adjunct infinitival clauses may have Nominative subjects:

(81)   a. [Al   cantarlo   **tú**]   empezó la fiesta.
           upon+the sing-inf.+CL you(Nom.) began   the party
           "Upon your singing it, the party began."
        b. [De ganar   **ellos**]   los   felicitaremos.
           of   win-inf. they(Nom.) CL(Acc.) congratulate-fut.1st.pl.
           "If they win, we will congratulate them."

1.3.3   Agreement

Most person/number suffixes are unambiguous. This is illustrated for a first conjugation verb *cantar* "to sing" in the present tense, where only 1st and 3rd person singular of the subjunctive are homophonous:

(82)   cantar   Indicative: Subjunctive:
        1st.sg.   canto   cante
        2nd.sg.   cantas   cantes
        3rd.sg.   canta   cante
        1st.pl.   cantamos   cantemos
        2nd.pl.   cantáis   cantéis
        3rd.pl.   cantan   canten

Finite clauses generally display person and number agreement between the clausal subject and the finite verb. Sentences with personal pronominal subjects show the same subject–verb agreement whether the pronoun is overt or covert. However, some sentences with covert subjects display invariant 3rd person singular agreement on the verb. One such case is constructions with the subject clitic *se*:

(83)   a. Se   trabaja   mucho en este curso.
           CL(nom) work-pr.3rd.sg. a lot in this course
        b. *Se trabajan   mucho en este curso.
           CL work-pr.3rd.pl. a lot   in this course
           "One works a lot in this course."

Constructions with non-referential subjects (corresponding to English *it*, *there*), also have invariant 3rd singular verb forms:

(84)   a. Parece   que los libros han llegado.
           seems-pr.3rd.sg. that the books have arrived
           "It seems that the books have arrived."
        b. *Parecen   que los libros han llegado.
           seems-3rd.pl. that the books have arrived

(85)   a. Es   obvio   que los libros han llegado.
           be-pr.3rd.sg. obvious that the books have arrived
           "It is obvious that the books have arrived."
        b. *Son   obvio(s) que los libros han llegado.
           be-pr.3rd.(pl.) obvious that the books have arrived
           "It is obvious that the books have arrived."

In some instances, "invariant" verb forms do alternate with agreeing forms. This is illustrated for existential constructions in (86), and atmospheric verbs in (87):

(86)   a. Había   tres   libros en la mesa.
           be-pr.3rd.sg. three books on the table
           "There were three books on the table."
        b. ?Habían   tres   libros en la mesa.
           be-pr.3rd.pl. three books on the table

(87)   a. Llueve   monedas del   cielo.   (Hurtado 1989a)
           rain-pr.3rd.sg. coins   from+the sky
           "It's raining coins from heaven."

    b. ?Llueven   monedas del   cielo. (=76a)
       rain-pr.3rd.pl. coins   from+the sky

Rightward agreement in existentials is fairly common, although it is considered substandard.

Copular sentences with an identificational interpretation require agreement with the predicative element:

(88)   a. El culpable [soy   yo].
           the culprit be-pr.1st.sg. I(Nom.)
           "The culprit is me."
        b. *El culpable es   yo.
           the culprit be-pr.3rd.sg. I(Nom.)

Passives generally display agreement between the finite verb and derived subject. This is shown for passives composed of *ser* "be" +participle and *se*+verb:

(89)   a. Esos libros fueron   vendidos.
           those books be-pa.3rd.pl. sell-pprt.m.pl.
           "Those books were sold."
        b. *Esos libros fue   vendido(s).
           those books be-pa.3rd.sg. sell-pprt.m(pl.)

(90)   a. Esos libros se   vendieron.
           those books CL(pas) sell-pa.3rd.pl
        b. *Esos libros se   vendió.
           those books CL(pas) sell-pa.3rd.sg.

The following pair has received various analyses:

(91)   a. Se   vende   flores.
           CL(pas) sell-pr.3rd.sg. flowers
           "Flowers sold/for sale."
        b. Se   venden   flores.
           CL(pas) sell-pr.3rd.pl. flowers

The fact that *se* may be a subject clitic, a passive morpheme, or an anti-causative (middle) morpheme leads to various possible analyses of (91b). A central issue that arises with respect to its analysis is that the verb agrees with *flores*, suggesting that this phrase is the grammatical subject. However, based on the fact that it is a bare plural (see 1.2.6), it must be in complement position. Example (91b) becomes ungrammatical if *flores* precedes the verb.

1.4   The predicate constituent

1.4.1   Tense and aspect

Verbal inflections express (a) tense (Past, Present, Future), (b) perfectivity (or telicity) of past events (Imperfect, Preterite Past) and (c) mood (Subjunctive, Indicative). Each of these is illustrated below. We then summarize periphrastic forms related to tense, aspect, modality and voice.

Indicative tenses include Future, Conditional, Present and two simple past tenses, Preterite and Imperfect Past. The Future tense is ambiguous between temporal future reference and a present modal of probability. This is illustrated by the pairs in (92) and (93):

(92)   a. ¿Dónde van   a estar   a las dos?
              where go-pr.3rd.pl. to be-inf. at the two
              "Where will they be at two o'clock?"
         b. Estarán   en casa a las dos.
              be-fut.3rd.pl. at home at the two
              "They will be at home at two o'clock."

(93)   a. ¿Dónde está María?
              where is   M.
              "Where's Maria?"
         b. Estará   trabajando, sin   duda.
              be-fut.3rd.sg. work-prt.   without doubt
              "(She) must be working, no doubt."

Notice in (92a) that temporal future reference is expressed by the periphrastic *ir a*+infinitive. This is the standard future construction, especially for near-future reference. In (93), the future tense does not locate an event in the future. It asserts a probability or likelihood in the present. On this reading, the future is most similar to non-indicative tenses, which generally do not assert an event's occurrence.

The conditional tense is sometimes referred to as a "past of the future," and indeed historically the Future and Conditional tenses evolved from Present and Imperfect forms of auxiliary *haber* based on its modal reading "have to V". The Conditional is still a grammatically [+PAST] counterpart of the "modal present" of probability:

(94)   Estarían   trabajando en ese momento.
         be-cond.3rd.pl. work-prt. at that moment
         "They must have been working at that moment."

The Conditional also behaves like a grammatical [+PAST] with respect to sequence-of-tense:

(95)   a. Te   prestarían   el   coche si lo   necesitaras.
            CL(Dat.) lend-cond.3rd.pl. the car   if CL(Acc.) need-pa.subj.2nd.sg.
            "They would lend you the car if you needed it."
        b. *Te   prestarían   el   coche si lo   necesitas.
            CL(Dat.) lend-cond.3rd.pl. the car   if CL(Acc.) need-pr.ind.2nd.pl.
            "They would lend you the car if you need it."

In (95b), the Conditional is incompatible with the present tense if-clause. In (95a), the Conditional is compatible with the past tense if-clause.[46] To refer to past time in counterfactual Conditionals, the compound perfect is required:

(96)   Te habrían   prestado el   coche si lo   hubieras
        necesitado.
        CL have-cond. lend.pprt. the car   if CL(Acc.) have-pa.subj.2nd.sg.
        need-pprt
        "They would have lent you the car if you had needed it."

(97)   *Te habrían   prestado el coche si lo   necesitaras.
        CL have-cond. lend-pprt. the car   if CL(Acc.) need-pa.subj.2nd.sg.

The contrast between (96) and (97) suggests that the Conditional is essentially modal or atemporal. Although the Conditional in (94) appears to order an event in the past, this reading is not possible without the adverb – unlike the adverbs in (92) and (93). Thus, while the Future tense is both temporal and modal, the Conditional may be exclusively modal, with only a formal feature for [+PAST] (as opposed to a semantic feature).

The Present Indicative potentially has present and future readings. Present readings for non-stative predicates are ambiguous between habitual (frequentative) and present-moment:

(98)   María estudia   geografía en la   biblioteca.
        M.   study-pr.3rd.sg. geography at the library
        "Maria studies geography at the library."
        "Maria is studying geography at the library."

Future readings are possible with non-statives such as (99a), but not with statives such as (99b):

---

[46] Notice that the grammatical feature [+PAST] does not necessarily correspond to semantic anteriority, as illustrated in (i):

(i)   Te prestarían el   coche mañana   si lo   necesitaras   hoy.
        CL lend-cond. the car   tomorrow if CL need-pa.subj. today
        "They would lend you the car tomorrow if you needed it today."

For discussion of construal of Past tense, see Iatridou (2000).

(99)   a. Salen   (esta noche).
             leave-pr.3rd.pl. this night
             "They're leaving/going out (tonight)."
         b. *María sabe   la lección a las tres.
             M.   know-pr.3rd.sg. the lesson at the three
             "María knows the lesson at three o'clock."

Indicative Past tenses refer to events and states which precede the "moment of speech." Spanish distinguishes further between Imperfect and "Preterite" Past. The distinction is similar to the distinction described by Vendler (1967) with respect to delimited and non-delimited events. Delimited events have an inherent endpoint, while non-delimited events (and states) do not. For example, *to walk* is not inherently delimited, but *to walk to the store* is, since once the goal is reached, the event necessarily ends. The Preterite and Imperfect Past tenses make an analogous distinction, but not with respect to events and states themselves; rather these tenses assert whether or not the interval during which an event or state occurs is delimited. This factor interacts with properties of the predicate, including adverbs, to provide inferences about the delimitedness of the event. To illustrate this point, let us first consider the Imperfect, which is often glossed as "was V-ing," "used to V":

(100)   a. Susana tocaba   la flauta.
             S.   play-imp. the flute
         b. "Susana used to play the flute."
         c. "Susana was playing the flute."

The interpretation in (100b) is frequentative or habitual: there is a past interval of non-specific duration, during which the activity of playing the flute is frequent or habitual. On the reading in (100c) there is a single event of playing the flute, which corresponds in duration to the interval of non-specific duration. What the two readings have in common is the occurrence of some event(s) during a non-delimited interval. An event may be neither frequentative within the interval nor correspond with the interval, as in (101):

(101)   Eran   las cinco.
         be-imp.3rd.pl. the five
         "It was five o'clock."

In (101) the event is the occurrence of five o'clock, which is punctual and delimited. The Imperfect is shown here not to define the duration of the event (or its delimitedness) but instead to refer to the non-delimitedness of the interval during which the event occurs. The Imperfect may have the effect of canceling the delimitedness of an event. Consider the two readings in (102):

(102)   a. (Yo) caminaba   a la tienda.
              I   walk-imp.1st.sg. to the store
          b. "I was walking to the store."
          c. "I used to walk to the store."

The predicate *walk to the store* is aspectually delimited. However, neither reading in (102) is delimited. On the single event reading in (102b), the goal is understood not to be reached. On the habitual reading in (102c), the plurality of occurrences produces a non-delimited interpretation.[47] Thus, in this example (unlike (101)), this potentially delimited event is non-delimited in the Imperfect.

Consider now the Preterite Past. By contrast, a delimited event such as (102) is understood to be completed:

(103)   (Yo) caminé   a la tienda.
              I   walk-pret.1st.sg. to the store

In the Preterite Past, the past interval itself is delimited. The endpoint of the interval corresponds with the endpoint of delimited events in the predicate. The Preterite Past typically adds a delimited reading to predicates which do not have them inherently. This is illustrated for states and activity predicates in (104):

(104)   a. Canté.
              sing-pret.1st.sg.
              "I sang."
          b. Fuiste   amable.
              be-pret.2nd.sg. kind
              "You were kind."
          c. Dibujé   círculos.
              draw-pret.1st.sg. circles
              "I drew circles."

The predicates in (104) do not express inherently delimited events or states. However in the Preterite Past, they have a delimited interpretation, by virtue of the delimitedness of the past interval during which they occur. The interval has a definite endpoint, and is followed by a subsequent interval during which

---

[47] The conversion of a (potentially) delimited event to a non-delimited one by "pluralizing" it, as in the frequentitive reading (102c), is analogous to the conversion of an Accomplishment to a non-delimited reading by pluralizing its complement:

(i)   a. dibujar un círculo (Accomplishment)
             "draw a circle"
        b. dibujar círculos (Activity)
             "draw circles"

In (ib), the plural has the effect of iterating events. The iterated sequence is non-delimited.

the event does not hold. For (104a), for example, if I sang (pret.), it is understood that I stopped singing and that some interval of non-singing is subsequent to the event of singing. By contrast, the Imperfect Past lacks this subsequent interval of non-singing. The Present Perfect lacks it as well, a point to which we return below.

Periphrastic tenses include a future construction consisting of *ir a* "go to" plus infinitive; *tener que* "have to" plus infinitive; and perfective and progressive constructions which are quite close to English counterparts in both form and interpretation. The perfect tenses are constructed with auxiliary *haber* "have" followed by a past participle. There is no change of auxiliary as is found in French, Catalan and Italian, nor does participle show agreement:

(105) a. Los niños han   lavado   la ventana.
          the kids   have-pr.3rd.pl. wash-pprt. the window-f.sg.
          "The kids have washed the window."
       b. Los niños la   han   lavado.
          the kids CL(f.sg.Acc.) have-pr.3rd.pl. wash-pprt.(m.sg.)
          "The kids have washed it."
       c. *Los niños la   han   lavada.
          the kids CL(f.sg.Acc.) have-pr.3rd.pl. wash-pprt.f.sg.

Unlike French and Italian, the Present Perfect does not serve as a simple past tense in main clauses:[48]

(106) *Los niños la   han   lavado   ayer.
        the kids   CL have-pr.3rd.pl. wash-pprt yesterday
        "The kids have washed it yesterday."

The standard approach to the interpretation of compound tenses is that they do not temporally locate the event relative to the time of the utterance. Instead, a "reference point" is located relative to the time of the utterance, and the event is in turn located relative to the reference point. In (105), the reference point is the present; the event of washing is anterior to the reference point. Positing the reference point allows the the present relevance of the event to be captured. The three points are differentiated in the Past Perfect (e.g., *Los niños la habían lavado* "The children had washed it").

---

[48] There is some variation with respect to the acceptability of past adverbs with the present perfect tense, at least among some peninsular speakers. For example, (i) is acceptable for some speakers, in contrast to *ayer* "yesterday," which is less so:

(i)   Los niños la   han lavado esta mañana.
       the kids   CL have washed this morning
       "The kids have washed it this morning."

It appears that for these speakers, a proximate/distant gradation may come into play.

The periphrastic progressive consists of auxiliary *estar* "be" followed by a progressive participle:

(107)   a. Estoy   leyendo   *El poema del Cid.*
             be-pr.1st.sg. read-prt. *El poema del Cid.*
         b. Estaba   leyendo   *El poema del Cid.*
             be-pa.1st.sg. read-prt. *El poema del Cid.*

(108)   María está   estudiando para dentista.
         M.   be-pr.3rd.sg. study-prt. for   dentist
         "María is studying to be a dentist."

The progressive refers to intervals of activities. As in English, it is not normally available with predicates that lack activity as part of the event structure:

(109)   a. *La caja está   conteniendo papeles.
             the box be-pr.3rd.sg. contain-prt. papers
             "The box is containing papers."
         b. *Está   pareciendo llover.
             be-pr.3rd.sg. seem-prt.   rain-inf.
             "It's seeming to rain."

1.4.2   Mood

Turning to expression of mood, we focus here on subjunctive morphology, which includes simple Present and Past (Imperfect) tenses, as well as subjunctive forms of the compound tenses and other periphrastic verbal constructions:

(110)   Marta lamenta ...
         M.   regrets ...
         a. que yo cante.
             that I   sing-pr.subj.1st.sg.
             "that I sing."
         b. que yo haya   cantado.
             that I   have-pr.subj.1st.sg. sing-pprt.
             "that I have sung."
         c. que yo cantara.
             that I   sing-pa.subj.1st.sg.
             "that I sang."
         d. que hubiera   cantado.
             that have-pa.subj.1st.sg. sing-pprt
             "that I had sung"
         e. que estuviera   cantando.
             that be-pa.subj.1st.sg. sing-prt.
             "that I was singing."
         f. que hubiera   estado   cantando.
             that have-pa.subj.1st.sg. be-pprt. sing-prt.
             "that I had been singing."

Mood is sometimes characterized as an expression of the speaker's attitude toward the factuality of an event or state expressed by a clause. In Spanish, indicative mood generally occurs in contexts which assert an event's occurrence (hence, factuality). Subjunctive occurs in contexts in which the event's occurrence is in doubt or unknown, and also in contexts such as (110), in which the event's occurrence or factuality is presupposed rather than asserted. However, optional alternations between subjunctive and indicative as a means of reflecting speaker's degree of certainty as to factuality are available only in ungoverned clauses, such as main clauses expressing possibility:

(111)   a. Quizás ya   hayas   comido.
           maybe already have-pr.subj.2nd.sg. eat-pprt.
           "Perhaps you have already eaten."
        b. Quizás ya   has   comido.
           maybe already have-pr.ind.2nd.sg. eat-pprt.

In (111), both sentences contain *quizás*, therefore express some degree of doubt or uncertainty as to the factuality of the proposition. The greater degree of certainty is associated with the indicative in (111b).

Although alternations of the type shown in (111) are possible in main clauses, they generally are not possible in subordinate clauses. There, the selection of subjunctive or indicative mood is determined by properties of the subordinate clause and its context. For example, adjunct clauses introduced by *cuando* "when" require the subjunctive if the subordinate predicate is interpreted as subsequent to the moment of speech:[49]

---

[49] Some adjuncts of place and time show alternations of subjunctive/indicative dependent on the specificity of the place or time indicated:

(i)   a. Lloraba   cuando estaba   triste.
                                                     (Campos 1993:151)
          cry-imp.ind.3rd.sg. when   be-imp.ind.3rd.sg. sad
          "S/he cried when s/he was sad."
       b. Llorará   cuando esté   triste.
          cry-fut.3rd.sg.   when   be-pr.subj.3rd.sg. sad
          "S/he'll cry when(ever) s/he's sad."
(ii)   a. Estudiará   donde estudia   su   novio.
          study-fut.3rd.sg.   where study-pr.ind.3rd.sg. her boyfriend
          "She'll study where her boyfriend is studying."
       b. Estudiará   donde estudie   su   novio.
          study-fut.3rd.sg.   where study-pr.subj.3rd.sg. her boyfriend
          "She'll study where(ever) her boyfriend studies."

These alternations appear to be analogous to contrasts in relative clauses, where subjunctive occurs if the relative clause antecedent is nonspecific. The examples in (i) and (ii) may in fact be relatives with a covert time or place antecedent.

(112)   a. Cenamos   cuando lleguen.
            dine-pr.1st.pl. when   arrive-pr.subj.3rd.pl.
            "We'll eat dinner when they arrive."
         b. Cenamos   cuando llegaron.
            dine-pa.1st.pl. when   arrive-pa.ind.3rd.pl.
            "We ate dinner when they arrived."

In argument clauses the mood of the subordinate clause is generally dictated by the lexical item which selects the clause, and mood alternations are generally impossible. Relative clauses are indicative, unless the antecedent has particular referential characteristics, such as a negative existential (*nadie* "nobody," *nada* "nothing," etc.) or a non-specific antecedent. That is to say, the appearance of subjunctive mood is conditioned by syntactic features of the context in which a clause occurs (see 1.6.2 on relative clauses). Theoretical issues related to mood include (a) the analysis of the temporal value of clauses whose verb appears in the subjunctive, and (b) the grammatical feature(s) which trigger the occurrence of the subjunctive.

1.4.3   Voice

Non-active voice morphology in Spanish includes passive and middle/passive constructions. Passives are formed with *ser* "be" followed by a passive participle:

(113)   Los argumentos   fueron   rechazados   (por el juez).
         the arguments-m.pl. be-pa.3rd.pl. reject-pprt.m.pl. by the judge
         "The arguments were rejected by the judge."

In (113), the finite verb agrees in person and number with the derived subject, the participle agrees in number and gender with the derived subject, and the agent may be expressed in a prepositional phrase headed by *por* "by." The derived subject may remain in post-verbal position. Both bare NPs and definite subjects appear between the participle and a locative complement:[50]

(114)   a. Fue encontrado oro en el Mar del   Norte.   (Bosque 1996:30)
            was found   gold in the sea of+the north
            "Gold was found in the North Sea."
         b. Fue encontrado el oro en el Mar del   Norte. (=114a)
            was found   the gold in the sea of+the north

---

[50] There are some restrictions on the occurrence of bare NPs in the post-verbal position of passives. See Bosque (1996:30), Contreras (1996:147).

Passivization is restricted to those arguments which correspond to Accusatives in the active voice. Neither indirect nor oblique complements can be passivized.[51]

Middle/passive constructions are formed with the clitic *se* with an active verb form. The clitic which appears in this construction is homophonous with reflexive clitics. Consequently, three readings of the clitic in sentences like (115) are possible – (a) transitive reflexive, (b) passive voice and (c) intransitive middle voice:

(115)   El   coche se   movió.
        the car   CL   move-pa.3rd.sg.
        a. "The car moved itself."
        b. "The car was moved."
        c. "The car moved."

In the middle/passive construction, the verb is active in form. It agrees in person and number with the derived subject, and the clitic agrees in person and number with the derived subject. For most speakers, optional agent phrases headed by *por* are impossible, both on passive and middle readings.

The middle and passive constructions are superficially identical, but the two can be differentiated on the basis of their argument structure and associated temporal properties. Passives, but not middles, have an implicit agent. This is shown by the fact that with agent-oriented adverbs and purpose clauses, only the passive interpretation is grammatical:

(116)   a. El   coche se   movió voluntariamente.
           the car   CL   moved voluntarily
           "The car was moved voluntarily."
           (not: "*The car moved voluntarily.")
        b. El   coche se   movió para evitar un accidente.
           the car   CL   moved to   avoid an accident
           "The car was moved to avoid an accident."
           (not: "*The car moved to avoid an accident.")

A related temporal property of passives, which also distinguishes them from middles, is the marginal status of simple present tense with definite subjects. Thus, the examples in (116) are ungrammatical in the present tense:

(117)   a. ?*El   coche se   mueve voluntariamente.
             the car   CL   moves voluntarily
             "The car is moved voluntarily."

[51] In "journalese", the indirect object of *preguntar* "ask" is sometimes passivized:

(i)   El representante fue preguntado si firmaría el acuerdo.
      "The representative was asked whether he would sign the agreement."

This does not generalize to other indirect objects.

b. ?*El coche se   mueve para evitar un accidente.
   the car   CL moves to   avoid an accident
   "The car is moved to avoid an accident."

An aspectual difference between passives and middles concerns the delimitedness of the underlying transitive predicate. Passive clitics may combine with transitives without regard to whether the transitive is a perfective (delimited) or an inchoative (nondelimited) predicate. The middle clitic appears to combine only with perfectives. Thus, *tocar* "to ring," an inchoative transitive (118a), takes only passive *se* (118b), not middle *se* (118c):

(118)   a. El   cura   toca   la   campana.
           the priest rings the bell
        b. La   campana se   tocó (voluntariamente).
           the bell   CL rang voluntarily
           "The bell was rung (voluntarily)."
        c. *La   campana se   toca.
           the bell   CL rings
           "The bell rings."

There are several issues to be addressed in analyzing the middle and passive constructions. One is whether or not the non-active sentences are related to corresponding active sentences by way of syntactic or (derivational) lexical processes. A second issue is the nature of the relationship between the transitivity of the predicates, voice, and temporal properties such as those noted above.

1.4.4   Modal verbs

The verbs *poder* "may; be able" and *deber* "must; should" are modal in meaning, but pattern syntactically with main verbs: they take a full range of tense, mood and person/number inflections; their position relative to negation and auxiliaries is identical to that of main verbs. On epistemic readings, these verbs do not occur in infinitives or in the compound perfect tense:

(119)   a. María parece deber   terminar el   proyecto.
           M.   seems should-inf. finish-inf. the project
           (=It seems that she should finish the project.)
           (*It seems that she must finish the project.)
        b. María parece poder   terminar el   proyecto.
           M.   seems may-inf. finish-inf. the project
           (=It seems that she is allowed/able to finish the project.)
           (*It seems possible for her to finish the project.)

(120)   a. Juan piensa poder   terminar el   proyecto.
           J.   thinks may-inf. finish-inf. the project

(=Juan thinks he is allowed/able to finish the project.)
(*Juan thinks it is possible he'll finish the project.)
b. Juan piensa deber   terminar el   proyecto
    J.   thinks should-inf. finish   the project
(=Juan thinks he is obliged to finish the project.)
(*Juan thinks it is necessary that he finish the project.)

(121)   a. Juan lamenta poder   terminar el   proyecto.
             J.   regrets may-inf. finish   the project
         (=Juan regrets he is allowed/able to finish the project.)
         (*Juan regrets it is possible he'll finish the project.)
         b. Juan lamenta deber   terminar el   proyecto.
             J.   regrets should finish-inf. the project
         (=Juan regrets he should finish the project.)
         (*Juan regrets it is necessary he finish the project.)

(122)   a. María puede haber   terminado el   proyecto.
             M.   may   have-inf. finish-pprt. the project
         (=It is possible M. has finished the project.)
         (=M. has been able/allowed to finish the project.)
         b. María ha podido   terminar el   proyecto.
             M.   has may-pprt. finish-inf. the project
         (=M. has been allowed/able to finish the project.)
         (*It has been possible that M. finished the project.)

(123)   a. Juan debe   haber   terminado el   proyecto.
             J.   should have-inf. finish-pprt. the project
         (=It is necessary that J. has finished it.)
         (=J. should have finished it.)
         b. Juan ha debido   terminar el   proyecto.
             J.   has should-pprt. finish-inf. the project
         (=J. should have finished it.)
         (*It has been necessary that J. finish it.)

These verbs pattern also with restructuring verbs (see 1.2.4), so that they form
a verbal complex with a following infinitive, and occur in construction with
the clitics associated with a following infinitive.

1.4.5   Negation

Negation is marked in the basic case by *no* "not":

(124)   Juan no cantó.
         J.   not sing-pa.3rd.sg.
         "Juan didn't sing."

Non-negation (affirmation) is unmarked except in contrastive contexts.
Contrastive contexts such as (125) and (126) show positive polarity marked
for a constituent by *sí* "yes," *sino* "but rather":

(125)   Juan sí llegó   anoche.
         J.   yes arrive-pa.3rd.sg. last night
         "Juan DID arrive last night."

(126)   María se   lo   regaló   no a Pedro sino   a
         Juan.
         M.   CL(Dat.) CL(Acc.) give-pa.3rd.sg. not to P.   but (rather) to
         J.
         "Maria gave it not to Pedro but to Juan."

Contrastive polarity is also possible with *sí* or *no* in a topic structure with clausal ellipsis:

(127)   Juana y   Susana llegaron,   pero José, no.
         J.   and S.   arrive-pa.3rd.pl. but J.,   not
         "Juana and Susana arrived, but José didn't."

(128)   Pedro no comió   pulpo, pero salmón, sí.
         P.   not eat-pa.3rd.sg. octopus but salmon, yes
         "Pedro didn't eat octopus, but salmon, yes."

In the second conjunct of (127) and (128), a constituent has been topicalized (left dislocated), and is followed by the focused polarity marker *sí* or *no*; the remainder of the second conjunct is ellipted.

No may be ambiguous in scope:

(129)   a. No comí la zanahoria cruda.
            not ate the carrot   raw
         b. "It is not the case that I ate the carrot raw (the raw carrot)."
         c. "I ate the carrot, but it wasn't raw."

On the reading in (129c), *no* has scope over the secondary predicate, while in (129b) *no* has scope over both the primary and secondary predicates, i.e., over the entire clause. Clausal negation – both main and subordinate – is distinguished in most cases by the presence of pre-verbal *no*. Negation of non-clausal constituents is more varied, both with respect to the form and position of negation. Let us take the two types in turn.

Clausal negation readings are possible when the morpheme *no* immediately precedes the verb inflected for finiteness. Only clitics intervene between *no* and the verb:

(130)   a. María no leyó ese capítulo.
            M.   not read that chapter
            "Maria didn't read that chapter."
         b. María no lo   leyó.
            M.   not CL(Acc.) read
            "Maria didn't read it."

c. María no lo   había leído.
M.   not CL(Acc.) had   read-pprt.
"Maria hadn't read it."

In each of the preceding examples, *no* precedes the verb inflected for tense (finiteness); in (130b) and (130c), a clitic intervenes between *no* and the verb. The following examples show that *no* also precedes non-finite verbs and the head of nominalized clauses:

(131)   a. Juan prometió ayer   [no   intervenir].
         J.   promised yesterday not meddle-inf.
         "Juan promised yesterday not to meddle."
         b. Pablo quería [no fracasar].
         P.   wanted   not fail-inf.
         "Pablo wanted not to fail."

(132)   a. [La no intervención] es admirable.
         the not meddling   is admirable
         "Not meddling is admirable."
         b. [El no soñar] es perder   mucho.
         the not dream is lose-inf. much
         "Not to dream is to miss a great deal."

Although adverbs may appear between *no* and the verb, this order (*no*-adverb-verb) produces constituent negation for the adverb:

(133)   Susana no siempre canta tangos (a veces canta boleros).
         S.   not always sings tangos (at times sings boleros)
         "Susana doesn't always sing tangos, she sometimes sings boleros."[52]

(134)   Pablo no sólo leyó ese periódico (además leyó dos libros).
         P.   not only read that paper   (also   read two books)
         "Pablo didn't only read that paper, (he) also read two books."

(135)   ?Juan no inmediatamente movió el   coche.
         J.   not immediately   moved the car
         "Juan didn't immediately move the car."

The fully grammatical sequences are those whose adverbs are quantifier-like in interpretation.

---

[52] Notice that constituent negation of *siempre* "always" is logically equivalent to propositional negation in this case: "It's not the case that (Susana always sings)." A similar effect is observable in (134) with *sólo* "only." This could be construed to imply that the sequence *no*-adverb-verb is structurally ambiguous between clausal and adverbial negation. If clausal negation were generally possible with this order, other adverbs should produce the same ambiguity. Example (135) shows that this is not generally true.

Subordinate clauses are not necessarily within the scope of negation of a main clause. Neither (136) nor (137) negates the subordinate clause:

(136) Juan no dijo que Pedro era inteligente.
       J.   not said that P.   was intelligent
       "Juan didn't say that Pedro was intelligent."

(137) Susana no lamenta que Pedro sea   inteligente.
       S.   not regrets that P.   is-subj. intelligent
       "Susana doesn't regret that Pedro is intelligent."

In these cases, the events of saying and regretting are negated independently of the polarity of the events of the complement clauses. However in Spanish as in other languages, there are specific classes of predicates which seem to "share" negation between subordinate and governing clauses (Bosque 1980). The following pairs are considered as more or less synonymous:

(138) a. Juan cree   que José no ha   llegado.
          J.   believes that J.   not has(ind.) arrived
          "Juan believes that José hasn't arrived."
       b. Juan no cree   que José haya   llegado.
          J.   not believes that J.   has(subj.) arrived
          "Juan doesn't believe that José has arrived."

As noted in Bosque (1980), the class of predicates which exhibit this phenomenon is not language-particular. It includes predicates of opinion, expectation, intention and volition, and of "perceptive approximation" (*seem, be likely*) – although individual lexical items may vary somewhat across languages. The phenomenon has been analyzed transformationally as involving "Neg-raising" from the subordinate to the higher clause. As Bosque's discussion indicates however, a movement analysis is problematic in various respects. The issue remains as to why these particular clausal arguments are interpreted as within the scope of the governing negation, while other complement clauses are not.

Multiple negation is possible, both in "Neg-raising" constructions and in simple sentences, although the latter is somewhat marginal, and is restricted to sentences with auxiliary-main verb sequences.[53] Multiple negation produces positive polarity:

---

[53] Spanish does not generally admit counterparts to English double negation supported by adverbs such as *really, exactly*:

(i)   ?*No exactamente no llueve.
          not exactly   not rains
       "It's not exactly not raining."

(139)   Juan no creía   que Pedro no   llegara.
        J.   not believed that P.   not arrived-subj.
        "Juan didn't believe that Pedro didn't arrive."

(140)   Susana no estaba no   estudiando la   lección.
        S.   not was   not studying   the lesson
        "Susana wasn't not studying the lesson."

1.4.6   Copular sentences: Ser and Estar

Both *ser* and *estar* are copular verbs meaning "to be." The category of complements possible with *estar*, PP and AP, is a subset of those which are possible with *ser*:

(141)   Complements of *ser*:
        a. ___ CP (clefts):
           Lo que piensa es [que debe practicar].
           "What she thinks is [that she should practice]."
        b. ___ DP (equational sentences):
           El siete es [un número impar].
           "Seven is [an odd number]."
        c. ___ NP (predicate nominals):
           María es [doctora].
           "Maria is (a) [doctor]."
        d. ___ AP:
           Susana es [alta].
           "Susana is [tall]."
        e. ___ PP:
           La reunión es [a las ocho].
           "The meeting is at eight o'clock."

(142)   Complements of *estar*:
        a. __ PP
           El lápiz está [en la mesa].
           "The pencil is on the table."
        b. __ AP
           Susana está [alta].
           "Susana is tall."

In many cases, the partition between *ser* and *estar* corresponds with the distinction between "individual-level" predicates and "stage-level" predicates. The former ascribe permanent qualities or properties, and the latter ascribe transient properties. Analyzing *estar* as the copula for stage-level predicates would account both for the narrower categorial selection of *estar*, for its use with locative PPs, and for the interpretation of adjectives which occur with it. For example the adjective *alta* "tall" in (141d) is understood as an individual characteristic of Susana; the adjective *alta* in (142b) is not interpreted as an individual-level property, but as a changed (recent) property, or a subjective attribution.

However, Sánchez and Camacho (1995) point out problems with this description of the partition. For example, *ser* is used with predicates of temporary condition such as expression of the time of day (e.g. (141e)) and the season. They explore the hypothesis that the basic distinction between the two is aspectual. The descriptive generalization which emerges is that *estar* is an inchoative predicate, while *ser* has no aspectual properties, and is transparent to those of its complements.

1.5   Main clauses

Main clauses may have different grammatical properties according to whether they function as declaratives, interrogatives (questions), imperatives (commands) or exclamatives. This section presents a brief overview of grammatical features that are particular to each of these types.

1.5.1   Declaratives

The constituents of declarative clauses have been described above. As noted previously, pronominal subjects are normally silent, and overt subjects may either precede the predicate or follow it. The order of constituents in declaratives is not fixed according to grammatical function (subject–predicate order), but may instead be determined in large part by the information load that constituents have in the discourse. To see this, consider first that unmarked order of constituents in declaratives may follow either of the patterns in (143):

(143)   a. Subject – Predicate
          b. (XP) – Predicate – Subject

In (143b), (XP) is an optional constituent other than the subject, such as the modifier in (144b):

(144)   a. Susana leyó el   diario esta mañana.
            S.   read the paper this morning
          b. **Esta mañana** leyó el   diario Susana.
            this morning read the paper S.

The fact that both orders are equally acceptable leads to several questions. First among these is whether, descriptively, Spanish should be analyzed as having a basic S-V-O order from which other orders are derived.

It has been argued in pre-generative as well as recent generative studies that an important concept that is relevant for determining constituent order in declarative sentences is the distinction between *presupposed* and *asserted* information (cf. Chapter 5, Section 5.2). Presupposed information is shared, or known, by the speaker and hearer. Asserted information is not. Other terms for this distinction are old (or given) versus new information, Theme versus Rheme, Topic versus Focus (or Comment). The mechanisms which derive surface order appear to be sensitive to the information content of clausal constituents. For example, the XP which precedes the predicate in (143b) may be a presupposed constituent (a Topic), as illustrated in (145a), or a Focus constituent, as in (145b):

(145)   a. [Susana]$_{TOPIC}$ [leyó el   diario esta mañana]$_{FOCUS}$.
                S.   read the paper this morning
          b. [Esta mañana]$_{FOCUS}$ [leyó el   diario Susana]$_{TOPIC}$.
             this morning   read the paper S.

Sentence (145a) illustrates a situation in which Susana is the Topic of the discourse, and the predicate contributes new information about her. Sentence (145b) illustrates a situation in which the speaker and hearer know that Susana has read the paper; the newly asserted information is that it was this morning that she read it. The intonation pattern of the sentence distinguishes between the two meanings. In both sentences, the Focus constituent contains the intonational peak (or main sentence stress). In (145a), this falls within the predicate; in (145b) it falls within the XP *esta mañana*.

The preceding discussion implies that the syntactic component of the grammar can be sensitive to features corresponding to information content, rather than to features related to subjecthood, as would be true of "fixed" word order languages like English or French. The freedom of position of the subject (see Section 1.3.1) may follow from the fact that the subject constituent may be either presupposed or asserted in most sentences, allowing derivations like those in (145a) or (145b). This generalization is supported by the fact that certain predicates have subjects that are not freely interpreted as presupposed, and the surface position of the subject is more restricted. (See Hatcher 1956, Contreras 1978, Suñer 1982 and references cited.) *Presentational predicates* are those which, as part of their meaning, introduce the existence or presence of the subject into the discourse. These predicates are not expected to have derivations corresponding to (145a). This is shown in a neutral context (146a), where no constituent is presupposed:

(146)   a. ¿Qué   pasó?
             What happened?

    b. Empezó la   resistencia.   (presentational)
       began   the resistance
       "The resistance began."
    c. ??La resistencia empezó.
    d. Salió   el   sol.   (presentational)
       came out the sun
       "The sun came out."
    e. ??El sol salió.

In (146b), the order V-S is the unmarked one for the presentational interpretation of the predicate. The entire sentence is understood as Focus (asserted). In (146c), the subject appears to the left of the verb, and the subject is analyzed as either the Topic, as in (145a), or a Focus constituent, with the predicate presupposed. Neither of these interpretations is compatible with the presentational interpretation, which asserts both the subject and predicate. Similarly, (146d) is presentational, but (146e) is not. The disfavored orders are perfectly grammatical in other contexts, where the predicate can be interpreted non-presentationally.

    In Chapter 5, the derivation of pre-verbal constituents in declaratives will be discussed in detail.

1.5.2 Interrogatives

    Direct questions include yes/no questions and *constituent questions*. Yes/no questions may be marked only by intonation, or by intonation and constituent order:

(147)   a. ¿Está María en casa?
            is   M.   at home
         b. ¿María está en casa?
            M.   is   at home?

The intonation of both sentences is distinct from declaratives, in that the tone remains level or rises after the main sentential stress, rather than falling, as in declaratives.

    Constituent questions, discussed briefly above in 1.2.5, normally display overt movement of an interrogative constituent (*Wh-phrase*) to clause-initial position. The subject must be post-verbal, unless the Wh-phrase is an adjunct (modifier) of a certain type. If the Wh-phrase is a modifier, the subject may be pre-verbal:

(148)   a. ¿Qué leyó Juan?
            what read J.
            "What did Juan read?"
         b. *¿Qué Juan leyó?

(149)   a. ¿Por qué Juan dice eso?
           why   J.   says that?
           "Why does Juan say that?"
        b. ¿Por qué dice Juan eso?
           why   says J.   that

(150)   a. ¿En qué medida la constitución ha contribuido a eso?
           in what way   the constitution has contributed to that
           "In what way has the constitution contributed to that?"
        b. ¿En qué medida ha contribuido a eso la constitución?
           in what way   has contributed to that the constitution

Multiple interrogatives are fully grammatical; one interrogative constituent moves to clause-initial position, others remain in-situ.[54]

One issue that has received attention in recent research concerns the derived position of the verb in interrogatives. Suñer (1994) has observed that the verb is not in the same position as in English, because other phrases can intervene between the Wh-phrase and the verb:

(151)   ¿A quién jamás ofenderías tú con tus acciones?
        PA whom never offend-cond. you with your actions
        "Who(m) would you never offend with your actions?"

(152)   ¿Qué idioma todavía estudia Pepita en su tiempo libre?
                                 (Suñer 1994:345)
        which language still   studies P.   in her time   free
        "Which language does Pepita still study in her free time?"

Since even the subject can precede the verb in examples like (149) and (150) above, the verb appears to be at some distance from the preposed Wh-phrase:

(153)   a. Wh-phrase (adverb) – Verb . . .
        b. Wh-phrase (subject) – Verb . . .

Wh-phrases have the same pattern of clitic-doubling as do other non-pronominal phrases. That is, Wh-phrases corresponding to indirect objects have a clitic double (see 1.2.4.), but those corresponding to direct objects do not. (See 1.7 for discussion of dialect variation.)

---

[54] Interrogative constituents also remain in-situ with a non-echo interpretation if the Wh-phrase is contained within an "island" – a syntactic constituent from which movement is impossible Arnaiz (1996). One type of island is the adjunct clause:

    (i).   a. ¿Juan llegaría [antes de saludar a quién]?
            J.   arrive-cond. before of greet-inf. PA who?
            "Juan would arrive before greeting whom?"
         b. ¿*A quién llegaría Juan [antes de saludar]?
            PA who arrive-cond. J.   before of greet-inf.
            "Who would Juan arrive before greeting?"

(154)   a. ¿Qué (*lo)   leyó Juan?
                what CL(Acc.) read J.
         b. ¿A quién (*lo)   vio Juan?
             PA whom CL(Acc.) saw J.
             "Whom did Juan see?"

Preposition stranding is never possible. Interrogatives within Prepositional Phrases move as a phrase:

(155)   a. ¿[Con quién] habló Susana?
             with whom spoke S.
             "With whom did Susana speak?"
         b. *¿Quién habló Susana con?
             whom spoke S.   with
             "Whom did Susana speak with?"

Chapter 6 discusses interrogatives, focusing primarily on the derived position of the Wh-phrase, the subject, and the verb.

1.5.3   Imperatives

Imperatives may be any person/number except first person singular. Positive and negative imperatives have distinct forms and syntax. Negative commands are identical to Present tense subjunctive forms, and show the same person/number endings as other verb forms:

(156)   Cantar "sing" Negative Imperative forms (=pr. subjunctive):
         a.   1st.pl.   No cant-emos
         b. 2nd.sg.   No cant-es   2nd.pl.   No cant-éis
         c. 3rd.sg.   No cant-e   3rd.pl.   No cant-en

The order of negation and clitics is the same as for other finite verb forms, with clitics preceding the verb:

(157)   No se   lo   mande.
         not CL(Dat.) CL(Acc.) send-I.
         "Don't send it to him/her."

Positive imperatives have unique forms in the second person, while the first and third person forms are identical to Present subjunctive forms:

(158) Cantar "sing" Positive Imperative forms:
         a.   1st.sg.   cant-emos
         b. 2nd.sg.   cant-a   2nd.pl.   cant-ad
         c. 3rd.sg.   cant-e   3rd.pl.   cant-en

In the 2nd person singular, the person ending -s is absent, and rather than a subjunctive form, the desinence is identical to the third person singular

Present indicative.[55] In the second person plural, the -*d* is unique to the imperative. Positive imperatives precede clitics:

(159)   a. ¡Cántalo!
             sing+CL(Acc.)
             "Sing it!"
          b. ¡Mándeselo!
             send+CL(Dat.)+CL(Acc.)
             "Send it to him/her!"

Imperatives exclude stative predicates and auxiliaries. Subject pronouns may be overt, but cannot precede the verb, unless separated by a pause.

Desideratives are expressions of wish or hope, formed with the Present or Past (counterfactual) subjunctive. The clause is introduced either by the complementizer *que* or by the expression *ojalá* (etymologically derived from an expression meaning "may Allah will it"). This phrase is optionally followed by *que*:

(160)   a. (Ojalá) que tengan   buen viaje.
                       that have-pr.subj.3rd.pl. good trip
             "May they have a good trip."
          b. (Ojalá) que estuvieran   aquí.
                       that be-pa.subj.3rd.pl. here
             "I wish that they were here."

1.5.4 Exclamatives

Exclamatives include the constituents shown in (161), where the initial XP is the focus of exclamation:

(161)   XP – (*que*) – V – (Subj.)

Que is the complementizer, and its distribution depends on the nature of the focus XP. The verb precedes the subject in exclamatives.

Adjectival and adverbial phrases in the XP position may be specified by *qué/cuán* "how" or by *lo*, the neuter determiner/pronominal, with degree interpretation:

(162)   a. ¡Qué/cuán lista   (que) es Miriam!
                how   smart (that) is M.
             "How smart Miriam is!"

[55] For first and second conjugation verbs, the indicative (third person singular) form is identical to the infinitive with its conjugation class or "theme"-vowel, minus the final consonant -*r*. Third conjugation verbs differ in this vowel, and show that the imperative is formed on the indicative. For example, *escribir* "to write," *escribe* "he/she writes," escrib-**e** "write!"

    b. ¡Lo   lista * (que) es Miriam!
       neut. smart that   is M. (=162a)

(163)   a. ¡Qué/cuan rápido (que) escribe Susana!
            how   quickly (that) writes S.
            "How quickly Susana writes!"
         b. ¡Lo   rápido *(que) escribe Susana!
            neut. quickly that   writes S. (=163a)

Adverbials of quantity in the XP position are expressed as *cómo/cuánto* "how/how much" or as *lo*. As in the preceding examples, *lo* requires that *que* be overt:

(164)   a. ¡Cómo/cuánto (que) escribe Juan!
            how (much)   (that) writes J.
            "How (much) Juan writes!"
         b. ¡Lo *(que) escribe Juan!
            neut. that writes J. (=164a)

Quantified NPs in the XP constituent are introduced by *cuántos/cuántas* "how many." In peninsular and some Latin American dialects, the quantified NP can be introduced by *qué* "what," or the feminine determiner *la*:

(165)   a. ¡Cuántos   premios (que) ganó Susana!
            how many prizes   (that) won S.
            "How many prizes Susana won!"
         b. ¡Qué de premios (que) ganó Susana!
            what of prizes   (that) won S.
            "What (a lot) of prizes Susana won!"
         c. ¡La de premios *(que) ganó Susana.
            the of prizes   that won S.
            "The (amount) of prizes Susana won!"

As the preceding examples show, *que* is optional where XP contains a form equivalent to the interrogative. *Que* is required where neuter *lo* or feminine *la* appears in XP. Note that the final two examples in (165) contain partitive NPs (introduced by *de*). The partitive form, as well as the feminine form of the determiner in (165c), suggests that the head of the NP is a non-overt feminine noun *cantidad* "quantity."

1.6   Subordinate clauses

1.6.1   *Argument clauses*

Argument clauses, sometimes called "nominal clauses," function as subject or complement (direct, indirect or prepositional) of a governing predicate. The complementizer *que* "that" precedes declarative subordinate clauses if the clause is finite (subjunctive or indicative). Infinitival clauses have no overt complementizer:

(166)   a. Quieren   [*(que) Sandra vaya   pronto].
                 want-pr.3rd.pl. that S.   go-pr.subj. soon
                 "They want *(that) Sandra go soon."
        b. Quieren   [(*que) ir   pronto].
                 want-pr.3rd.pl. that go-inf. soon
                 "They want (*that) to go soon."

Campos (1993:63) observes that clauses which are complements of certain verbs (of fear, will and desire) allow omission of *que*, but only if there is no overt pre-verbal subject:

(167)   a. Temo   [estén   enojados].
                 fear-pr.1st.sg. be-pr.subj.3rd.pl. angry
                 "I'm afraid (they) are angry."
        b. *Temo   [ellos estén   enojados].
                 fear-pr.1st.sg. they be-pr.subj.3rd.pl. angry

Complementizer omission is subject to dialectal variation and to varied judgments according to register. For some speakers, (167a) is impossible in colloquial Spanish.

Argument clauses may contain an indirect question or exclamative if the governing predicate so selects:

(168)   Me pregunto   [(que) por qué salió   María].
             CL wonder-pr.1st.sg. (that) why   leave-pa.3rd.sg. M.
             "I wonder (that) why Maria left."

(169)   Mira [qué alta   (que) estás].
             look-I how   tall (that) be-pr.2nd.sg.
             "Look at how tall (that) you are!"

Notice in both (168) and (169) the complementizer *que* is optional. In (169) the complementizer follows the XP focus of exclamation. This mirrors the pattern for direct exclamations discussed in the previous subsection. The pattern in (168), however, differs from direct questions, where the complementizer does not surface.[56]

Argument clauses exhibit case markers (prepositions) parallel to corresponding NP arguments. Subject clauses are never preceded by prepositions,

---

[56] Plann (1982) shows that under certain verbs of communication such as *decir* "say," the overt complementizer is necessary for a true interrogative interpretation. Under such verbs, if *que* is suppressed, the interpretation is pseudo-interrogative.

nor are clauses which occur as direct objects of a verb, in standard dialects.[57] Clauses which function as the indirect object of a verb are preceded by the Dative preposition *a*. These clauses are not clitic-doubled:

(170)   (*Le)   obligaron   a   Pedro [a   terminar el
         proyecto].
         CL(Dat.) obliged-pa.3rd.pl. PA P.   to(Dat.) finish-inf. the
         project
         "They forced Pedro to finish the project."

Clauses which are complements of adjectives and nouns are preceded by *de* "of," parallel to NP counterparts:

(171)   a. Patricio está orgulloso *(de) su hermana.
            P.   is   proud *(of)   his sister.
         b. Patricio está orgulloso *(de) que su hermana hizo   un gol en
            P.   is   proud (*of)   that his sister   made a goal in
            ese partido.
            that game
            "Patricio is proud (*of) [that his sister scored a goal in that game]."

1.6.2   Relative clauses

Relative clauses, traditionally called adjective clauses (because they function as modifiers of nouns), have been analyzed as sharing certain basic properties with interrogatives. Compare (172a), (172b):

(172)   a. ¿A   quién conoció Juan?
            PA whom met   J.
            "Whom did Juan meet?"
         b. la persona [a   quien conoció Juan][58]
            the person PA whom met   J.
            "the person whom Juan met"

In (172a), the interrogative *a quién* is understood as the complement of the verb, and fills a "gap" corresponding to the missing complement. Likewise, in (172b), the relativized phrase *a quien* is related to a direct object gap within the relative clause. The central difference between the two constructions, of course, is that the relative pronoun has an antecedent, *la persona*, while interrogative

[57] In some dialects, the preposition *de* "of" is inserted before clauses which are direct complements of verbs. This phenomenon, called *dequeísmo*, is considered substandard.

[58] By convention, the interrogative forms are orthographically differentiated by an accent on the stressed syllable when they are homophonous with relative pronouns or the complementizer *que*. The convention does not signify a difference in strong versus weak (clitic) status.

phrases do not. Consequently, the manner in which reference is derived differs in the two constructions.

There are two significant grammatical differences between interrogatives and relative clauses in Spanish. One concerns constituent order, illustrated in (173):

(173)   a. *¿A quién Juan vio?
             PA whom J.   saw
             "Whom did Juan see?"
          b. la persona [a   quien Juan vio]
             the person   PA   whom   J.   saw

As noted previously, sentences with interrogatives corresponding to arguments of the verb require subject–verb inversion; as shown in (173b), relatives do not.

The second difference concerns the form (including overtness) of relativized constituents, as opposed to corresponding interrogative phrases. The form of relativized constituents varies depending on: (a) whether the relative clause is restrictive or non-restrictive, (b) the grammatical function of the relative phrase within the relative clause, and (c) the features (gender, number, definiteness and, in some cases, [$\pm$HUMAN]) of the antecedent. The following discussion will summarize properties of relatives with overt antecedents, where the relativized constituent corresponds to an argument.[59]

Consider first a restrictive relative in which the relativized phrase is the subject of the relative clause:

(174)   a. el hombre [que   trabaja aquí]
             the man   that works here
          b. *el hombre [quien trabaja aquí]
             the man   who   works here

The relative pronoun *quien* is impossible as subject; this contrasts with the relativized object above in (173b), and also with the relativized subject of a non-restrictive relative:

(175)   ese hombre, [quien/que trabaja   aquí]
          that man,   who/that work-pr.3rd.sg. here
          "that man, who/*that works here"

For some speakers, *quien* is preferred in non-restrictive relative clauses.

Direct object relativization of a [+HUMAN] argument has the forms in (176):

_____

[59] For discussion of other relative clause types, including infinitival relatives and free relatives, see Campos (1993:97ff.), Plann (1980).

(176)   a. el   hombre [**que** conocí   ayer]
              the man   that meet-pa.1sg. yesterday
              "the man that I met yesterday"
        b. el   hombre [**a   quien**   conocí   ayer]
              the man   PA whom-sg. meet-pa.1sg. yesterday
              "the man whom I met yesterday"
        c. el   hombre [**al   que** conocí ayer]
              the man   PA+the that met.1sg. yesterday
              "the man that I met yesterday"
        d. el   hombre [**al   cual** conocí   ayer]
              the man   PA+the which meet-pa.-1st.sg. yesterday
              "the man that I met yesterday"

Notice in (176a) that *que* is not preceded by personal *a*, but other forms in
(176) are. This suggests that (176a) contains a covert form of *a quien*, and that
que is the complementizer. For some speakers, non-restrictive relatives pattern
the opposite way, disallowing covert *a quien*:

(177)   esos hombres, [a   quienes conocí   ayer]
        those men,   PA whom meet-pa.1st.sg. yesterday
        "Those men, that I met yesterday"

(178)   (*)esos hombres, [que conocí   ayer] (=177)
             those men   that meet-pa.1st.sg. yesterday

The relative forms in (176) are not sensitive to the definiteness of the antecedent (cf. *un hombre que conocí* "a man that I met"; *un hombre a quien conocí*
"a man whom I met").[60]

Recall that the Spanish definite determiners show number/gender agreement. In sentences whose antecedent is invariant with respect to
number/gender features (e.g., algo "something," *nada* "nothing") the neuter

---

[60] None of the relative constructions are sensitive to Case-matching of the gap with
    the antecedent. In the following examples, Accusative/Nominative and Nominative
    /Accusative are paired:

    (i)   El   hombre [al   que conocí   ayer]   presentó su
          trabajo hoy.
          the man   PA+the that meet-pa.1st.sg. yesterday   presented his
          paper today
          "The man that I met yesterday presented his paper today."
    (ii) Esta mañana conocí   al   hombre que presentó su trabajo
          ayer
          this morning meet-pa.1st.sg. PA+the man   that presented his paper
          yesterday
          "This morning I met the man that presented his paper yesterday."

form *lo* replaces the definite article (cf. *No dijo nada con lo cual yo esté de acuerdo* "He didn't say anything with [*lo+*] which I agree").

Restrictive relativization of [-HUMAN] direct objects requires *que*; personal *a* is absent, and forms with *quien, el que* and *el cual* are impossible:

(179)　　a. el　cuaderno [que　Juan perdió]
　　　　　　the notebook　that　J.　　lost
　　　　　b. *el　cuaderno [al/el　　　que Juan perdió]
　　　　　　the notebook　PA+the/the　that J.　　lost
　　　　　c. *el　cuaderno [al/el　　　cual　Juan perdió]
　　　　　　the notebook　PA+the/ the　which Juan lost

(180)　　a. *un cuaderno [el　que Juan perdió]
　　　　　　a　notebook　the that J.　　lost
　　　　　b. *un cuaderno [el　cual Juan perdió]
　　　　　　a　notebook　the that J.　　lost

Relative constituents corresponding to indirect objects and other prepositional phrases require a preposition. An unspecified covert relative pronoun is possible only with [-HUMAN] antecedents; compare (181d), (182):

(181)　　a. la　persona　　[de quien hablamos]
　　　　　　the person-f.sg. of whom speak-pa.1st.pl
　　　　　　"the person of whom we spoke"
　　　　　b. la　persona　　[de la　　que hablamos]
　　　　　　the person-f.sg. of the-f.sg. that speak-pa.1st.pl.
　　　　　　"the person that we spoke of"
　　　　　c. la　persona　　[de la　　cual　hablamos]
　　　　　　the person-f.sg. of the-f.sg. which speak-pa.1st.pl.
　　　　　　"the person that we spoke of"
　　　　　d. *la　persona　　[de que hablamos]
　　　　　　the person-f.sg. of that speak-pa.1st.pl.
　　　　　　"the person that we spoke of"

(182)　　a. la　cuestión　[de que hablamos]
　　　　　　the issue-f.sg. of that speak-pa.1st.pl.
　　　　　　"the issue that we spoke of"
　　　　　b. la　cuestión　[de la　　que hablamos]
　　　　　　the issue-f.sg. of the-f.sg. that speak-pa.1st.pl.
　　　　　　"the issue that we spoke of"
　　　　　c. la　cuestión　[de la　　cual　hablamos]
　　　　　　the issue-f.sg. of the-f.sg. which speak-pa.1st.pl.
　　　　　　"the issue that we spoke of"

As in other constructions, the indirect object generally requires a clitic double, e.g. *la persona [a la que *(le) mandé la carta]* "the person to whom I sent the letter."

Relativization of possessives is shown in (183). The relative pronoun agrees in number and gender with the object possessed, rather than with the antecedent:[61]

(183)   a. el   hombre [cuya   esposa   está en Cuba]
            the man   whose-f.sg. wife-f.sg. is   in Cuba
            "the man whose wife is in Cuba"
         b. el   artículo   [a cuyos   autores   conocí
            ayer]
            the article-m.sg PA whose-m.pl. authors-m.pl. meet-pa.1st.sg.
            yesterday
            "the article whose authors I met yesterday"
         c. el   curso   [para cuyos   exámenes estudiaron   mucho]
            the course-m.sg. for whose-m.pl. exams   study-pa.3rd.pl. a lot
            "the course for whose exams they studied a lot"

The selection of subjunctive versus indicative mood in relative clauses depends on features of the antecedent. Non-existing, negated and non-specific antecedents trigger a subjunctive relative clause; otherwise the relative clause is indicative. This is illustrated below for a negative antecedent (184a), which triggers subjunctive, versus an indefinite specific antecedent (184b), which triggers indicative:

(184)   a. No conozco   (a) nadie   que hable   diez
            idiomas.
            not know-pr.1st.sg. PA anybody that speak-pr.**subj.**3rd.sg. ten
            languages
            "I don't know anyone who speaks ten languages."
         b. Conozco   a   alguien   que hab**la**   diez idiomas.
            know-pr.1st.sg. PA someone that speak-pr.ind.3rd.sg ten languages
            "I know someone that speaks ten languages."

1.6.3   Temporal adjunct clauses

Finite temporal clauses introduce secondary relationships of ordering between events. A simple finite main clause expresses a relation between the occurrence of a state or event and a deictic moment "now," often referred to as "Speech-time," following Reichenbach (1947). For example, in (185),

(185)   María cantó/canta/cantará el sabado.
         M.   sang/sings/will sing Saturday.

[61] There is also a possessive relative with *que su* instead of *cuyo*:

    (i)   el   artículo que sus   autores los conocí   ayer
           the article   that their authors CL meet-pret.1st.sg. yesterday
           "the article whose authors I met yesterday"

the event of Maria's singing precedes, coincides with or follows Speech-time. Temporal adjunct clauses do not alter or further specify the tense interpretation of the simple clause, but instead order the event in relation to other events:

(186)　a. María cantó antes de que llegáramos.
　　　　M.　　sang before of that arrive-pa.subj.1st.pl.
　　　　"Maria sang before we arrived."
　　　　b. María cantó mientras escribía.
　　　　M.　　sang while　　write-pr.ind.3rd.sg.
　　　　"Maria sang while he/she wrote."
　　　　c. María cantó después de que llegamos.
　　　　M.　　sang after　　of that arrive-pa.ind.1st.pl.
　　　　"Maria sang after we arrived."

The clauses in (186) exhibit sequence-of-tense, that is both clauses bear a [+PAST] tense. Although Spanish differentiates present and future tense morphology, sequence-of-tense requires only agreement with respect to [±PAST]:

(187)　a. María cantará mientras escribo.
　　　　M.　　sing-fut. while　　write-pr.ind.1st.sg.
　　　　"Maria will sing while I write."
　　　　b. *María cantará después de que salí.
　　　　M.　　sing-fut. after　　of that leave-pa.ind.1st.sg.
　　　　"María will sing after I left."

Temporal clauses may also express an ordering relationship between an event's onset or end and a secondary event:

(188)　a. Estudian　　　　　español desde hace　　　　　un año.
　　　　study-pr.ind.3rd.pl. Spanish since do-pr.ind.3rd.sg. one year
　　　　"They have studied Spanish for a year."
　　　　b. Conozco　　　　a Susana desde mi niñez.
　　　　know-pr.ind.1st.sg. PA S.　　since my childhood
　　　　"I've known Susana since my childhood."

In (188), the temporal clause specifies a time which marks the onset of the main clause activity or state. In the following example, the endpoint of the main clause event is modified by the temporal clause:

(189)　No acepto　　　　　la propuesta hasta que me　　　escuches.
　　　　not accept-pr.ind.1st.sg. the proposal　until that CL(Dat.) listen-
　　　　pr.subj.2nd.sg.
　　　　"I won't accept the proposal until you listen to me."

In (189), the time of the event of the temporal clause marks the end of the predicate *no acepto la propuesta*.[62] A similar interpretation results if the temporal clause is introduced by *mientras (que)* "as long as":

(190)   No acepto   la propuesta mientras (que) no me
         escuches.
         not accept-pr.ind.1st.sg. the proposal   while   that not CL(Dat.)
         listen-pr.subj.2nd.sg.
         "I won't accept the proposal as long as you don't listen to me."

In (190) as in (189), the time at which *me escuches* "you listen to me" occurs marks the termination of not accepting the proposal.

1.6.4   Gerundive and participial adjuncts

Gerundive clauses contain a verb in the form of a present participle, i.e., bearing the non-agreeing affix *-ndo* "*-ing*." The participle appears in clause-initial position:

(191)   a. habiendo terminado la   reunión
            have-prt. finish-pprt. the meeting
            "having finished the meeting"
         b. *la reunión habiendo terminado

The predicate of gerundive clauses may contain any elements normally possible for non-finite verb phrases, including a full range of auxiliaries, negation, subject-oriented adverbs and clitics. As in other constructions, clitics follow the non-finite verb:[63]

(192)   a. leyéndolo   cuidadosamente
            read-prt.+CL(Acc.) carefully
            "reading it carefully"
         b. *lo leyendo cuidadosamente

---

[62] By inference the polarity of the main clause is reversed at the point in time marked by (the completion of) the adjunct clause event. For further discussion of negation in Italian counterparts to these contexts see Tovena (1996).

[63] The occurrence of clitics shows that the verb is not nominalized. Clitics do not occur with derived nominals:

(i)   a. María lo   leyó.
            M.   CL(Acc.) read
            "Maria read it."
         b. su lectura   del   poema
            her reading-f.sg. of+the poem
            "her reading of the poem"
         c. *su lo   lectura
            her CL(Acc.)   reading
            "her reading it"

Overt subjects of gerundives are Nominative, never Genitive, and must be post-verbal:

(193)   a. estando tú   en la   sala
            be-prt. you(Nom.) in the room
            "you being in the room"
         b. *tú estando en la sala
         c. *estando tuyo   en la   sala
            be-prt. your(Gen.) in the room
            "your being in the room"

As adjuncts, gerundive clauses may be more or less closely linked to the main predicate. In the following examples, "#" represents obligatory pause intonation:

(194)   a. Fuimos   a cenar [hablando de la   película].
            go-pa.1st.pl. to dine   speak-prt. of the film
            "We went to eat talking about the film."
         b. Fuimos   a cenar# habiendo salido   el   sol.
            go-pa.1st.pl. to dine   have-prt. come-out the sun
            "We went to eat, the sun having come out."

In sentence (194a), which does not require pause intonation, the subjects of the clauses are coreferential and the event of the gerundive clause temporally includes the event of the main clause. The gerundive clause in (194a) might be described as a subject-oriented secondary predicate. In (194b), the subjects of the two clauses are not coreferential, and the adjunct event does not (necessarily) temporally include the main clause event.

Participial clauses, like gerundive clauses, contain a clause-initial participle and a Nominative subject. However, the participle in this instance is a past participle, and these participles show number/gender agreement with the subject:

(195)   a. terminada   la   reunión
            finish-pprt.f.sg. the meeting-f.sg.
            "the meeting finished"
         b. *la reunión terminada[64]
         c. *[terminado   la   reunión]
            finish-pprt.m.sg. the meeting-f.sg.

As (195b) shows, the subject cannot precede the participle; failure of agreement in (195c) is also ungrammatical.

Participial clause predicates do not display full Verb Phrase structure. The

[64] Bello ((1847) 1971:315, para.1178e) notes that the subject may in exceptional cases precede the participle, as in *Esto dicho* "that said."

participle may not be negated, it does not bear clitics, and auxiliaries are not possible:

(196) a. *[No terminado el proyecto], Juan siguió trabajando.
          not finish-pprt. the project, J. continued working
       b. *mandádole el paquete (a Juan)
          send-pprt.-CL(Dat.) the package (to(Dat.) Juan)
       c. *habido terminado el proyecto
          have-pprt. finish-pprt. the project
       d. *sido publicado el artículo
          be-pprt. publish-pprt. the article

Number/gender agreement makes participial clauses appear to be formed on the passive rather than the past participle. The verbs which appear in participial clauses, however, include both those which can be passivized and others which cannot. Perfective predicates, those which effect a change of state or location which delimits the event, can appear in participial clauses. Example (197) illustrates the contrast between transitive predicates with affected and those with non-affected arguments:

(197) a. vendidas las flores
          sell-pprt.f.pl. the flower-f.pl.
       b. pintada la casa
          paint-pprt.f.sg the house-f.sg.
       c. roto el vaso
          break-pprt.m.sg. the glass-m.sg.
       d. ?vista María
          see-pprt.f.sg. M.
       e. ?reconocido el extranjero
          recognize-pprt.m.sg. the foreigner-m.sg.
       f. *amada María
          love-pprt.f.sg. M.

A similar contrast is observed among unaccusative verbs (those verbs whose subjects behave as though they are generated as objects). Participial clauses may be formed only on those verbs which effect a change of state or location:

(198) a. ?venidos los huéspedes
          came-pprt.m.pl. the guest-m.pl.
       b. ?llegados los estudiantes
          arrive-pprt.m.pl. the student-m.pl.
       c. ?salida María
          leave-pprt.f.sg. M.
       d. *faltados los comestibles
          lack-pprt.m.pl. the foodstuff-m.pl.
       e. *quedadas las tortillas
          remain-pprt.f.pl. the tortilla-f.pl.

Participial clauses are temporally related to the main predicate, albeit indirectly. The participial clause describes a state which precedes the onset of the main clause event. However, this temporal connection is not strict. Consider for example (199):

(199)   [Vendido   el   coche],   salimos   a   celebrar.
        sell-pprt.m.sg. the car-m.sg. go(out)-pa.1st.pl. to celebrate-inf.
        "[The car sold], we went out to celebrate."

The event of selling the car precedes (and triggers) the event of going out to celebrate. However, the two events seem to be independent of each other, at least in the sense that they are viewed as distinct intervals, rather than as parts of a single interval. There are arbitrarily many other events that could occur between the two.

1.6.5   Infinitival adjuncts

Infinitival adjunct clauses are complements of prepositions, a "upon; on," de "of," con "with" and sin "without":

(200)   a. [Al   encontrar el   artículo], lo leí.
           on+the find-inf.   the article CL(Acc.) read
           "On finding the article, I read it."
        b. [De venir   María], haremos   paella.
           of come-inf. M.   make-fut.1st.pl. paella
           "If Maria comes, we'll make paella."
        c. [Con protestar   tú], no ganan   nada.
           with protest-inf. you not gain-pr.3rd.pl. anything
           "With you protesting, they won't gain anything."
        d. [Sin   saberlo   yo], los niños   salieron   a la calle.
           without know-inf.CL I   the children go-pa.3rd.pl. to the street
           "Without my knowing it, the children went out in to the street."

Clauses introduced by a (which is contracted with determiner el to form al) are temporal or aspectual modifiers of the main clause. For some speakers, they may also express cause. The event of the infinitival clause precedes the onset of the event of the main clause (or causes it). The infinitival event must be non-stative, if it is a temporal modifier, as in (201a); if it is a causal modifier, a stative is possible, as in (201b):

(201)   a. *[Al   parecer   que iba   a llover], nos quedamos   en casa.
             on+the seem-inf. that go-pa. to rain   CL stay.pa.1st.pl. at home
             "On seeming that it was going to rain, we stayed home."
        b. [Al   ser francés Juan], no le pidieron   pasaporte.
           on+the be French J.,   neg. CL ask.pret.3rd.pl. passport
           "As Juan is French, they didn't ask for his passport."

When the subject of the adjunct is not overt, it may be understood as coreferential with the main clause subject. However, coreference is not obligatory, as shown in (202):

(202)   [Al   dejar   de llover]   salimos   a caminar.
        on+the stop-inf. of rain-inf. leave-pa.3rd.pl. to walk-inf.
        "Since it stopped raining, we went out to walk."

The predicates of *a* clauses display characteristics of full Verb Phrase structure, including the possibility of adverbs, clitics and passive morphology:

(203)   a. [Al   ser   publicado   el   artículo], se   lo   mandamos   a
        Julio.
        on+the be-inf. publish.pprt. the article   CL CL send.pret.1st.pl. to
        J.
        "On the article's being published, we sent it to Julio."
        b. [Al   mandárselo   José],   lo   leyó.
        on+the send-inf.+CL(Dat.)-CL(Acc.) J.,   CL read.pret.3rd.sg.
        "On José's sending it to him/her, he/she read it."

Copular verbs are possible, perhaps with a preference for a causal interpretation:

(204)   a. ?[Al   ser piloto (Roberto)] hicimos   un viaje.
        on+the be pilot   make.pret.1st.pl. a trip
        "On (Robert's) being a pilot, we took a trip."
        b. Al   ser piloto Roberto, pudo   salvar   el   avión.
        on+the be pilot   R.   manage.pret. save-inf. the airplane
        "Since Roberto was a pilot, he managed to save the airplane."

De-clauses, as in (200b) above, are conditional in interpretation. These clauses may have overt or non-overt subjects, and coreference between the adjunct and main clause subject is not obligatory:

(205)   [De haber   público], actuaremos.
        of have-inf. audience perform-fut.3rd.pl.
        "If there's an audience, we'll perform."

The predicate of *de*-clauses shows characteristic elements of the Verb Phrase: it may be negated and accepts clitics and auxiliaries: *de no haberlo entendido* "if s/he hasn't understood it."

De-infinitival clauses alternate with relativized degree phrases:

(206)   María se   enfermó   de   lo   mucho que comió.
        M.   CL-(inc.) sicken-pa.3rd.sg. from that much   that eat-pa.3rd.sg.
        "Maria got sick from how much she ate."

The finite clause may have a non-coreferring subject, and may or may not be intonationally separated from the main clause:[65]

(207)   María se   deprimió (#)   de   lo   mucho que llovió.
        M.   CL depress-pa.3rd.sg. from that much that rain-pa.3rd.sg.
        "Maria got depressed from how much it rained."

Infinitivals introduced by *con* are described by Campos (1993:175) as concessives (having a negative conditional "despite" interpretation). They typically co-occur with the adverb *aun* "even," or with a negated main clause:

(208)   [(Aun) con estudiar] no aprendes   mucho.
        even with study-inf. not learn-pr.2nd.sg. a lot
        "Even if you study, you don't learn a lot."

Con-infinitivals admit overt nominative subjects, as shown in (209):

(209)   [Aun con protestar   tú]   no tendrás   éxito.
        even with protest-inf. you(Nom.) not have-fut.2nd.sg. success
        "Even if you protest, you won't succeed."

Non-overt subjects of *con*-infinitivals are necessarily coreferential with that of the modified clause, as shown by the degraded status of (210):

(210)   ?*Aun con hacer buen tiempo, no llegué   a la   oficina a
        tiempo.
           even with make good weather not arrive-pa.1st.sg. to the office on
           time
        "Even with the good weather, I didn't arrive at the office on time."

The predicate of *con*-infinitivals shows characteristics of full Verb Phrase structure, accepting clitics and auxiliaries, as shown in the following example from Campos (1993:175):

(211)   (Aun) con haberse   levantado temprano
        even with have-inf.CL(3rd.sg.) arise-pprt. early
        "(even) having gotten himself up early"

Infinitivals introduced by *sin* "without" alternate with finite clauses. The infinitive is selected if the clausal subjects are coreferential; otherwise a finite clause occurs:

[65] *De* also introduces an adjectival small clause with similar interpretation:

(i)   a. [de   lo   tan contento que estaba]
         from that so happy   that be-pa.3rd.sg.
         "from how happy s/he was"
      b. [de   lo   contento que estaba]
         from that happy   that be-pa.3rd.sg.

(212)   a. Saqué   el   libro [sin   mirarlo].
            take(out)-pa.1st.sg. the book without look(at)-inf.+CL(Acc.)
            "I took out the book without looking at it."
         b. Saqué   el   libro [sin   que Juan lo   mirara].
            take(out)-pa.1st.sg. the book without that J.   CL(Acc.) look(at)-
            pa.subj.3rd.sg.
            "I took out the book without Juan's looking at it."

The predicate of *sin*-infinitivals shows full structure of a verb phrase; the predicate may include auxiliaries and clitics. Because *sin* is a negative element, an additional negation is possible only with contrastive stress:

(213)   ?Sin   NO   conversar, nos entendemos.
         without NOT talking,   we get along.
         "We get along without NOT talking."

1.7   Syntactic dialects

This section summarizes several forms of dialectal variation found in Latin American Spanish, drawing on data summarized in Lipski (1994). Some information on syntactic variation in peninsular dialects is found in Alvar (1996).

1.7.1   Clitic-related variation

Latin American dialects display several variations in the grammar of clitics. In all dialects, pronominal and anaphoric direct object full phrases co-occur with a clitic, which is referred to as a clitic "double":

(214)   a. María lo   vio   a   él.
            M.   CL(Acc.) saw-pa.3rd.sg. PA him(Acc.).
            "Maria saw him."
         b. María se   vio a   sí misma.
            M.   CL(Acc.Refl.) saw PA Acc.refl-3rd.sg.
            "Maria saw herself."

In some dialects, clitic-doubling occurs with non-pronominal direct objects, including inanimate objects, as in (215b):

(215)   a. Lo   conozco   a   Juan.   (Argentina; Lipski 1994:174)
            CL(Acc.) know-1st.sg. PA J.
            "I know Juan."
         b. Tú lo   tienes   la   dirección.
                                            (Bolivia; Lipski 1994:191)
            you CL(Acc.m.sg.) have-2nd.sg. the address(f.sg.)
            "You have the address."

The example cited in (215b) has a non-agreeing clitic double: the clitic has the unmarked masculine singular form, although the full phrase direct object is feminine. Non-agreement of clitics seems to occur commonly in areas of direct object clitic doubling. These are found in the Río de la Plata region of Argentina and Uruguay, in Bolivia, Ecuador, Peru and Mexico. For discussion of direct object clitic doubling, see Jaeggli (1982), Luján (1987), Suñer (1988), Kayne (1994) and references cited.

Another clitic-related phenomenon that overlaps with direct object clitic-doubling is the absence of clitics in contexts where they are normally required, such as preposed phrases, as in (216), and ordinary pronominals, giving rise to "null objects," as in (217):

(216)   Su bebito también [lo]   tenía.   (Perú; Lipski 1994:325)
         her baby   also   [CL(Acc.)] had-imp.3rd.sg.
         "She also had her baby."

(217)   (Aquí están los medicamentos.) ¿Cómo ø   has traído?
                                                  (Bolivia; Lipski 1994:191)
         "Here are   the medicines.   How   have you brought (them)?"

In (217), the antecedent of the null direct object is a definite NP. This type of null object is found in Andean Spanish (Bolivia, Colombia, Ecuador and Perú). In other dialects, the clitic would be required in (217). Null objects are generally possible only if they are indefinite, as in (218b):

(218)   a. ¿Compraste café?
            "You bought coffee?"
         b. Sí,   compré.
            "Yes, I bought (some)."

A third phenomenon related to clitics concerns the use of the direct object clitic as a double with prepositional or clausal complements:

(219)   a. Se   lo   fue   de viaje.   (Honduras Lipski 1994:272)
            CL(refl.) CL(Acc.) went   of trip
            "(S)he left on a trip."
         b. Lo   temo   que se   muera.
                                                 (Nicaragua Lipski 1994:292)
            CL(Acc.) fear-1st.sg. that CL(refl.) die-subj.3rd.sg.
            "I'm afraid that he will die."

The use of clitics as doubles of PPs and clauses has been recorded in northern Latin American regions: Colombia, Honduras, Nicaragua and Mexico.

One final clitic-related phenomenon that Lipski mentions in his survey is the "reduplication" of clitics in contexts where they could appear in one position or another:

(220)   a. No la   he   podido   conocerla.   (Bolivia; Lipski 1994:191)
         not CL(Acc.) have been able know-inf.+CL(Acc.)
         "I haven't been able to meet her."
         b. Me   está castigándome.   (Perú; Lipski 1994:191)
         CL(Acc.) is   punish-prt.+CL(Acc.)
         "(S)he is punishing me."

1.7.2 Negation-related variation

Three types of negation-related variation have been attested in different areas. In the Río de la Plata region of Argentina and Uruguay, pre-verbal negative phrases like nadie "nobody" co-occur with negation:

(221)   Nadie no   está.
         nobody(not) is-pr.3rd.sg.
         "Nobody is there."

As discussed in 1.2.7 above, the co-occurrence of *no* "not" with such phrases is standardly possible only if the negative phrase is post-verbal: *No está nadie*, but *Nadie está* "Nobody is there."

A second negation-related form of variation is the "reduplication" of *no*:

(222)   a. No hablo   inglés   no.
                              (Colombia (Pacific coast) Lipski 1994:215)
         not speak-1st.sg. English not
         "I don't speak English."
         b. Nosotros no   vamos   no.   (Dominican Republic Lipski 1994:242)
         we   not go-1st.pl. not
         "We're not going."

This phenomenon is said in Lipski (1994:242) to be frequent in vernacular Dominican Spanish.

A third type, noted in Bosque (1980), is null negation with *hasta* "until," attested in Colombia and Mexico:

(223)   Vamos hasta que termine.
         go-pret.1st.pl. until that end.pr.subj.3rd.sg.
         "We won't go until it ends."

1.7.3 "Intensive ser"

The phenomenon referred to as the "intensive *ser*" construction is illustrated in (224):

(224)   a. Lo   hice   fue   en el   verano.
                                        (Colombia Lipski 1994:215)
         CL(Acc.) do-pa.3rd.sg. be-pret.3rd.sg. in the summer
         "I did it in the summer."

b. Lo   conocí   fue   en la fiesta.
                                        (Panama Lipski 1994:301)
CL(Acc.) meet-pret.1st.sg. be-pret.3rd.sg. at the party
"Where I met him was at the party."
c. Me   fijaba   era   en la luz.
CL(1st.sg.) pay attention-imp.1st.sg. be-imp.3rd.sg. to the light
"What I was paying attention to was the [traffic] light."
                                        (Panama Lipski 1994:301)

The glosses given for (224b) and (224c) suggest that intensive *ser* is a form of cleft sentence marker. Kany (1951) documents the phenomenon as occurring in Colombia and Ecuador as far back as the mid nineteenth century. Lipski mentions it as a recent phenomenon in Venezuela, and as becoming quite frequent in Panama City.

1.7.4 Possessives

It was noted in Section 1.2.2 above that the Spanish genitive construction is marked either by a possessive form (*mis libros, los libros mios* "my books") or by a possessive phrase introduced by *de* (*el retrato de Josefina* "Josefina's portrait"). Dialectal variation takes various forms:

(225)   a. de la María su casa   (Bolivia Lipski 1994:194)
            of the M.   her house
            "Maria's house"
         b. mi casa mía   (Honduras Lipski 1994:272)
            my house my
            "my house"
         c. hijo de un su papá   (El Salvador Lipski 1994:259)
            son of a his father
            "his father's son"

In (225a), the *de*-phrase co-occurs with possessive *su*.[66] Note that the *de*-phrase precedes the genitive pronoun. In (225b), there is doubling of the possessive marker, and in (225c), the possessive form co-occurs with an indefinite article. This last type of co-occurrence is noted in Lipski to occur in El Salvador, Guatemala and in southern Mexico.

1.7.5 Subject-related variation

Several forms of variation related to the clausal subject are prevalent in the Spanish of the Caribbean. The two most common phenomena are the

---

[66] For discussion, see Camacho, Paredes and Sánchez (1995).

occurrence of pre-verbal pronominal subjects in Wh-questions, as in (226), and in infinitives, as in (227):

(226)   ¿Qué tú   quieres?   (Cuba Lipski 1994:233)
          what you(Nom.) want-2nd.sg.
          "What do you want?"

(227)   a. antes de yo   salir   de mi país
                                                    (Colombia Lipski 1994:215)
          before of I(Nom.) leave-inf. of my country
          "before I leave my country"
          b. para yo   hacer eso   (Puerto Rico Lipski 1994:335)
          for   I(Nom.) do-inf. that
          "for me to do that"

These phenomena are common in Cuba, the Dominican Republic, Puerto Rico and Venezuela, and are also found in Panama. Pre-verbal subjects of infinitives are found in these same areas, as well as in Colombia and sometimes in Ecuador.

One analysis of this dialectal difference is in terms of the clitic status of subject pronouns. As described earlier, overt pronouns in most Spanish dialects are strongly stressed, and behave in all syntactic respects like full Noun Phrases. It has been suggested (Lipski 1977; Contreras 1989) that, in Caribbean Spanish, subject pronouns have unstressed variants which behave like clitics, as is true of French subject pronouns.

However, Suñer (1994) presents data which suggest that, at least for some speakers, the absence of inversion is not restricted to pronominal subjects. For these speakers, sentences like (228) are not completely ungrammatical:

(228)   ¿Qué libro María quiere?   (Suñer 1994)
          which book M. want-pr.3rd.sg.
          "Which book does Maria want?"

The role of weakened verbal inflection in Caribbean dialects has also been discussed in relation to properties of the subject (Suñer 1986; Toribio 1993, 1996).

As noted earlier, the phenomena discussed here are dialect variants of Latin America. Some of these variants occur also in peninsular dialects. For example, negative doubling like that in (221), and possessive doubling with definite article + possessive form (la mi vaca "the my cow") are found – among other variants – in Leonese Spanish (Alvar 1996:156).

2

The Noun Phrase

2.1 Introduction

This chapter will examine the structure of the category traditionally referred to as the Noun Phrase (NP). We will consider the NP from two perspectives. First, from a phrase-external perspective, we will discuss the distribution of NP, and present a brief overview of the principles of grammar which account for this distribution. These matters are taken up in 2.2 for argument NPs, and in 2.3 for predicative NPs. We then turn to examination of the internal structure of NP. In 2.4, general structural properties of phrases which are established by X'-theory are introduced. This includes relations between the head and its complements and adjuncts, and the general properties of these constituents. Then in Sections 2.5–2.7, we will focus on specifiers of NP. In 2.5, the structure and function of NP determiners will be discussed; in 2.6, we examine elements that are traditionally referred to as "pre-determiners" and "post-determiners." Section 2.7 finishes the discussion of specifiers with an overview of specifiers of predicative NPs. Section 2.8 will address one of the central issues with respect to constituent order within NP: the order of the head, complements and adjuncts relative to each other. Finally, Section 2.9 will summarize the general conclusions of the chapter.

2.2 The distribution of argument NPs

Principles of X'-theory allow us to infer the presence of NP whenever a noun is present (since all NPs are headed by nouns, and every noun (N°) projects X' structure (NP)). Therefore, in the following examples, the italicized nouns head NPs:

(1)   a. *Juan* hizo *pan.*
         "Juan made bread."
      b. *Maria* es *doctora.*
         "Maria is (a) doctor."

The NPs in (1) do not all have the same status with respect to their function in the sentence. Consider the contrast between the post-verbal NPs, *pan* in (1a) and *doctora* in (1b). In (1a), the two NPs in the sentence (*Juan, pan*) have separate, independent reference; in (1b) however, the two NPs (*María, doctora*) do not have separate reference. The NP headed by *doctora* does not refer to an individual, but instead is a property of the NP *María*.

The contrast between the post-verbal NPs in (1a) and (1b) can be described as a distinction between *arguments* and *predicates*. In (1a), $[_{NP} pan]$ is an argument of *hizo*; in (1b), $[_{NP} doctora]$ is not an argument of some predicate, but is a predicate itself. Only arguments are capable of independent reference. Consequently, *pan* can be understood as having reference distinct from *Juan*, but *doctora* cannot be understood as having reference distinct from *María*. In this section, we will focus on the distribution of argument NPs. Below, the discussion will begin with a descriptive summary of contexts in which argument NPs can occur; then we will review two subtheories of grammar which account for this distribution. Predicative NPs will be discussed in 2.3.

2.2.1   The descriptive generalizations

NP cannot function as anything other than an argument or predicate. This is shown by the impossibility of an adjunct NP in (2a):

(2)   a. *Juan hizo   pan   piloto.
            J.   made bread pilot
         b. Juan hizo   pan   descalzo.
            J.   made bread barefoot

In (2a), the "extra" NP *piloto* is neither an argument nor a (primary) predicate, and its presence makes the sentence ungrammatical. Example (2a) cannot be understood as meaning that Juan, who is a pilot, made bread. This contrasts with (2b), with an Adjective Phrase, *descalzo*, as adjunct.[1]

We have assumed that the presence of a noun indicates the presence of NP, and that an NP is interpreted either as an argument or a predicate. NP cannot be arbitrarily inserted in a sentence such that it has no status as either an argument or a predicate. This implies that in those cases where an NP is possible, there are specific semantic and/or grammatical relations that make the

---

[1] Certain adjuncts appear to be NPs:

(i)   Juan hizo   pan   **ayer**.
         "Juan made bread yesterday."

Larson (1985) has argued, for similar examples in English, that what appear to be NPs functioning as adverbs (predicates) are PPs headed by a covert preposition.

appropriate interpretation possible. To see this more clearly, consider again (1a) versus (1b). In (1a), *pan* can only be interpreted as an argument, not as a predicate, while in (1b), *doctora* can only be interpreted as a predicate. However, this is clearly not due to inherent characteristics of these nouns, as a change in context shows:

(3)   a. Hay piloto en el   avión.
          is   pilot   in   the   plane
          "There is a pilot in the plane."
      b. La masa se hizo pan.
          "The dough became bread."

In (3a), *piloto* refers to an individual; in (3b), *pan* is predicative. It does not have reference independent of *la masa*. The interpretation of a given NP as an argument or a predicate is therefore not due to lexical properties of the NP itself, but depends on the context in which the NP occurs.

In subsequent sections, it will be useful to distinguish argument NPs from predicative NPs, since, as we will see, the difference in function can affect the internal composition of the phrase. With this in mind, let us look briefly at how phrase-external factors determine the status of NP as an argument or predicate.

2.2.2   Theta-theory

Traditional grammars describe the distribution of arguments in terms of the "transitivity" of the predicate to which an argument is related. Intransitive predicates select only a single argument, transitives select two arguments, and ditransitives select three arguments. These are illustrated below with verbal predicates:

(4)   INTRANSITIVES
      a. Juan durmió.
          "Juan slept."
      b. Los niños bailan.[2]
          "The children dance."
      c. Llega el tren.
          "The train is arriving."

(5)   TRANSITIVES
      a. María compró pan.
          "Maria bought bread."

[2] Note that the verb *bailar* "dance" appears to be a transitive verb in examples like: *María bailó el tango* "Maria danced the tango." The NP *el tango* does not have the same status as the complements of transitive verbs such as those in (5). It is a "cognate object," i.e., a phrase which repeats the meaning of the verb itself.

b. Susana construyó una casa.
"Susana built a house."
c. Los estudiantes saben la respuesta.
"The students know the answer."

(6)   DITRANSITIVES[3]
a. Pedro le mandó un paquete a José.
"Pedro sent a package to José."
b. El perro le dio un mordisco al hueso.
"The dog gave the bone a bite."

Informally stated, the notion of transitivity describes the number of arguments that are required for completeness of the meaning of the predicate. For example, the ditransitive verb *mandar* "send" in (6a) requires one individual to carry out the action (*Pedro*), another to undergo the action (*el paquete*), and a person or location indicating an endpoint of the sending (*José*). The number of arguments that a given predicate requires is a lexical property of the predicate. This means that the number of arguments that will be required (as in (4)–(6)), is not predictable from anything other than the meaning of the particular lexical item itself. The lexical entry for each predicate includes specification for transitivity, often called *predicate argument structure*, or simply *argument structure*. A lexical item's argument structure specifies the number of required arguments. The item's argument structure must be satisfied when it is inserted in a syntactic derivation, ensuring that the predicate is not used in structures in which there are too few or too many arguments.[4]

In the Principles and Parameters framework, argument structure is expressed in lexical entries in terms of one or more semantic roles assigned by

---

[3] The term "ditransitive" is normally used for predicates that have both a direct and an indirect object, as well as a subject. There are also predicates that occur with a direct object and a locative prepositional phrase, such as *Susana dejó el lápiz en la mesa* "Susana left the pencil on the table," which have three arguments, but are not traditionally considered ditransitives.

[4] In early versions of transformational grammar (Chomsky 1965), argument structure was given in the form of subcategorization frames. Predicates comprise subcategories according to the contexts in which they can be inserted, as in (i):

(i)   a. dormir: __
        b. comprar: __ NP
        c. mandar: __ NP PP

Subcategorization frames of the type in (i) do not give the subject argument, only the VP-internal arguments. The subject was assumed to be provided automatically by phrase-structure rules. Current proposals differ as to whether or not the subject (external argument) is distinguished in some way in lexical entries.

a given predicate. For example, a ditransitive verb such as *mandar* "send" assigns an Agent role (the sender), a Theme or Patient (the thing sent) and a Goal (the endpoint); the intransitive verb *bailar* selects only an Agent, etc.:

(7)   a. mandar "send":   Agent, Theme, Goal
        b. bailar "dance":   Agent
        c. comprar "buy":   Agent, Theme
        d. saber "know":   Experiencer, Theme

The specification of these roles, called *Thematic Roles*, or *Theta-roles*, indicates in the lexical entry both the number of arguments required by a predicate, and also the particular semantic role that each argument has in relation to the predicate. For this reason, a given NP such as *María* in (8) can have different semantic roles, depending on the particular Theta-role assigned to the NP by some predicate:

(8)   a. María bailó.   (=Agent)
           "Maria danced."
        b. María sabe la respuesta.   (=Experiencer)
           "Maria knows the answer."
        c. Juan le mandó un paquete a María.   (=Goal)
           "Juan sent a package to Maria."

In each sentence, there must be a "match" between the roles specified in the lexical entry of the predicate (e.g. (7a)) and the number of positions in the syntactic structure to which a role could be assigned. In the sentences in (8), each verb has the number of arguments that matches the number required in the verb's lexical entry. If there is a mismatch, ungrammaticality results:

(9)   a. *María le sabe la respuesta a Juan.
           "Maria knows the answer to Juan."
        b. *Juan mandó.
           "Juan sent."

To account for the status of (8) versus (9), it is assumed that lexical insertion of some item into a syntactic derivation involves the assignment, or "discharge," of the Theta-roles associated with the lexical entry. At some level(s) of syntactic representation, it is necessary to check the context in which a predicate occurs against its lexical entry. The derivation will be well formed in relevant ways if every Theta-role of a predicate is assigned to some NP (or other argument category, such as a clause), and if every NP is assigned a Theta-role. The sentences in (8) satisfy this requirement, because every NP present has a role specified in the lexical entry. The sentences in (9) fail because there are missing NPs or extra NPs.

Theta-roles are assigned under sisterhood.[5] Theta-role assigners include the head of phrase (V, in (10)), and higher bar-level projections of the head. A Theta-role assigned by the head is its "internal argument"; a Theta-role assigned by V′ is an "external argument."

(10)   a.

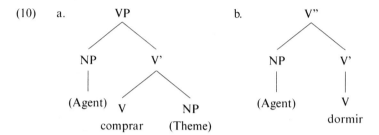

In (10a), the Theta-role "Theme" is assigned to the sister of the verb *comprar*, so this internal argument NP is interpreted as having the semantic function of Theme of *comprar*. The role of the "external argument" (the Agent in (10a) and (10b)) is assumed (e.g., in Chomsky 1981) to be assigned compositionally by the verb together with any objects. This implies that it is assigned by the V′ node to its sister, rather than by the verb alone.[6]

---

[5] The "sisterhood" relation can be formalized as mutual c-command. A node x c-commands a node y if the first branching node which dominates x also dominates y. In (i),

(i)

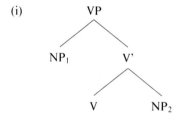

the verb c-commands NP_2 but not NP_1. It c-commands NP_2 because the first branching node which dominates the verb (V′) also dominates NP_2. NP_2 c-commands the verb also, because the first branching node that dominates NP_2 also dominates the verb. Therefore the verb and NP_2 are in a relation of mutual c-command. The verb does not c-command NP_1, because the first branching node which dominates the verb, V′, does not also dominate NP_1. NP_1 is c-commanded by V′.

There may be exceptions to mutual c-command as a condition on Theta-role assignment. One case is Theta-role assignment to the complement of ditransitive verbs, to be discussed in Chapter 3 (Section 3.6).

[6] Evidence for the compositionality of Theta-role assignment is based on pairs like the following:

It follows from the above assumptions that an NP that is interpreted as an argument can be generated only in those positions to which a Theta-role can be assigned. These positions are called argument positions, or *A-positions*. An NP could not be generated in a position other than an A-position and be interpreted as an argument, since it would have no semantic role, or relation to any predicate. Thus, the structure (11b) corresponding to (11a) cannot be well formed.

(11)   a. *el libro Juan compró
        "the book Juan bought"

    b.

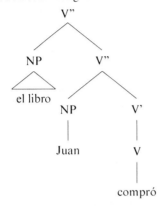

(i)   a. John rolled down the hill.   (John=Patient)
        b. John rolled the ball down the hill.   (John=Agent)
(ii)   a. John broke his arm.   (John=Patient)
        b. John broke the glass.   (John=Agent)

In (ia), intransitive *roll* assigns Patient to its subject, but in (ib), transitive *roll* assigns Agent to its subject. The status of external arguments as assigned a "compositional" Theta-role is in a sense problematic, because it is inconsistent with the view that Theta-roles are an idiosyncratic property of lexical items. Compositionality of assignment implies that a particular semantic role cannot be determined on the basis of knowledge of the lexical entry alone. One solution to this problem is the idea that knowledge of the semantic role assigned to a given argument does not derive exclusively from lexical items, but is based in part on a primitive set of relations known as the "thematic hierarchy." For example, (iii) shows a partial hierarchy:

(iii)   Agent < Theme < Experiencer < Goal

If a lexical item assigns Theme to its internal object, it can then only assign to its external argument a role that is higher on the thematic hierarchy, not a role that is lower. The thematic hierarchy is, on this view, a universal set of restrictions on possible lexical items. It follows that the full array of Theta-roles does not have to be specified for each predicate in the lexicon, and compositionality is to be expected. The thematic hierarchy then participates in predicting both the content of particular roles and the distribution of roles relative to each other (the "mapping" of roles) in syntactic structure. For discussion of the thematic hierarchy, see Jackendoff (1972).

In (11b), the NP *el libro* is not in a position to which a Theta-role could be assigned, consequently it cannot be interpreted as an argument of *compró*. The lexical properties of the predicate are not matched, or satisfied, by this structure.

So far, we have looked only at examples in which A-positions are filled by argument NPs. Suppose, however, that a verb does not assign any Theta-role to an A-position. Such a position can be occupied by an NP, but that NP is not related to a predicate, hence cannot have reference. Examples are the non-referential or "pleonastic" elements in the English examples in (12):

(12)   a. **It** seems that the apples are ripe.
        b. **There** were unicorns in the garden.

Pleonastics are typically invariant morphologically, and may be present only to satisfy structural or other grammatical requirements in a derivation. Corresponding sentences in Spanish never have an overt pleonastic, but the presence of a covert pleonastic is suggested by invariant agreement on the verb:

(13)   a. Parece/*n que las manzanas están maduras.   (=12a)
        b. Había/*n unicornios en el jardín.[7]   (=12b)

Summarizing to this point, we have seen that argument NPs are generated only in positions to which a Theta-role could be assigned (A-positions). If a role is actually assigned, NP is interpreted as an argument with a particular semantic role in relation to the predicate that assigns the Theta-role; if no role is assigned, NP is pleonastic, and has no reference. Argument NPs cannot be generated in non-A-positions, since they will have no semantic interpretation in relation to any predicate.

2.2.3   Abstract case

The above brief description of argument NPs describes only the "basic" or "original" position of NPs – the position in which NP receives its interpretation as semantically related to a predicate. Other processes can move NPs, so that the "derived" position of NP may differ from its basic, or canonical, position. The moved, or "derived," positions of NPs may be forced by other NP licensing requirements. One such requirement for NPs is (abstract)

---

[7] Some dialects of Spanish allow plural agreement in examples like (13b), parallel to English (12b). The occurrence of agreement with the post-verbal NP suggests that the pleonastic is a temporary "placeholder" for the semantic subject of the clause, and that the features of the semantic subject are raised to subject position in the course of the derivation.

Case, such as Nominative or Objective Case. The idea behind "abstract" Case is that, just as pronominals have different forms (*yo, me, mí*) according to their grammatical function, so also do other NPs have an "abstract" feature which identifies their grammatical function – even though the NP does not overtly express this feature. Case theory has undergone several revisions, so that recent formulations differ significantly from earlier ones. In the course of our discussion in subsequent chapters, the conditions under which Case is assigned will be considered in more detail. For the moment, it will suffice to outline two Case-theoretic generalizations: (A) that Case is assigned by certain heads, in part determined by the category of the head, and in part by lexical properties of the head. Verbs and prepositions assign Objective Case, and the finite head of the clause, INFL, assigns Nominative Case. Not every member of these categories has a Case feature to assign, as we will see below. (B) Objective Case, assigned by V or P, is assigned to an NP that the head governs, which is usually a sister constituent.[8] In a sequence like: *compró el libro* "bought the book" or *con un amigo* "with a friend," the head (V or P) assigns Case to its sister. INFL, however, assigns Case to the NP in its Specifier (i.e., the subject of the clause). These preliminary generalizations are summarized in (14):

(14)   Case Assignment (Simplified):
        a. lexical heads (V and P) assign Case to a sister
        b. INFL assigns Case to an NP in the Specifier of IP

This early formulation of Case theory assumed that only phonetically overt NPs require Case, and the requirement for Case was analyzed as a filter operating in the phonological component of the grammar. More recent versions of Case theory have considered Case to be realized also on covert NPs, and the Case filter has been reinterpreted as a component of the syntactic licensing of NPs.

---

[8] Theta-roles (discussed above in 2.3.2) were also described as assigned to a sister constituent. In note 5 this relation was described technically as mutual c-command. Case assignment is more "liberal," in that the NP that is assigned Case need not c-command the Case-assigning head. This is illustrated in (i), where the bracketed phrase is the sister of the verb:

(i)   Consideran $[_{AP}$ a María muy inteligente].
       "They consider Maria very intelligent."

The bracketed phrase is an adjective phrase (or "small clause") which is assigned a Theta-role by the verb under mutual c-command. The verb also assigns Case to the NP. Here, however, mutual c-command does not obtain: the verb c-commands NP, but NP does not c-command the verb, because the first branching node which dominates NP (AP) does not dominate the verb. Case-assignment in such instances is referred to as "exceptional Case marking" (ECM).

It was noted above that the requirement for Case can trigger movement of NPs from the position in which they are assigned a Theta-role. This type of NP movement is illustrated for the boldfaced NPs in (15a), (16a):

(15)   a. [e] fue obligada **ella** a   salir
                  was forced   she to leave
         b. **[ella]** fue obligada – a salir
              she   was forced   to leave

(16)   a. [e] parece [**ella** haber   salido]
                  seems   she to have left
         b. **[ella]** parece [– haber   salido]
              she seems   to have left

In the (a) examples above, the NP *ella* is not governed by a verb that can assign Objective Case; neither the passive participle *obligada* in (15) nor the verb *parece* in (16), for example, assigns Objective Case. This is due to morphological or lexical properties of these items. (See Chapter 3, Sections 3.5 and 3.7.) Consequently, NP must move to the Specifier of IP, where it can be assigned Nominative Case by the Inflectional head of the clause.

Summarizing, argument NPs originate in A-positions, the position in which NP receives a semantic role as an argument of a predicate. This role must be made visible by abstract Case, with the consequence that sometimes NP must move in order to satisfy its Case requirement. Similarly, an interrogative NP must move to satisfy its visibility as an operator. As we have seen, NPs cannot be generated arbitrarily in "satellite" positions since, in such cases, NP will fail to have a Theta-role, and will not have any type of argumental interpretation. Since every constituent of a sentence must have an interpretation, derivations with such unrelated NPs will not be grammatical.

2.3   Predicative NPs

The preceding discussion of predicate argument structure focused on NPs as arguments. NPs can also have the distribution and interpretation of predicates, similar to other predicate categories such as Adjective Phrases:

(17)   a. María es inteligente/doctora.
              M.   is intelligent/(a) doctor
         b. Los estudiantes parecen inteligentes/genios.
              the students   seem   intelligent/geniuses
         c. Los profesores consideran inteligente/genio   a   Juan.
              The teachers   consider   intelligent / (a) genius PA J.
              "The teachers consider Juan intelligent/a genius."

In (17a) and (17b), the post-verbal NPs/APs lack independent reference. Their interpretation is predicative, rather than argumental. In (17c), the phrase *intel-igente/genio* is also predicative, but the phrase *a Juan* is not. The predicative NPs and APs in (17) assign a Theta-role to an NP, such as *Juan*, in (17c), which is interpreted as the subject of the predicate. This implies that predicative NPs are not generated in A-positions, since they assign, rather than receive a Theta-role. The distribution of predicative NPs (and other predicate categories) is then complementary to that of arguments. The visibility of the predicate category is licensed through its syntactic association with an A-position. This relation is referred to as *Predication*. To illustrate the licensing of the elements of predicative NPs, (17a) derives from a structure like (18).

(18)

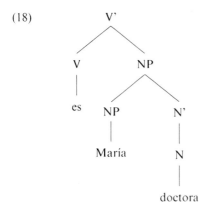

In (18), NP consists of the predicate N' and its single argument, the NP *María*. Both the predicate and the argument must satisfy grammatical licensing requirements that make them "visible" for interpretation. The argument NP, *María*, is assigned a Theta-role by N', and is made visible by abstract (Nominative) Case, once it moves to the position of clausal subject. The predicate N' satisfies its lexical requirement by assigning a Theta-role to the NP *María*. The predicate is licensed by the relation of *Predication*. In essence, Predication "completes" the interpretation of the predicate by associating it with its subject.[9] Predication is shown as coindexing of the subject and predicate.

[9] The semantic basis for the Predication requirement is that predicates express sets of individuals, and Predication identifies members of that set. For example, in (i),

(i)   María es inteligente
        M.   is intelligent

The predicate *inteligente* is understood as the set of individuals with the property of being intelligent. Predication identifies *María* as asserted to be a member of that set.

(19)

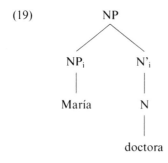

In (19), Predication is satisfied because there is an NP with which the predicate A'/N' is coindexed. If no NP were present as a sister to A'/N', Predication would fail and the derivation would be impossible.[10]

Predicative NPs are not standardly analyzed as requiring Case. Abstract Case has been considered to have a function in relation to the "visibility" of Theta-roles. Predicative NPs would not be expected to require Case, since they are not theta-marked. Examples like those in (20) support this claim:

(20)   a. Juan es (*a) mi mejor amigo.
           J.   is PA my best   friend
           "Juan is my best friend."
        b. Soy   yo/*mí.
           be-1st.sg. I/*me
           "It is I/*me."

Example (20a) shows that predicative NPs do not co-occur with "personal a." This is expected if predicative NPs are not assigned Case, since "personal a" is restricted to Objective contexts. In (20b), the predicative pronoun yo takes Nominative form. This appears to indicate that the predicative NP has Case; however, an alternative is that the predicative yo in (20b) agrees in Case with the (covert) subject of the clause. Both sentences in (20) have a subject that is assigned Nominative Case by the inflectional head of the clause. In (20a), the subject is $Juan$; in (20b), the subject is the covert pleonastic pronoun corresponding to English it. The occurrence of Nominative as the form of post-verbal predicative NP then suggests that the predicate "shares," or agrees with, the Case of its subject, rather than being assigned a separate Case by an independent governor.[11]

---

[10] Williams (1982) argues that NP does not have a phrase-internal subject. That is, NP has no A-position specifier.

[11] The assumption that predicate NPs do not require Case leaves unanswered one fact about their distribution. That is, as was noted in Section 2.2 above, Predicative NPs cannot occur as secondary predicates – that is, in adjunct positions, as illustrated by the ungrammaticality of sentences like $Juan\ hizo\ pan\ piloto$ "Juan, a pilot, made bread." If predicative NPs required Case, these sentences would be automatically excluded, since there is no Case assigner for the secondary predicate.

Notice that the verb agrees in person/number with the predicative NP, not with the covert pleonastic *it*.

Summarizing, the distribution of predicative NPs is complementary to argument NPs. Predicative NPs do not occur in A-positions, but occur in positions that can be linked to A-positions. The licensing process by which this linking occurs is Predication. Predicative NPs are not assigned an independent Case. Their morphological Case forms can be derived by agreement with the clausal subject.

2.4   The constituents of NP

In this section, we will introduce several types of constituents that co-occur with a noun to form a Noun Phrase. We will focus on the distinctive properties of these constituents. Subsequent sections will examine in closer detail some of the "finer structure" associated with them. Let us begin with a preliminary structural description of the phrase, and of three types of constituents that can be generated with a head noun: complements, adjuncts and specifiers. Let us look first at a phrasal "skeleton" which shows several types of nodes within NP.

(21)

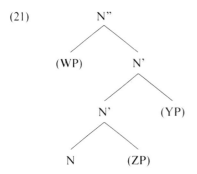

In (21), N (or N°) is the category label of a lexical item that constitutes the head of phrase N''.[12] N' and N'' are projections of the head – that is, non-lexical category nodes which share the category features of the head. Because these nodes are projected from N°, they could not be present in the absence of a head noun. In other words, there can be no phrase without a head. Also, because these nodes share categorial and other features of the head, the phrasal node N'' (= NP) is necessarily the same category as the head. Thus, all

---

[12] N can also have internal structure, for example in compounds. Internal structure can also represent sub-lexical morphological relations.

phrases are *endocentric*. An NP can only be headed by a noun, an AP can only be headed by an adjective, etc.

The N' and N'' nodes may branch so as to dominate additional constituents – in (21), the optional elements WP, YP and ZP. It has been argued (Kayne 1981) that a node may have a maximum of two branches, so phrase markers observe a condition of maximal *binary branching*. The optional constituents in (21) are in different configurations relative to the head and to the phrase as a whole. ZP is a sister of the head; because this is a position to which a Theta-role can be assigned, ZP is an argument or complement position. YP is in a position to which a Theta-role could *not* be assigned, and YP could therefore only be a non-argument. YP is in a position occupied by *adjuncts* (optional modifiers). Notice that YP is both a sister of N' and is dominated by N'. The "duplication" of a bar-level projection such as this marks an adjunction structure. A constituent YP is *adjoined* to N' by a process of copying the N' node, creating a position for an additional branch. (There is no intrinsic limit on the number of adjuncts in a phrase, so N' could be duplicated further, creating a more complex NP.) WP is in the *Specifier* of XP – the position dominated by the maximal projection of the phrase. The following subsections present a preliminary overview of these constituent types.

2.4.1   *Complements*

A noun may have a complement, in other words an argument that is assigned a Theta-role by the head noun. As noted above, a complement could occupy the position of ZP in (22), but not the position of YP, since YP is not a sister of the head.

(22)

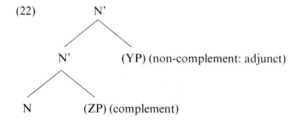

Examples of noun complements are the bracketed constituents in (23):

(23)   a. la destrucción [de la ciudad]
          the destruction of the city
        b. tu   creencia [en la justicia]
          your belief   in the justice
          "your belief in justice"

c. el   deseo [de llegar   temprano]
   the desire of to arrive early
   "the desire to arrive early"
d. la   apariencia [de que ganamos   el   partido]
   the appearance of that win.1st.pl. the game
   "the appearance that we're winning/we won the game"

Notice that in (23), the bracketed phrases are complements of the nouns *destrucción, creencia,* etc. This is independent of the status of the whole NP, which is normally an argument of another predicate. For example, the phrase *la destrucción de la ciudad* in (23a) could be the complement of a verb: *Vieron la destrucción de la ciudad* "They saw the destruction of the city." The whole phrase is the argument of the verb; within NP, the phrase *de la ciudad* is the argument of *destrucción.*

Notice also in (23) that all of the complement constituents are introduced by a preposition – in these examples, *de* or *en.* The occurrence of the preposition can be related to the Case licensing of the complement. Recall from 2.2 that a theta-marked complement must be assigned Case; unlike verbs, nouns are not Case assigners, or at least do not assign Case directly to a complement, but do so via a prepositional Case marker. Notice that the verbal counterpart of (23a), for example, does not have the preposition: *Destruyeron (*de) la ciudad* "They destroyed (*of) the city."[13]

Looking still at the bracketed complements in (23), we see that, in addition to the preposition, these complements contain either NP (23a,b) or a clause

---

[13] Chomsky (1986), proposes that Nouns (and Adjectives) do assign Case to their complements, but the nature of the Case that is assigned differs from that assigned by Verbs, Prepositions and INFL. Nouns and Adjectives are suggested to assign "inherent" Case, a Case that is linked to Theta-role assignment. This contrasts with the "structural" Cases, which can be assigned to an NP, without it being theta-marked by the Case assigner. This is illustrated in (i):

(i)   Consideran [inteligente a   Pedro].
      consider   intelligent PA Pedro
      "They consider Pedro intelligent."

In (i), the verb theta-marks the bracketed constituent, an adjectival small clause. The adjective theta-marks *Pedro,* the external argument of the small clause. The verb assigns Case to this NP, as is shown by the occurrence of Personal *a.* We will see below that small clauses do not occur as complements of nouns, a fact which can be attributed to the hypothesis that a noun can only "inherently" Case-mark – that is, assign Case in conjunction with Theta-role assignment.

Notice that example (23b) does have a preposition in the verbal counterpart: *creer en la justicia* "to believe in justice." This illustrates that some verbs do not assign Case to their complement, but instead select a complement type that contains a Case assigner, namely the preposition.

(23c,d). Nouns do not freely select complements of other categories. This is illustrated below by contrasts between the (a) and (b) examples:

(24)   a. Pedro se   siente [$_{AP}$ contento].
        P.   CL feels   happy
        "Pedro feels   happy."
        b. *el   sentimiento contento
        the feeling happy

(25)   a. Consideran   [a Juana inteligente].
        consider.3rd.pl PA J.   intelligent
        "They consider Juana intelligent."
        b. *la   consideración [a/de   Juana inteligente]
        the consideration PA/of J.   intelligent

(26)   a. Vi   [llegar a   Pedro].
        saw.1st.sg. arrive PA P.
        "I saw Pedro arrive."
        b. *la   vista de llegar a/de   Pedro
        the sight of arrive PA/of P.
        "the sight of Pedro arrive"

The verbs in (24a) and (25a) select AP and adjectival small clause complements, in (26a), a verbal small clause (cf. 1.3.1). The corresponding nominals disallow these complements.

Not all nouns assign Theta-roles. Those which do are of the following types: (a) nouns derived from verbs or adjectives, illustrated in (27a), and "picture" nouns, illustrated in (27b):

(27)   Theta-assigning nouns:
        a. Deverbal and de-adjectival nouns: destrucción (destruir)
        "destruction (cf. destroy)"; prueba (probar) "proof (prove)";
        apelación (apelar) "appeal (appeal)"; fidelidad (fiel) "faithfulness
        (faithful)"; claridad (claro) "clarity (clear)"
        b. "Picture" nouns: foto "picture, photograph"; retrato "portrait"; libro
        "book"; artículo "article"; historia "story"; idea "idea"

The nominals in (27a) select arguments that correspond to those of the related verb or adjective. If the verb or adjective theta-marks a PP complement, that complement is typically headed by a unique preposition, and the complement of the nominal will also be a PP headed by the same preposition (e.g. *creer en* "to believe in" *creencia en* "belief in"; *apelar a* "to appeal to" *apelación a* "appeal to"). If the related verb theta-marks an NP, then the complement of the noun selects the "default" preposition *de* (e.g., *destruir la ciudad* "destroy the city" *destrucción de la ciudad*). The argument structure of picture nouns can be attributed to their relational meaning. The entities which they denote (pictures) have the characteristic of "representing" objects. These nouns can take as a complement a phrase which expresses the represented object. Other types of common and proper nouns do not have argument structure.

2.4.2   Adjuncts

As noted above, adjuncts are assumed to be generated as sisters of N', in the position of YP in (22), repeated below.

(22)

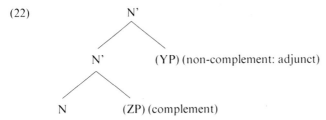

The following types of constituents occupy this position:

(28)   Adjective Phrase:
    a. una comida [muy buena]
      "a very good meal"
    b. un color [exquisito]
      "an exquisite color"
    c. un político [fiel a los principios democráticos]
      "a politician faithful to democratic principles"

(29)   Prepositional Phrase:
    a. la solución [en ese libro]
      "the solution in that book"
    b. un regalo [para Juan]
      "a gift for Juan"
    c. el estudiante [de Caracas]
      "the student from Caracas"
    d. una máquina [para reparar]
      a   machine for to fix
      "a machine to fix"

(30)   Clause:
    a. el libro [que leímos]
      "the book that we read"
    b. una ciudad [que María ha visitado]
      "a city that Maria has visited"

(31)   Small Clause:[14]
    a. una persona [respetada por todos]
      "a person respected by everyone"
    b. los niños [jugando en la calle]
      "the children playing in the street"

These adjunct constituents are licensed by predication. The subject of the predication is the noun, or a higher projection of it. For example, in (29a), the adjunct *en ese libro* "in that book" is predicated of *solución* "solution"; in the sequence *la solución correcta en ese libro* "the correct solution in that book" the PP could be predicated either of the head noun or of the noun together with its adjunct.

Adjectival adjuncts differ from the others listed above in two respects. One is that adjectives agree with the head noun in number and gender. Second, some adjectives occur in positions within the Noun Phrase other than the "canonical" adjunct position discussed above. They may be pre-nominal, as in (32):

(32)   Adjective Phrase (pre-nominal):
    a. un mero soldado
      a mere soldier
    b. un viejo amigo
      an old friend
    c. la pura fantasía
      the pure fantasy

They also occur between the head noun and its complement:

(33)   a. la destrucción completa de la ciudad
      the destruction complete of the city
    b. tu creencia absoluta en la justicia
      your belief absolute in justice

The position in which an adjective appears depends both on the nature of the adjective itself – the subcategory of adjective – and on the adjective's interpretation in a given NP. A few adjectives, such as *mero* in (32a), are always pre-nominal. A large class of adjectives, called "qualitative" adjectives, such as *viejo* and *puro* in (32b,c), can be either pre- or post-nominal. Qualitative adjectives differ in their interpretation depending on their position. In pre-nominal position, they are appositive. For example in (32b), *un viejo amigo* is someone who is old as a friend (i.e., a long-time friend), not necessarily someone who is old. In post-nominal position, these adjectives are restrictive: *un amigo viejo*

---

[14] The participial and gerundive adjuncts illustrated here are sometimes referred to as "reduced relatives." Their interpretation is analogous to full relative clauses (e.g., *los niños que están jugando en la calle* "the children who are playing in the street").

is someone who is a friend and is old. A third class of adjectives, "relational" adjectives, which express relations of various types, such as origin (e.g. *un estudiante mexicano* "a Mexican student") or material composition (e.g. *una sustancia química* "a chemical substance") are always post-nominal.

Notice that the order of constituents shown in the examples in (33) is not predicted to be possible as a basic order. This is so because the complement is not the closest constituent to the head, and is therefore not a sister of it so it could not be assigned a Theta-role. The order: head–adjunct–complement in these examples implies that a constituent has been displaced from its D-structure position. This topic will be taken up in Section 2.5.

2.4.3   Distinguishing complements from adjuncts

It is often not obvious at first glance whether a post-nominal PP is a complement of the noun or an adjunct. Consider the examples in (34), (35):

(34)   a. una silla [de   Francia]
           a   chair from France
    b. una silla [en el   jardín]
           a   chair in the garden
    c. una silla [para José]
           a   chair for   J.

(35)   a. un estudiante [de sintaxis]
           a   student   of syntax
    b. un estudiante [de   pelo negro]
           a   student   with hair black
           "a student with black hair"
    c. un estudiante [de   México]
           a   student   from Mexico

Unfortunately, there are no straightforward syntactic diagnostics that differentiate complements of a head noun from adjuncts. The preceding discussion has provided some tools that can help to deduce the status of a PP in examples such as these. Recall from 2.4.1 that only certain types of nouns have argument structure: derived nominals and picture nouns. With this in mind, we may suppose that, in (34), none of the bracketed phrases are complements of the noun, because the head noun *silla* is not of the type which has arguments. The noun *estudiante* in (35), however, could have a complement, if it is a deverbal nominal related to the verb *estudiar*. But not all of the PPs in (35) are complements of the head. One way to decide whether any of these PPs is a complement is to "convert" the nominal to its verbal form, and compare the interpretations. In (36b), the PP has the same relation to the nominal *estudiante* as the NP *sintaxis* has to the verb *estudiar* in (36a):

(36)   a. estudiar sintaxis
           to study syntax
        b. un estudiante de sintaxis
           a   student   of syntax

In both cases, the complement is the Theme of the head, i.e., the object of study. In (35b) and (35c) on the other hand, the PP is not interpreted as something that undergoes study, but instead indicates an additional property of the noun. By this criterion (a semantic one), only the PP in (35a) is a complement of the head. A second criterion that supports this analysis is the "typical" order of constituents if more than one is present:

(37)   a un estudiante de sintaxis de México
        b. un estudiante de sintaxis de pelo negro
        c. ??un estudiante de México de sintaxis
        d. ??un estudiante de pelo negro de sintaxis

Examples (37c) and (37d) show "marked" orders. They are improved by adding pause intonation between the PPs. These examples are revealing of the status of the PPs, because complements are generated as sisters of the head, and should therefore be expected to appear as the closest constituent to the head, unless some additional operation has altered the order. Such operations could derive sequences in (37c,d), but, in doing so, the intonation would change. Based on the contrast between (37a) and (37c), it is possible to claim that *de México* is an adjunct, while *de sintaxis* is a complement. Likewise, *de pelo negro* is an adjunct in (37b), given the contrast with (37d).

It is perhaps useful to point out a contrast between English and Spanish with respect to diagnostics for noun complements. In English, *one*-pronominalization replaces only N', which means that adjuncts can be sisters of *one*, but complements cannot:

(38)   a. the student from Argentina and the one from Mexico
        b. *the student of phonology and the one of syntax

Example (38b) is ungrammatical because *one* has replaced only the head, and not the complement; (38a) is well formed because *from Mexico* is an adjunct, i.e., a sister of N', which *one* has replaced. In Spanish, there is no overt proform corresponding to English *one*, but there is an analogous construction with an ellipted N' (or a covert proform):

(39)   el estudiante de   Granada y   el de   México
        the student   from Granada and the from Mexico
        "the student from Granada and the (one) from Mexico"

This construction does not, however, replace N' exclusively, as is shown by the grammaticality of (40):

(40)   el   estudiante de sintaxis y   el   de física
          the student   of syntax and the of physics

Because complements and adjuncts behave identically under ellipsis, this construction does not provide evidence supporting the structural distinction between the two.

2.4.4   NP specifiers

In early work on X'-theory, it was shown that there is a third type of constituent which can accompany the head of a phrase. These elements are "specifiers," a heterogeneous class of constituents which are typically phrase-initial, and which differ from complements and adjuncts in certain ways. A summary of Specifiers of NP is given in (41):

(41)   a. Possessives: mi libro "my book," tu chaqueta, "your jacket"
          b. Demonstratives: ese vaso "that glass," esta película "this movie"
          c. Definite determiners: el cine "the movies," los aviones "the airplanes"
          d. Indefinite determiners: un cuchillo "a knife," unas guerras "some wars"
          e. Cardinals: dos capítulos "two chapters," cien pesos "(a) hundred pesos"
          f. Quantifiers: algún estudiante "some student," toda persona "every person"
          g. Interrogatives: cuáles niños "which children," cuántos libros "how many books"

Although many of the items in (41) are similar to certain types of adjuncts, particularly adjectives, specifiers of NP must be differentiated from typical adjuncts (modifiers), in that, in certain contexts, NP must have some type of specifier:

(42)   a. Mi/un libro está en la   mesa.
             my/a   book is on the table
          b. *Libro está en la   mesa.
             book is on the table

The obligatoriness of the specifier suggests that it has some function for the licensing of NPs, a point to which we return in 2.5. In recent years, there have been considerable advances in analyzing the syntax of these specifiers. Sections 2.5–2.7 discuss these constituents and their analysis in detail.

Summarizing the main points of this section, we have seen that X'-theory makes several claims about the structure of Noun Phrases. Every NP is headed by a noun, and may contain other types of constituents: complements, adjuncts and specifiers. Complements are sisters of the head, and are PPs or clauses. Adjuncts typically follow complements, although adjectival complements can also be pre-nominal or post-nominal. Specifiers are a heterogeneous class, whose structure will be discussed below.

2.5   Determiners of argument NPs

We turn now to discussion of the Specifiers of argument NPs. Recall from 2.2 that NP can function either as an argument or as a predicate, and its distribution and licensing vary accordingly. It was noted there that the status of NP as an argument or predicate can also affect the internal structure of the phrase. As we will see, the determiner system is centrally affected. In this section and in 2.6 below, specifiers of argument NPs will be discussed. We then return to predicative NPs in 2.7.

2.5.1   Distribution of specifiers

Argument NPs allow all of the specifier types listed in (41) above:

(43)   a. Mi/ese/el/un libro está en la mesa.
           "My/that/the/a book is on the table."
       b. Dos libros están en la mesa.
           "Two books are on the table."
       c. Algunos libros están en la mesa.
           "Some books are on the table."
       d. ¿Cuántos libros están en la mesa?
           "How many books are on the table?"

Specifiers that have definite interpretations (possessives, demonstratives and definite determiners) cannot co-occur with each other in pre-nominal position:

(44)   a. *el mi libro
           "the my book"
       b. *ese su libro
           "that his book"

Based on the uniqueness of the pre-nominal specifier position for these determiners, earlier versions of X'-theory analyzed NP as having a unique "Determiner" position as a daughter of X", the maximal phrasal projection (see (45)). This structure generally predicts that any NP will have a single position for specifiers, which occurs as the first (leftmost) constituent of the phrase. However, determiners of the first subclass can co-occur if one is post-nominal with strong stress:

(45)

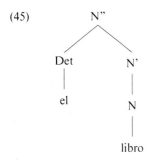

(46) a. el   libro tuyo
      the book   your
      "the book of yours"
      b. el   libro ese
      the book   that
      "THAT book"

The grammaticality of sequences in (46) shows that it is not the items themselves that must be unique within NP, but rather that there is a single prenominal position in which a determiner of this class can surface. This is problematic for a purely phrase structure account of the distribution of determiners as in (45) since, in order to generate sequences like (46), the category *Det* must be possible in post-nominal positions, as shown in (47):

(47)

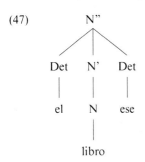

Given this possibility, additional constraints are needed to exclude phrases with only a post-nominal determiner (*libro ese).

Another issue is that Specifiers of other types can co-occur pre-nominally. Consider the sequences in (48), which contain "pre-determiners" and "post-determiners" in boldface:

(48) a. los **varios** libros
      the several books
      b. **todos** esos libros
      all   those books

c. unos **tres** libros
some three books
d. **cuáles** de mis libros
which of my books
e. **ninguno** de esos libros
none of those books

Traditional (and generative) accounts of these sequences have typically analyzed the "extra" specifiers as modifiers of a separate category, such as "predeterminer," Quantifier or Adjective. Under this approach, the Determiner position is unique, but it can co-occur with modifiers that specify quantity. For example, (48a) and (48b) might have the structures shown in (49a) and (49b).

(49)   a.

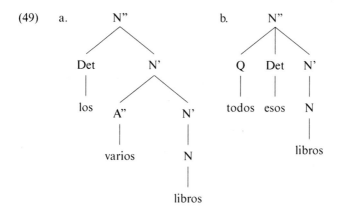

Notice that *varios* in (49a) is analyzed as an Adjective, based on its position between the determiner and the noun – a position where adjectives may typically appear – while *todos* is analyzed as a Quantifier. *Todos* could not be an adjective, since adjectives cannot appear before a Determiner (**buenos los* *libros* "good the books"). An analysis based on the category of these specifiers does account for (a) their distribution, and (b) their co-occurrence with Det. However, one generalization remains unexpressed: the fact that these items can also satisfy the requirement for a determiner. That is, they can also appear without a separate determiner, unlike other optional modifiers:

(50)   a. Varios libros están en la mesa.
several books are on the table
b. *Buenos libros están en la mesa.
good books are on the table

Another issue is that this approach does not account for the appearance of the Case marker *de* in examples like (48d), (48e). We return to the topic of "pre- and "post-determiners" in Section 2.6.

Summarizing to this point, we have seen that specifiers of NP are not strictly optional, like other modifiers of nouns. This suggests that specifiers have a particular function in licensing the NP, so that, without a specifier, the NP is not fully interpretable as a phrase. However, we have seen that the specifier "function" cannot be accounted for simply by positing a Determiner position as in (45), since certain subclasses of specifiers can co-occur with each other as pre- and post-nominal constituents, and others can co-occur pre-nominally. In 2.5.2 and in 2.6, we will consider ways of accounting for these co-occurrences.

There is one further point to be noted with regard to the distribution of specifiers: the obligatoriness of specifiers of argument NPs depends on phrase-internal as well as phrase-external factors. Phrase-internally, the choice of noun is relevant; unmodified proper nouns do not co-occur with specifiers in most dialects of Spanish:

(51)   *el Juan llegó.
         "The Juan arrived."

Phrase-external factors are also relevant. Argument NPs in certain positions in a sentence can lack a specifier:

(52)   a. Cantaron canciones toda la   noche.
            sang   songs   all the night
            "They sang songs all night."
         b. *Canciones fueron cantadas toda la   noche.
            songs   were   sung   all the night
            "Songs were sung all night."

In (52a), *canciones* is the object of the verb; in (52b), it is the subject of the passive sentence. The possibility of an "absent" specifier thus depends on the surface position of NP. There are two possible analyses of NPs without overt specifiers. One is that there is simply no Det position present; the other is that there is a Det position present filled by an empty (covert) specifier. One argument supporting the latter analysis is that NPs lacking overt determiners such as (52a) have essentially the same interpretation as though a specifier were present – in this case, the indefinite determiner *unos* "some." If the NP has an interpretation other than indefinite, an appropriate specifier must be present:

(53)   Cantaron *(las) canciones que aprendieron en Málaga.
         sang   *(the) songs   that learned   in Malaga
         "They sang the songs that they learned in Malaga."

In (53), where the object NP has a definite interpretation, the Det position must be filled. This points to an analysis of (52a) in which the specifier position is filled by a covert specifier.

2.5.2   The DP hypothesis

We saw above that there are two limitations of the analysis of specifiers in (45) above, where specifiers are generated under a Det node as a daughter of N''. One problem is that specifiers are not strictly optional, but the analysis in (45) predicts that the Det node, like other adjunct positions, should be optional. The second problem is that, although the specifier is in some cases unique, there are also instances of co-occurring specifiers. These problems (and related ones) have been addressed in recent years under a theory of functional categories, which explores structural and grammatical relations between the lexical categories (nouns, verbs and adjectives) and related grammatical or functional elements such as specifiers. A foundational work in this vein is Abney (1987), which proposes that D (=determiner) heads a phrase DP (Determiner Phrase). D selects NP as its complement, as shown in (54).

(54)

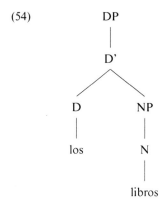

This structure posits a head–complement relation between Det and NP; however, because D is a functional category rather than a lexical category, it does not select NP as a complement – NP is not theta-marked by D. Here, the head–complement relation is a "functional" relation. This function can be thought of in the following way: assuming the NP itself to be basically predicative, the determiner function "translates" the NP into an expression which has reference, i.e., refers to definite or indefinite individuals.[15]

---

[15] Higginbotham (1985) proposes a mechanism by which this function is carried out, which he terms "theta-binding." This mechanism is a form of variable binding. Recall that the licensing of predicative NPs (2.3) was stated in terms of Predication, the syntactic relation between subject and predicate. Theta-binding is similar to Predication in certain respects: both processes "complete" or "saturate" the predicate via a grammatical relationship with a constituent external to the predicate. The processes differ at least syntactically, in that Predication operates between full

The DP hypothesis accounts for the failure to co-occur of definite, indefinite and demonstrative specifiers, on the assumption that these are all generated under D, with features of either [+DEF(INITE)] or [-DEF]. The DP hypothesis also provides a means of accounting for the co-occurrence of definite determiners with post-nominal, but not pre-nominal, possessives and demonstratives:

(55)   a. los libros esos/míos
             the books those/mine
         b. *los esos/mis libros
             the those/ my books

This contrast can be accounted for on the assumption that "strong" (stressed) and "weak" (unstressed) forms differ structurally, and perhaps categorially. Suppose, for example, that weak forms are simple determiners, and are always generated in the head of DP. This head is a non-lexical category, and items inserted there may be devoid of word-level stress. Strong forms must therefore be generated elsewhere, perhaps as adjuncts, as shown in (56).[16]

(56)

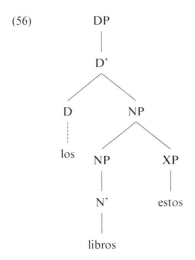

It is possible that XP (the category of the post-nominal strong form) is also DP, and that, due to its position within NP, it can inherit phrasal stress associated with the NP.

phrases, while theta-binding is a relation between a (functional) head and a lexical head.

[16] The structure shown in (56) distinguishes NP (a noun phrase) from N', in line with the traditional three levels of structure of phrases assumed under X'-theory. It is frequently assumed in more recent work that lexical categories have only two projections, the head and X' level, so that X' is non-distinct from "phrase."

The structure (56) accounts for the surface order and co-occurrence of demonstratives and possessives with definite determiners, but does not explain why the phrase is well formed with two specifiers. Here, however, the more articulated structure of DP, which has a specifier position of its own, is useful. We may suppose that the definite determiner *los* in (56) is a purely formal element, akin to pleonastic pronouns. In recent work, it has been proposed that such elements must be eliminated in the course of a derivation, because they have no semantic interpretation. If they were to remain, the sentence would contain a semantically uninterpretable element. This replacement must occur at an abstract level of representation referred to as "Logical Form," which is the form of a sentence which provides the input to semantic interpretation. If a "pleonastic" determiner occurs then, it must be eliminated in favor of a true determiner. In (56), the post-nominal strong form is such an element. The manner in which it "becomes" the determiner in Logical Form is by movement to the Specifier of the higher DP "leaving a trace" (t) in its original position, as shown in (57).

(57)

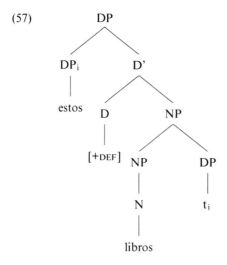

Here, the post-nominal demonstrative DP has moved to the Specifier position of the higher DP. Once there, its presence allows the pleonastic to be eliminated.

The notion of "replacement" of definite determiners may also provide a basis for explaining the absence of determiners with proper names. Compare (58a,b):

(58)   a. los libros
              the books
          b. *el   Juan
              the J.

This contrast suggests that another means of replacing a definite determiner is by movement of the head noun to the head of DP (see (59)).

(59)

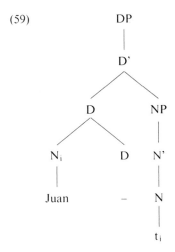

Here, the head of NP has moved, adjoining to D. There are various possible explanations for the fact that common nouns do not undergo this movement. These might appeal either to differences in the inherent features of common versus proper nouns, or to differences in the structure associated with the two types of nouns.[17] For example, some proper nouns may be inherently definite singular, while common nouns are not inherently specified for definiteness or for number. It must be borne in mind, however, that the explanation for the contrast must be language-specific, or even dialect-specific, as is the contrast between (58a) and (58b).

Summarizing to this point, we have seen that the DP hypothesis makes two significant claims about the structure of determiners in relation to NP. First, DP, like other categories, has full phrasal structure, including its own Specifier, head and complement positions. Second, the structural relationship between the determiner and NP is a head–complement relation. Movement out of the NP complement is possible, both for XP and X° (phrases and heads). On the hypothesis that some functional elements must be eliminated, the order and co-occurrence of determiners with definite interpretations can be accounted for.

---

[17] Notice that the movement of a specific subcategory of nouns (proper nouns) is similar to the phenomenon of V-movement in English, where only the subcategory of Aux can move to INFL. The movement analysis of proper nouns is due to Longobardi (1994).

2.6   Pre- and post-determiners

The theory of functional categories discussed above has led to the investigation of other specifiers as heads of functional phrases. This implies that the actual structure of NP – now DP – may contain further phrasal projections between DP and NP, a possibility that remains under investigation. One candidate is a phrase associated with expressions of number and quantity that we will refer to as a Quantifier Phrase (QP).[18] The hypothesis that QP is a separate phrase between DP and NP may account for the co-occurrence of definite and indefinite determiners with specifiers of quantity. One such specifier is the cardinals, such as in (60), generated as in (61).

(60)   a. unos tres   libros
              some three books
         b. estos tres   libros
              these three books

(61)

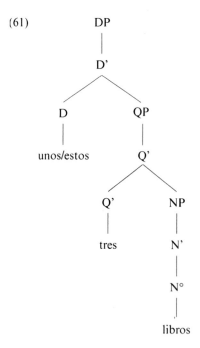

[18] The Quantifier Phrase is proposed for Italian in Giusti (1991). (The analysis presented in the text departs from Giusti's proposal, both with respect to the hierarchical position of QP and with respect to the analysis of "post-determiner" quantifiers.) In addition to the Quantifier Phrase, it is argued by Ritter (1991) that there is a separate phrase for number (NumP), under which the plural affix is generated. For analysis of the NumP in Spanish, see Parodi (1994).

If cardinals were generated as heads of D, rather than Q, it would be impossible to account for sequences in which both are present, such as (60). On the other hand, if cardinals were generated simply as adjuncts (for example, as adjectives) it would be difficult to account for the fact that cardinals can "act alone" as determiners. However, if cardinals are analyzed as functional items, their distribution can be accounted for along lines similar to those of determiners discussed in 2.5.

(62)   [Tres libros] están en la mesa.
         three books are on the table

(63)

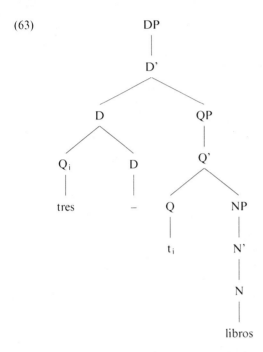

In (63), the Q *tres* has adjoined to D, replacing the determiner. Notice that DPs such as *tres libros* in (62) must be analyzed as having a determiner of some type, rather than simply a pre-nominal adjunct. This is so since the pre-verbal subject position is one which disallows "bare NPs," i.e., DPs without any overt determiner. This is shown by the contrast between (62) and (64):

(64)   *[buenos libros] están en la mesa.
         good books are on the table

Elements such as *varios* "several," *muchos* "many" and *pocos* "few," which may either appear alone as determiners or co-occur with a definite or indefinite determiner, are other candidates for heads of QP.

The structure of QP may also account for the distinctive properties of *todos*, as opposed to quantifiers like *varios* and *pocos*. Recall that *todos* behaves like a "pre-determiner," in that it precedes rather than follows a determiner, as in (65), and co-occurs with other quantifiers, as in (66):

(65)   a. todos los/estos libros
        b. *los/estos todos libros

(66)   todos los diez / muchos libros que   compraste
        all   the ten / many   books   that (you) bought

These generalizations are reminiscent of the co-occurrence of definite determiners discussed above in 2.5. Recall that there it was suggested that these co-occurrences can be accounted for on the assumption that functional elements can be generated either as a head or as a full phrase. Let us extend that analysis to quantifiers. Suppose QP has a specifier position in which a phrasal expression of quantity can be generated. Let us take *todos* to be such a specifier of QP.

(67)

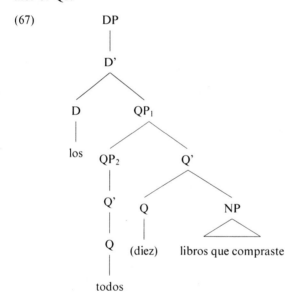

In (67), QP_1 can be headed by a quantity expression, such as *diez* "ten," underlying (66), or by an abstract [+Q] head, as in the structure underlying (65a). To derive the surface order of (65a) or (66), *todos* moves to the specifier of DP, as shown in (68).

Under the assumptions adopted so far, there are several types of evidence that *todos* is generated as QP_2 in (68), that is, as a specifier of QP_1, rather than as the head of QP_1. One type of evidence is the co-occurrence of *todos* with

(68)

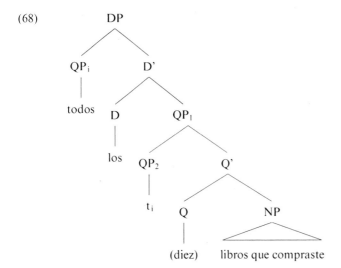

both D and Q, as in (68). This implies that there is a separate phrasal node dominating *todos*.[19] Another type of evidence is the phenomenon of quantifier float, or *Q-float*. This is illustrated in (69):

(69)   **Los estudiantes** dicen **todos** que el   examen fue difícil.
       the students   say   all   that the test   was difficult
       "The students all say that the exam was difficult."

In (69), *todos* appears separated from the DP (*los estudiantes*) with which it is interpreted. Assuming that *todos* is generated together with DP, its separability can be accounted for on the basis of XP (phrasal) movement: the QP dominating *todos* can move from the Spec of DP to other Specifier positions in the clause.[20] Q-float is impossible for heads of QP, which undergo only head movement, and cannot move to phrase-level specifier positions:[21]

(70)   *los estudiantes dicen varios/tres   que ...
        the students   say   several/three that ...
        "The students several/three say that..."

---

[19] The evidence which supports analyzing *todos* as a Specifier of QP is also consistent with the possibility that *todos* is generated directly as a Specifier of DP, instead of QP.
[20] For discussion of Q-float, see Kayne (1975), Sportiche (1988).
[21] *Ambos* "both" behaves like *todos* with respect to Q-float:

(i)   Los estudiantes dijeron ambos que el   examen fue difícil.
      the students   said   both that the exam was difficult
      "The students both said that the exam was difficult."

It is also like *todos* in lacking a partitive form: *ambos de los libros* "both of the books." Unlike *todos*, *ambos* cannot precede the definite article: *ambos los libros* "both the books."

A third type of evidence supporting a structural distinction between *todos* and other quantifiers is the distribution of the partitive construction:

(71)   a. muchos/varios/cinco de los libros
             many/few/five   of the books
         b. *todos de los libros
             all   of the books

In (71a), those specifiers that were analyzed as heads of QP in (61) above can be followed by a *de*+DP, rather than NP. As (71b) shows, *todos* cannot occur in this construction. This contrast may follow from the structural difference between *todos* and other quantifiers discussed before, shown in (68) above. Notice that quantifiers other than *todos* are transitive (not in the sense that they assign a Theta-role, but in the sense that they select an NP complement). *Todos*, on the other hand, is a Specifier of QP, which does not select a complement NP.[22] There are several possible ways of analyzing the structure of partitives, of which we will briefly consider one. Suppose that in the partitive construction the *de*-phrase is not in complement position, but that complement is instead occupied by a covert NP, understood as "*ones*" (see (72)).

(72)

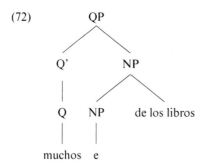

This structure accounts for the absence of an overt NP following the quantifier in the partitive construction. The impossibility of a null NP following *todos* in (71b) would then be related to the fact that *todos* is not a head that selects a complement, therefore it cannot select the null NP "ones."[23]

In summary, the postulation of QP as a phrase that can intervene between DP and NP accounts for the possibility that certain sequences of NP determiners are possible. Additionally, the phrasal structure of QP, with an

---

[22] *Cada* "each" behaves like *todos* in this respect. It lacks a partitive (**cada de los estudiantes* "each of the students" versus *cada estudiante* "each student"), but it differs from *todos* in other respects. It does not precede a determiner, and does not undergo Q-float.

[23] As an alternative, it may be possible to analyze the partitive phrase as a specifier, or external argument of the quantifier:

independent specifier position, accounts for a number of contrasts between the "pre-determiner" *todos* and other quantifiers.

2.7   Specifiers of predicative NPs

The preceding discussion presented the structure in (73) for specifiers of NP.

(73)

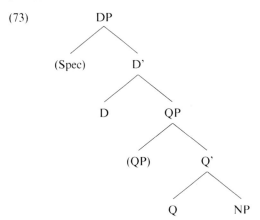

DP is assumed to be obligatory, and QP is optional. (Therefore, DP can select either a QP or an NP as its complement.) DP is the locus of specification for

(i)

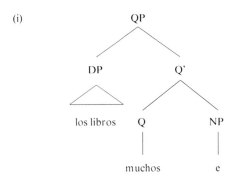

The correct surface order would result from movement of Q to D:

(ii) $[_{DP}$ muchos$_i$ $[_{QP}$ de los libros t$_i$ $[_{NP}$ e]]]

An analysis like (ii) correctly predicts that the partitive construction is incompatible with sequences of a definite or indefinite determiner followed by *muchos* (*esos muchos de los libros*). Notice also that in (ii), *de* is a marker of partitive Case assigned by the quantifier, unlike the adjunct analysis, where *de* is the head of a true prepositional phrase.

(in)definiteness, and QP is the locus of expressions of quantity or amount. Recall also from the preceding discussion that expressions of quantity are in fact determiners, in the sense that they move to D or DP. In this section, we consider the distribution of determiners and quantifiers in predicative NPs.

Under the DP hypothesis described above in 2.5, recall that there is a functional relation between D and its complement NP which "converts" the predicative category NP to a referring expression. Given this view of determiners, predicative NPs might be expected to differ from argument NPs with respect to the necessity of a determiner, since predicative NPs do not refer, but are predicated externally of a subject, as discussed in 2.3.1. As we will see below, predicative NPs do not generally require determiners; however determiners do surface in predicate NPs under specific conditions. We will also see that predicative NPs do not allow as broad a range of determiners as are possible for arguments.

Recall that instances of predicative NPs are the boldfaced items in (74):

(74)   a. María es **doctora**.
            M. is (a) doctor
         b. Ese estudiante parece   **genio**.
            that student   seems (a) genius
         c. Consideran **amigo** a   Juan.
            consider (a) friend PA J.
            "They consider Juan a friend."
         d. Eligieron a   Juan **presidente**.
            elected   PA J.   president
            "They elected Juan president."

Notice that these singular ([-plural]) items are not preceded by a determiner. This contrasts with corresponding singular argument NPs, which generally require a determiner of some type:

(75)   a. María reconoció a *(una) doctora.
            M.   recognized PA (a)   doctor
         b. Ese estudiante conoce a *(un) genio.
            that student   knows PA *(a) genius

The contrast between (74) and (75) suggests that predicative NPs are in fact NPs, not DPs. Predicative NPs may, however, appear with a determiner, if one is needed independently, for example to support a comparative:

(76)   a. *Juan es mejor   amigo.
            J.   is better/best friend
            "Juan is a better / the best friend."
         b. Juan es el   mejor amigo que tengo.
            J.   is the best   friend that have.
            "Juan is the best friend that I have."

    c. Juan es mi mejor amigo.
       J. is my best friend.
    "Juan is my best friend."

In (76), the comparative *mejor* induces a requirement for an overt determiner. Several approaches might be pursued in accounting for the contrast between modified and unmodified predicative NPs. One is that they differ in their interpretation, and this difference is reflected in their category: DP versus NP. Alternatively, it may be that both are DPs, and that the presence or absence of an overt D is determined by phrase-internal relations.

Let us turn now to those determiners that have been analyzed as generated under QP. This class of determiners is uniformly absent for predicative NPs, whether modified or not:

(77)   a. Ellos son (*muchos/varios/pocos/tres) pilotos.
           they are many/several/few/three   pilots
        b. Ellos son los (*muchos) pilotos que   conocí ayer.
           they are the many   pilots that (I) met yesterday

Finally, notice that it appears at first glance that the QPs *todos* and *ambos* can co-occur with predicative NPs:

(78)   Ellos son todos/ambos pilotos.
        they are all/both   pilots

Although the position occupied by *todos* in (78) appears to be a specifier of the predicative NP, notice that *todos* is related to *ellos*, not *pilotos*. That is, (78) is a variant of (79):

(79)   Todos ellos son pilotos.
        all   they are pilots
        "All of them are pilots."

The discontinuity of [*todos ellos*] is then a result of Q-float. This is confirmed by the fact that where the subject NP has its own quantifier, *todos* becomes impossible:

(80)   *Muchos de ellos son todos pilotos.
         many   of them are all   pilots

To summarize, we have seen above that predicative NPs have overt determiners only if modified, and do not take any QPs.

2.8   Constituent order within NP

The last topic that we address with respect to NP concerns the order of adjectival adjuncts in NP relative to the head and complements. Recall from

2.4 that the preliminary phrasal "skeleton" introduced there, repeated below as (81), generates the basic order summarized in (82).

(81)

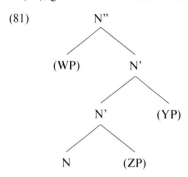

(82)   Head – Complement – Adjunct

Most adjuncts, including PPs, APs, clauses and small clauses occupy the "canonical" adjunct position at S-structure. APs, however, have greater freedom of position with respect to the head and complements. Certain APs may be pre-nominal as well as post-nominal, as illustrated in (83):[24]

(83)   a. una comida muy buena
            a   meal   very good
        "a very good meal"
        b. una muy buena comida
            a   very good   meal

Furthermore, APs can also appear between the head noun and a complement:

(84)   la destrucción completa de la ciudad
        the destruction complete of the city

In this section, we will consider how these orders are derived.

Let us take as a starting point the alternative orders in (83), and consider several ways of generating these two orders. One possible analysis is that each order is base-generated in the same order that appears on the surface. That is, each order is generated from a separate D-structure, which implies that adjuncts can have more freedom of position than was given in the basic phrasal "skeleton" in (81). Suppose instead that adjuncts could be generated either before or after the N' to which the adjunct is adjoined, as shown in (85):

[24] Pre-nominal APs cannot contain complements:

(i)   a. un competente pianista
            a   competent   pianist
        b. *un competente en jazz pianista
            a   competent   in jazz pianist

This generalization also holds in English, as noted in Emonds (1976). This is shown by the ungrammaticality of the gloss for (ib).

(85)

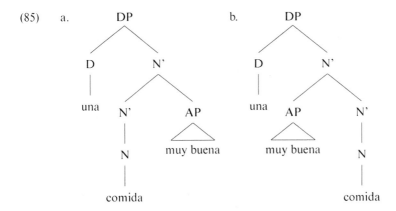

On this analysis, the contrast in order between complements (which must follow the head) and adjuncts (which can precede or follow the head) could derive from theta-theory: theta-marking by the head may be from left to right in head-initial languages. However, this analysis has several drawbacks. First, it does not account for the fact that adjuncts other than APs must be post-nominal. Consequently, the structure shown in (85b) would generate ungrammatical sequences, for example with pre-nominal PPs or other types of adjuncts. Second, recall from Section 2.4 that qualitative adjectives (those which can be both pre-nominal and post-nominal) have different interpretations depending on their order. Post-nominally, they are restrictive, while pre-nominally their interpretation is appositive. The analysis in (85) does not provide any way of accounting for this difference in interpretation.

A variation of this analysis overcomes the last drawback noted above. Pre-nominal APs (with an appositive interpretation) can be analyzed as Specifiers of NP (daughters of N″) rather than as adjuncts. Example (85b) would then have the structure shown in (86).

(86)

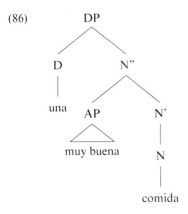

The idea underlying this analysis is that the level at which a non-argument is attached plays a role in determining how the constituent is interpreted in the phrase. Jackendoff (1977) argued that restrictive modifiers are lower in the structure than are non-restrictive modifiers. A restrictive modifier may be assumed to receive its restrictive interpretation via the adjunction structure – from the additional N' that is present. A non-restrictive modifier is simply a specifier, without an additional N'.

Let us now return to the third position in which APs can occur – between the head and its complement, illustrated in (84), repeated below:

(84)   la destrucción completa de la ciudad
        the destruction complete of the city

Consider first the possibility that this order is base-generated (in other words, that the surface order is the same as the D-structure order). If we continue to assume that only binary branching is permitted, the structure would be as in (87).

(87)

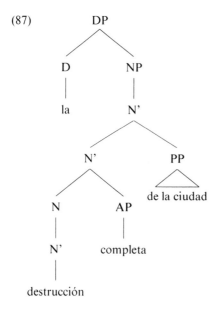

Here, the AP *completa* is a post-nominal adjunct, and the complement PP is – incorrectly – also adjoined. This structure cannot be correct, because the PP is not a sister of the head, and therefore cannot be theta-marked.

A plausible alternative to base-generating the structure shown above is to suppose that the complement has undergone rightward movement from a D-structure position adjacent to the head (see (87)).

(88)

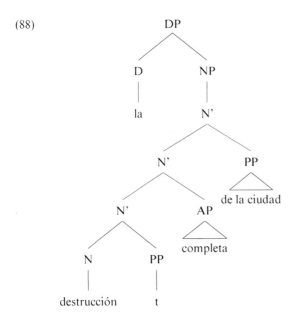

On this analysis, the PP is a sister of the head at D-structure, and can be theta-marked by it.

Although the preceding analysis achieves an adequate description of the surface order of constituents in NP, it has been questioned on several grounds, both theoretical and empirical. One theoretical point that is a topic of ongoing inquiry is whether there is any rightward movement at all (Kayne 1994). Leaving aside this issue, which takes us beyond the matter at hand, let us consider two related empirical issues. First, the possibility for noun–adjective–complement order is common, not just in Spanish, but in Romance generally, and differs from other languages and language families, as can be illustrated easily in English, which disallows: *the destruction complete of the city. This cross-linguistic contrast suggests that there is a syntactic parameter at work. Since parameters are not construction-specific, but involve general lexical properties of the language, it would be desirable to account for this particular order in as general a manner as possible. Furthermore, notice that the Romance/English parameter is not restricted to Noun Phrases, but is reflected also in the order of constituents in clauses:

(89)   a. Destruyeron   completamente la   ciudad.
          destroyed.3rd.pl. completely   the city
          "They completely destroyed the city."
       b. María escribió ayer   una carta.
          M.   wrote   yesterday a letter
          "Maria wrote a letter yesterday."

(90)   a. *They destroyed completely the city.
         b. *Maria wrote yesterday a letter.

The sentences in (89) show that, in Spanish, an adverb can intervene between a verb and its complement, while corresponding examples in (90) show that in English, this order is ungrammatical. Presumably, the account of NP constituent order should generalize to clausal constituent order. In fact, research on clausal word order has led the way to a unified analysis of these phenomena. Following Emonds (1978), the contrast in (89) versus (90) is due to the movement of main verbs to the inflectional head of the clause – INFL, shown in (91).

(91)

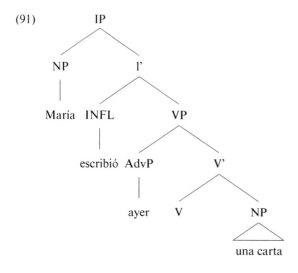

On this derivation, which will be discussed in Chapter 4, an adverb is generated in the specifier of VP, and the verb moves to its left. The absence of verb movement in English is confirmed by the impossibility of fronting a verb in questions (e.g., *Wrote Mary a letter?).

Likewise, it has been proposed that the position to which nouns move must be the head of a functional category that is associated with NP (Mallén 1989; Cinque 1992). That category must be lower than the DP structure – because the noun is still to the right of any determiners. The functional category in question has been argued to be associated with the noun's inflectional features of number and gender. We will refer to these features as an Agreement Phrase (AgrP), since these features are shared by the noun and its agreeing modifiers. On this analysis, the structure of (84) is as shown in (92).

(92)

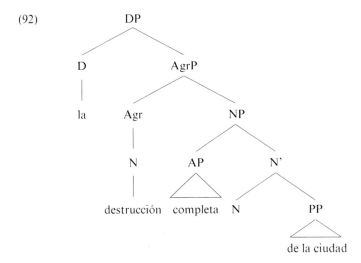

The noun is not in its original position – the position in which it theta-marks its complement. It has moved to a higher (functional) head that is associated with the noun's inflection. It has been argued that the relative "richness" or "strength" of agreement in Romance languages explains why this order is possible in Spanish (as in other Romance languages) but not in English. In English, the "weakness" of the Agreement Phrase does not attract the noun to this position (except at the level of logical form). Consequently, the order noun–adjective–complement does not occur in English.

As a final point, let us return briefly to the analysis of the pre-nominal adjective position, illustrated in (93):

(93)　　a. la　completa destrucción de la　ciudad
　　　　　　the complete destruction of the city
　　　　b. una　muy　buena　comida
　　　　　　a　　very　good　meal

Recall that the structure of (93b), shown in (86) above, was analyzed as having an adjective in the NP specifier position. Assuming now that there is an AgrP above NP, there are now two possible ways of deriving pre-nominal adjective order. One possibility is that the noun is in its base position, rather than in the head of AgrP, and the adjective is in the NP specifier. On this analysis, movement of the noun to Agr is optional. A second possibility, however, is that the noun has moved to the head of AgrP, and that the adjective has also moved, to the specifier of AgrP.

Summarizing the main points of this section, we have seen that there is a subclass of adjective, qualitative adjectives, that can be generated in two positions: (a) in standard post-nominal adjunct position, where they are interpreted as restrictive modifiers; and (b) in specifier of NP position, where they receive an appositive interpretation. The order head–adjective–complement cannot be generated directly from a D-structure in which the adjective follows the head since, on this derivation, shown in (87) above, the head could not theta-mark its complement. Two ways of deriving this order by movement were considered. One analysis is rightward movement of the complement; a second analysis, which unifies NP constituent order with clausal constituent order, is leftward movement of the noun. As in clauses, the position to which the noun moves has been proposed to be a functional category associated with inflection (here, nominal inflection for number and gender). Differences between English and Romance with respect to this order have been explained in terms of the relative richness or "strength" of nominal inflection in the two language families.

2.9   Summary

In this chapter, the noun phrase has been examined from two perspectives. From the phrase-external perspective, we considered the distribution and interpretation of NP, as well as the principles that license NPs. In 2.2 and 2.3, two types of NPs were discussed: argument NPs and predicative NPs. Argument NPs are licensed by Theta-role assignment and by Case. Since the heads that assign Theta-roles are not necessarily Case assigners, NP may move in the course of a derivation to satisfy a requirement for Case. Predicative NPs are not licensed by Theta-roles, but are predicates that are interpreted via Predication. Section 2.4 introduced preliminary characteristics of the internal structure of the phrase. These include (a) the relations between the head and the phrase (headedness, endocentricity), and (b) the types of constituents that co-occur with a noun to form a Noun Phrase: complements, adjuncts and specifiers. Sections 2.5–2.7 focused on the determiner system. In Section 2.5, the distribution of determiners and their analysis as DPs was introduced. Section 2.6 then discussed "pre-determiners" and "post-determiners": constituents that can co-occur with determiners, or can function as determiners themselves. These elements were analyzed as functional elements generated in a Quantifier Phrase. Section 2.7 summarized the determiner system of predicative NPs, which has overt determiners when modified, but cannot have independent quantifiers. Section 2.8 returned to "lower" NP structure, and considered the derivation of NPs that contain pre-nominal APs as well as APs that intervene between the head and its complement. These orders have been analyzed in terms of movement of the head noun to the left – to the head of a functional category that we have called AgrP. This category bears inflectional features of number and gender, and is analogous to the inflectional head of clauses. A noun phrase such as (94) then may include the functional projections shown in (95):

(94) todas estas varias interesantes categorías estudiadas
      all   these several interesting categories studied

(95)

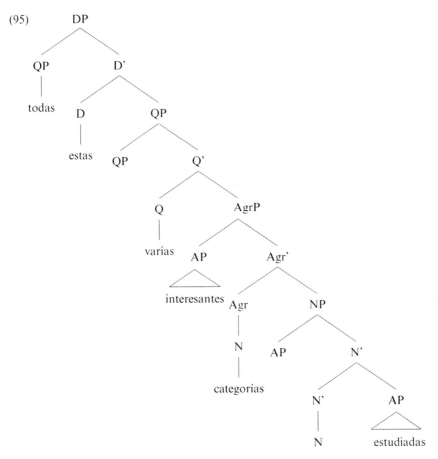

3

The Verb Phrase

3.1 Introduction

In Chapter 2, we studied the Noun Phrase from two points of view. First, from a phrase-external perspective, we discussed the contexts in which NP is found, and introduced subtheories that account for NP distribution. We then examined the internal structure of the phrase, describing the basic structural and functional relations among constituents that co-occur with a noun to form NP (or DP). In this chapter and in Chapter 4, we will consider these same issues with respect to the Verb Phrase (VP). We will begin the discussion in this chapter with an overview of the distribution of VP, and provide a preliminary description of principles that account for this distribution (Section 3.2). We will see that there are two grammatical relations that restrict the distribution of VP: the relation between VP and the clausal subject, and the relation between VP and Tense. Subsequent sections of this chapter will be concerned with relations between the head of the phrase and its arguments. Section 3.3 discusses the external argument, or subject; Sections 3.4–3.7 describe complements or internal arguments. Although we will not provide a detailed account of the properties of verbal arguments, we will see that the subtheories introduced in Chapter 2 provide a means of structurally distinguishing verbal arguments from non-arguments. In Chapter 4, we will take up several additional issues related to the structure of the Verb Phrase, including how clitics and auxiliary verbs are related to the verb and its arguments.

3.2 The distribution of VP

This section is concerned with the contexts in which Verb Phrases are found. We begin in 3.2.1 with a summary of environments in which VP is generated, and then discuss in 3.2.2 two factors that determine this distribution.

118

3.2.1 VP as primary predicate of the clause

Consider first the contrast between sentences (1a) and (1b):

(1)   a. Susana descansó.
            "Susana rested."
         b. *Susana cansada
            "Susana tired"

These sentences differ in the category of their main predicate. In (1a), the predicate is the VP headed by the verb *descansó*, while in (1b), assuming that no verb has been ellipted, the main predicate is an Adjective Phrase headed by *cansada*. This contrast in grammaticality illustrates the first generalization with respect to the distribution of VP, namely that a VP – and only VP – occurs as the primary predicate in clauses.[1] Notice that this contrast would be difficult to account for on semantic grounds, since adjectives and verbs are both predicative categories that can describe states, and they can be similar in their argument structure. The difference between VP and AP (likewise, NP and PP) must be a syntactic difference. A simplified (surface) structure for (1a) is shown in (2a), and the distributional generalization is given as (2b). In (2), the clause is IP (Inflectional Phrase), whose head, INFL, contains features for Tense (and Agreement), and VP is the sister of the INFL node. Let us refer to this position as the "primary predicate" of the clause.

(2)   a.

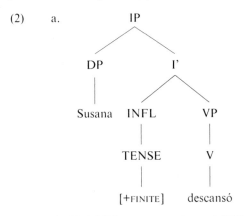

b. (Only) VP occurs as a sister of INFL (as "primary predicate" of a
   clause).

---

[1] This generalization is common cross-linguistically. Some languages, however, such as Japanese, appear to allow categories other than VP as main clausal predicates.

As we will see below, VP does not occur in adjunct positions, where it corresponds to a "secondary predicate" of a clause, as in (3), where there is a VP in an adjunct position (VP_2) that is not contained in a separate clause. Adjuncts can of course contain VPs, but, in such cases, there is evidence that the VP is a sister of a separate IP node, so that the VP within the adjunct conforms to (2b). This is illustrated by the contrast between (4a) and (4b):

(3)

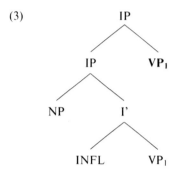

(4)   a. Susana dejó la sala [cansada].
        "Susana left the room [tired]."
        b. *Susana dejó la sala [descansaba/descansar]
        "Susana left the room [(she) rested/to rest]"

In (4a), there is a clausal adjunct or secondary predicate, the AP *cansada*. In (4b), the secondary predicate is a VP, which is ungrammatical in both finite and non-finite form. Notice that (4b) becomes grammatical if the adjunct is introduced by a preposition like *para* "in order":

(5)   a. Susana dejó la sala para descansar.
        "Susana left the room in order to rest."
        b. Susana dejó la sala para que José descansara.
        "Susana left the room in order that José rest."

Para selects as its complement a clause, as is shown by the presence of the overt complementizer *que* in (5b). In this context, either an infinitive or finite (subjunctive) form of the verb is possible, because VP is again related to an IP in the subordinate clause.

We have seen that VP is obligatory as the primary predicate of the clause, or IP, as shown in (1) above. VP is impossible as a secondary predicate of a clause, as shown by the contrast in (4) above. A VP may appear within an adjunct only if, within that adjunct, it is the primary predicate of a separate IP node. There are certain adjuncts, such as those illustrated in (6), that superficially resemble VPs rather than full clauses:

(6)   a. Llegado José, empezó la fiesta.
        "José arrived, the party began."
        b. Habiendo terminado la lección, Susana salió.
        "Having finished the lesson, Susana left."

These participial adjuncts might appear to be a constituent closer in structure to VP than to IP. However, comparable Italian constructions are argued in Belletti (1990) to have clausal structure. One argument supporting this conclusion concerns the order of the participle relative to an overt subject, such as *José* in (6a). An overt subject of a participial clause must follow the participle:

(7)   *José llegado, empezó la   fiesta.
        José arrived, began   the party

Belletti (1990) argues that the order participle–subject can be explained on the assumption that the participle has undergone head movement to an empty complementizer position, as shown in (8) (with a simplified structure):

(8) $[_{CP}$ llegado $[_{IP}$ José $[_{VP} -]]]$

The presence of the complementizer position as a landing site for verb movement then provides indirect evidence that the structure is a clause, just as the overt complementizer indicates clausal structure in (5b).

There is one quite clear exception to the generalization that VP appears only as a primary predicate. In clauses with auxiliary verbs, sequences of VPs are possible, as in (9b):

(9)   a. Los niños comieron.
        "The children ate."
        b. Los niños han comido.
        "The children have eaten."

Assuming both the auxiliary and the participle to be verbs, (9b) must have two VPs, one dominating each verb. There have been numerous proposals in the literature as to the structure of sequences with auxiliaries, and we will defer fuller discussion of their structure and function until Chapter 4. Here, the point of interest is that, if such sequences contain two verbs (and therefore two VPs), but only one INFL node, it follows that one of these VPs is in some position other than that of primary predicate. Two possible analyses of the structural relation between an auxiliary and the following participle are shown in (10).

In (10a), the VP dominating the auxiliary is structurally the primary predicate (sister of INFL), and the participle is also the sister of a head – but the

(10)

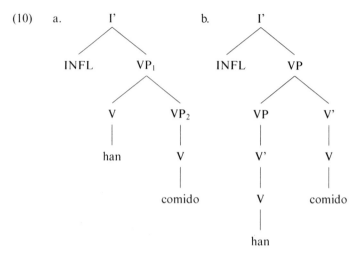

head is the auxiliary verb. In (10b), the auxiliary VP is analyzed as a specifier of the participle, the latter being in primary predicate position. Both of these structures require some "loosening" of the description of VP distribution. Either the VP can occur as the sister of (a) INFL or (b) an auxiliary verb (structure (10a)); or VPs headed by certain verbs – auxiliaries – may be specifiers or adjuncts of a primary predicate. Finally, note that any analysis of auxiliaries must be able to accommodate multiple auxiliaries:

(11)   Esta manzana puede haber estado siendo comida.
         "This apple may have been being eaten."

Another possible exception to the distribution of VP as a primary predicate is constructions with verbs that are informally described as "semi-auxiliaries." These verbs are main verbs according to standard diagnostics (for example, unlike auxiliaries, they select their own arguments). However, when followed by an infinitival complement, the sequence of verb+infinitive behaves syntactically like sequences of auxiliary followed by main verb. These predicates include aspectual and volitional verbs like (12), and causative and perception verbs such as (13):

(12)   a. María lo   quiere cantar.
            M.   CL(Acc.) wants to sing
            "Maria wants to sing it."
         b. Pedro lo   volvió   a copiar.
            P.   CL(Acc.) returned to copy
            "Pedro copied it again."

(13)   a. Juan se lo hizo escribir (a Pedro).
            J. CL(Dat.) CL(Acc.) made write (to P.)
            "Juan made him (Pedro) write it."

b. María lo   vio pasar.
   M.   CL(Acc.) saw happen
   "Maria saw it happen."

Predicates of the type in (12), referred to as "Restructuring" predicates, continue to be topics of investigation. Although there has been controversy as to the underlying structure of these sequences, there is consensus that in the superficial structure (and the logical form) of these sentences, the infinitive behaves like a constituent of the matrix clause. (See Chapter 6, Section 6.5.)

Summarizing, we have seen above that the contexts in which VP occurs are restricted: the principal context is as a sister of INFL, i.e., as the primary predicate of a clause. VP does not occur as an independent adjunct. The clearest exception to this generalization is auxiliary verbs.

3.2.2   Licensing VP

In this section, we will restrict our attention to VP as primary predicate, that is, in the position of sister of INFL, as shown in (14).

(14)

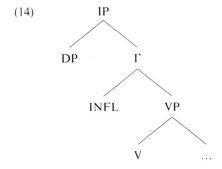

Here, VP is licensed both by its relation to the subject DP and by its relation to INFL. Let us consider these in turn. The relation between VP and the subject is via Predication. Recall from Chapter 2 that a predicative NP is licensed by Predication – a relation between the NP and an argument that is interpreted as its subject. Likewise, VP is predicated of a subject. In (14), VP is in a configuration that satisfies Predication. Although the VP and the subject DP are not mutually c-commanding, (Chapter 2, Section 2.2.2), they satisfy a slightly "looser" configurational requirement: mutual m-command.[2]

---

[2] M-command is defined as in (i):
   (i) α m-commands β iff α does not dominate β and every maximal projection that dominates α dominates β.
   In (14), the subject and VP m-command each other, since neither dominates the other and the only maximal projection that dominates one dominates the other – the IP.

The principle that enforces Predication for VP is referred to as the *Extended Projection Principle* (*EPP*), which states that every clause must have a subject. Because VP is the primary predicate in clauses, the EPP "enforces" Predication for VP.

Although the subject of a clause is not always overt, different types of clauses provide evidence that a subject constituent is present.[3] This can be illustrated for finite clauses in Spanish, which – unlike in English – allow "covert" subjects – subjects that lack phonetic content:

(15)   a. Mary walked.
        b. *Walked.

(16)   a. María caminó.
        "Maria walked."
        b. Caminó.
        walk.past.3rd.sg.
        "You/she/he walked."

The contrast between the grammaticality of (16b) and the ungrammaticality of (15b) in English is described in terms of the presence versus absence of "null subjects." Although one might be tempted to analyze (16b) as lacking a subject DP, there is evidence that (16b) has a DP in the specifier of IP which simply lacks phonetic content, as shown in (17).

(17)

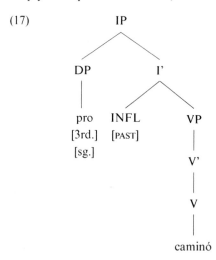

---

[3] It is well beyond the scope of the present discussion to show that clauses must have subjects. We will touch on this topic in Chapter 4. In-depth discussion is to be found in Rothstein (1983).

Here, the subject position is occupied by a DP that has syntactic features, but no overt phonetic features. One type of evidence supporting this analysis is that the VP in (16b) is interpreted as an event performed by an Agent, which means that a Theta-role has been assigned to some constituent. There are also features carried by DPs – beyond the person and number features that are overtly marked on the verb. These are semantic features such as [+HUMAN], which allow the DP to satisfy the semantic selectional restrictions of the predicate. The features of the subject constituent also allow it to participate in various grammatical processes. For example, the subject can serve as the antecedent of a reflexive (e.g., *Hablaba consigo mismo* "He talked to himself"). If an appropriate antecedent for a reflexive is not present in the structure, the sentence becomes ungrammatical, as in: *El problema fue resuelto por sí mismo* "The problem was solved by himself."

Returning to the main point, the obligatoriness of the clausal subject under the EPP has the effect of ensuring that VP will be licensed by Predication. However, this does not by itself automatically account for the ungrammaticality of VP as an adjunct, since predicative adjuncts also undergo Predication. The restricted distribution of VP must therefore be accounted for on some other basis. There is, as noted above, another constituent in IP with which VP is related: the head, INFL, bears Tense features that are related to the inflectional morphology of the verb. Although the precise nature of the relationship between INFL and V is a topic of ongoing research (and is a point to which we return in Chapters 4 and 5), we can describe the relation here in informal terms. The Tense features of INFL ([±FINITE], [±PAST]) participate in determining the interpretation of VP, because these features provide a "temporal specification" or temporal "location" for the event expressed by the VP. It is possible to think of these features of INFL as a type of determiner for VP. On this view, we might draw an analogy between the INFL/VP relation in (14) and the Det/NP relation that was discussed in Chapter 2. In fact, IP is standardly analyzed as a functional category, although, as noted above, the precise nature of its functional relation to VP is under active investigation.

We have considered here the conditions that account for the occurrence of VP in primary predication contexts. Recall, though, that VP can also occur as a sister of certain verbs, including auxiliaries and semi-auxiliaries. To unify these contexts with those discussed above, it may be possible to analyze these auxiliary verbs as having grammatical features that are similar in relevant ways to Tense features. This would allow them to provide a "temporal specification" for VP just as INFL does. In other words, these verbs might be analyzed as functional categories that share certain crucial properties with INFL. These issues will be taken up in Chapter 4. Below, we will turn to consideration of one facet of phrase-internal syntax, namely the relations between the verb and its arguments.

3.3   The external argument of VP

We saw above in 3.2 that, due to the EPP, a subject constituent must be present in the Specifier of IP and, once that constituent is present, Predication co-indexing occurs. In this section, we will take a closer look at the derivation of the subject. We will see below that the interaction of theta-theory and Case theory determines the position of the subject at *D-structure* (the initial syntactic representation, or "deep" structure) and *S-structure* (the representation after overt movement, or "surface" structure). One issue that we will be concerned with is the conditions under which a subject is assigned a Theta-role by the predicate. Recall from the discussion of theta-theory in Chapter 2 that a DP is an argument (i.e., can have reference) only if it is assigned a Theta-role. As is illustrated by the contrast between (18a) and (18b), not all predicates assign a Theta-role to a subject:

(18)   a. Los niños leyeron los libros.
            "The children read the books."
         b. Parece que los niños leyeron los libros.
            "(It) seems that the children read the books."

In (18a), the VP headed by *leyeron* assigns a Theta-role (Agent) to the DP *los niños*. In (18b), the VP headed by *parece* does not assign any Theta-role to the subject, and the covert pronoun can only be interpreted as pleonastic (non-referential). This pleonastic pronoun is grammatically necessary to satisfy the EPP (and hence, Predication). The VPs headed by *leyeron* "read" and *parece* "seem" differ with respect to their argument structure: only the former has the lexical property of assigning a thematic role to an "external" or subject argument. The first topic that we will address below in 3.3.1 is the relationship between this lexical property and the D-structure syntactic representation. We will then see how theta-assignment interacts with Case to derive the S-structure representation. Then, in 3.3.2 we will consider a variant of (18b) in which a pleonastic has not been inserted, as shown in (19):

(19)   Los niños parecen haber leído los libros.
         "The children seem to have read the books."

In (19), the main clause has an S-structure referential subject, *los niños* – despite the fact that the predicate *parece* does not assign any external Theta-role.

3.3.1 *Theta-role assignment and Case assignment to the external argument*

To explore Theta-role assignment to the external argument, consider again predicates such as *leer* which assign a Theta-role, setting aside for the moment predicates like *parecer*, which do not. As noted above, the assignment of Theta-roles by individual verbs is largely idiosyncratic. The fact that argument structure is not predictable means that it must be specified in the verb's lexical entry. The lexical entry for *leer*, for example, would include the role "Agent" (*los niños* in (18a)), and the role "Theme" (*los libros* in (18a)). Furthermore, the lexical entry must specify a structural context in which each role is assigned. The verb *leyeron* assigns the role "Theme" to its complement (or "internal argument"), and the role "Agent" to its subject (or "external argument"). These roles are not interchangeable. We cannot say: *los libros leyeron (a) los niños*, meaning that the children read the books. The lexical entry for *leer* must not only specify the roles assigned by the verb, but must also differentiate its external from its internal role(s). This can be specified in the lexical entry as shown in (20):

(20)   leer: V   Theme Agent(External)

In (20), the Agent role has been identified as an "external" argument. Arguments not so specified are "internal" arguments, or complements of the verb.

Theta-theory characterizes the configuration in which Theta-roles such as those in (20) are syntactically realized on, or assigned to, a constituent. Internal arguments are generated usually as sisters of the verb; their Theta-role is assigned by a head to a sister of the head (see (21)). We will see in later sections that Theta-role assignment is not restricted to sister constituents, but is possible as long as the head *c-commands* the complement. The head c-commands the complement if the first branching node dominating the verb (here, V′) also dominates the complement. Constituents that are sisters both c-command each other. In (21), DP also c-commands the head, because the first branching node that dominates DP also dominates V. Mutual c-command is not essential to theta-marking, but the head that assigns a Theta-role must c-command the constituent to which the Theta-role is assigned.

(21)

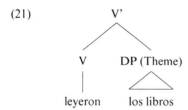

But what about the external argument's Theta-role? In earlier versions of transformational grammar, it was assumed that the subject of a clause was generated in the specifier of IP, in which case it is structurally distant from the verb – more distant even than adjuncts of VP. More recently, it has been argued that the external argument of the verb is generated within the VP. In particular, the external argument position is analyzed as generated in the Specifier of VP, as shown in (22). Here, there is no DP in the specifier of the IP in D-structure; the Agent role is assigned to a DP that is in the specifier position of VP. This position is distinct from complement position, in that the Agent DP is not a sister of the head. It was noted above that the verb assigns a Theta-role to a sister constituent. In (22), the external argument is a sister of V′, and Chomsky (1986) has suggested that external Theta-roles are actually assigned by V′ – that is, compositionally by the verb together with its sister constituent.[4] If this is correct, then all Theta-roles are assigned to a sister: in (22), the Theme role is assigned by the verb to its sister; the Agent role is assigned by V′ to its sister in the Specifier of VP. This analysis of theta-assignment to the external argument is referred to as the "VP-internal subject hypothesis."

The structural conditions under which Theta-roles are assigned then determine the position of the external argument at D-structure. Let us now consider the derivation to S-structure. Recall from Chapter 2 that DP must be also assigned Case. The verb does not by itself assign Case to its external argument. The Case of a subject (Nominative Case) is instead assigned by the head of the clause, INFL, to a DP in its specifier position. Consequently, the external argument in the Specifier of VP must move to the Specifier of IP (see (23)). This movement then produces a surface structure in which the subject is in its

---

[4] As noted in Chapter 2, external roles are assigned compositionally, as illustrated in (i):

(i)   a. John broke the window.   (External role: AGENT)
       b. John broke his arm.   (External role: THEME)

These sentences illustrate that the role of the subject of the verb *break* can vary depending on features of the complement.

(22)

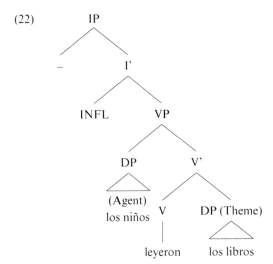

"canonical" position, i.e., the Specifier of IP. Note that, unlike English, the clausal subject in Spanish does not always precede the verb in declaratives, a difference that might be attributed to a parametric difference in Case assignment. (See also Chapter 5 on clausal constituent order.)

(23)

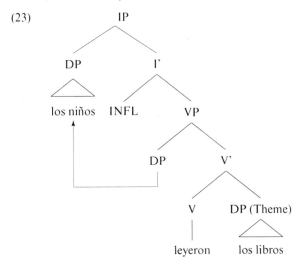

Summarizing to this point, we have differentiated two types of Theta-roles: internal roles, assigned to complement positions, and external roles, assigned by V' to an argument in the Specifier of VP. Movement of that argument to the position of "clausal subject," or Specifier of IP, is triggered by Case, because INFL is the assignor of Nominative Case.

3.3.2   Subject-to-subject raising

The derivation of the clausal subject discussed above characterizes the external argument as related to two different constituents. It is "theta-related" to V′ (i.e., is assigned its Theta-role by V′); and it is "Case-related" to INFL (i.e., is assigned Case by INFL). At S-structure then, the subject does not occupy just a single position, but forms a *chain* consisting of two DP positions: the Specifier of VP (the position to which a Theta-role is assigned), and the Specifier of IP (the position to which Case is assigned). Analyzing the derivation of the clausal subject in this way provides a natural account for alternations like (24a) versus (24b):

(24)   a. Parece que los niños leyeron los libros. (=18b)
        b. Los niños parecen haber leído los libros.
        "The children seem to have read the books."

In (24a), the subject of the main clause is the covert pleonastic pronoun corresponding to English *it*. As noted above, this pronoun has no reference because *parecer* does not assign any Theta-role to it. Nevertheless, in order to satisfy the EPP (and Predication), the covert pronoun is inserted in the Specifier of IP, where it is assigned Case, and where it also triggers subject–verb agreement. The main clause in (24a) has a "grammatical" subject – one that has grammatical features, and Case, but it has no semantic content, which follows from the fact that it is not assigned a Theta-role. Now consider (24b). The subject of the main clause *does* have semantic content, which means that it must bear a Theta-role. However, this role cannot have been assigned by *parecer*, which we have seen in (24a) does not assign an external role. How can the role in (24b) have been assigned? Notice that a verb in the subordinate clause assigns an Agent role. Notice as well that in (24b), unlike (24a), the subordinate clause is not finite. What these facts suggest is that the Agent DP is generated in the Specifier of the VP of the subordinate clause, and it has moved to the Specifier of IP in the main clause, where it is assigned Case. The D-structure of the subordinate clause is shown in (25a), the S-structure in (25b):

(25)   a. [parece [$_{IP}$ – INFL [$_{VP}$ los niños [haber [leído los libros]]]]]
        b. los niños INFL [parecen [$_{IP}$ – INFL [$_{VP}$ [haber [leído los libros]]]]]

The construction illustrated in (25) is referred to informally as "Subject-to-subject Raising" or simply "Raising," because the external argument of a subordinate clause has undergone movement to a higher clause (i.e., has "raised"). This movement of DP is triggered by Case: the DP moves from its theta-position in the lower clause to the Specifier of the matrix IP where it is assigned Nominative Case. This movement also satisfies the EPP for the main clause, since, once this movement has taken place, the matrix IP has a subject. Finally, notice that Raising cannot occur in structures like (24a), where the subordinate clause is finite, although we will not explore here the reasons why it is impossible. Notice, however, that if movement were to occur, the moved NP would have Case twice: the Nominative Case from its original position in the subordinate clause, and the Nominative Case from INFL of the main clause.

3.4   Complements of V: prepositional complements versus adjuncts

We turn now to the structural position that is closest to the verb, namely the sister of the head, or complement position, shown as XP in (26):

(26)

V   XP (complement; sister of V)

This is a position that is theta-marked by the verb. It can be occupied by complements of different categories, such as those illustrated in (27):

(27)   a. Pedro dijo **que los niños leyeron los libros.**   (CP) (=clause)
           "Pedro said **that the children read the books.**"
       b. Susana pateó **la pelota.**   (DP)
           "Susana kicked **the ball.**"
       c. Juan habló **con el vecino.**   (PP)
           "Juan talked **with the neighbor.**"

All of the complements in (27) are generated in the position XP in (26), which is the position that is theta-marked by the verb. One of the first questions that arise concerning the analysis of complements is simply: how do we know whether a constituent that follows the verb is a complement at all? On what basis are complements differentiated from adjuncts? To illustrate the problem, consider the PPs following the verb *hablar* in (28):

(28)   a. Juan habló de política.
           "Juan spoke about politics."
       b. Juan habló de nuevo.
           Juan spoke of new
           "Juan spoke again."

As we will see below, there are diagnostics that can be applied to a given constituent to determine its relation to the head. These will show that in (28a), the

PP *de política* is a complement of *habló*; in (28b), the PP *de nuevo* is an adjunct, which is a sister of V'. Their respective structures are shown in (29a,b).

(29)   a.

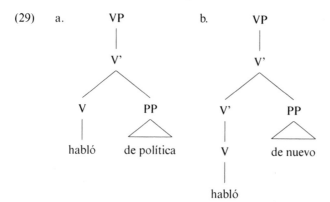

Diagnostics which distinguish PP complements from PP adjuncts include: (a) *hacerlo* "do so" replacement, and (b) substitutability of the preposition. *Hacerlo* is a proform which replaces a V' constituent, i.e., the head and its complement. Let us illustrate this first with the verb *patear* and its DP complement:

(30)   Pedrito pateó la pelota y José lo hizo también.
        "Pedrito kicked the ball and José did so too."

In the second conjunct of (30), *lo hizo* is a proform that has replaced a second occurrence of the constituent *pateó la pelota*. The antecedent of this proform is the V' (*pateó la pelota*) in the first conjunct. Like English *do so*, *hacerlo* may also replace a higher V', one which dominates V' and an adjunct. To see this, consider first (31a), whose VP structure contains two V' nodes, as shown in (31b).

(31)   a. Pedrito pateó la pelota con entusiasmo.
           "Pedrito kicked the ball with enthusiasm."

        b.

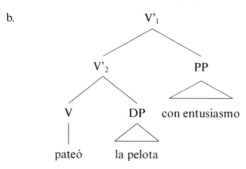

Hacerlo can replace either of the V′ constituents in (31b) as shown by the two examples in (32), where the antecedent of *hacerlo* is boldfaced:

(32)   a. Pedrito **pateó la pelota** con entusiasmo pero José lo hizo distraídamente.
        "Pedrito **kicked the ball** with enthusiasm but José did so distractedly."
       b. Pedrito **pateó la pelota con entusiasmo** y José lo hizo también.
        "Pedrito **kicked the ball with enthusiasm** and José did so too."

In (32a), based on the understood antecedent of *hacerlo*, we can say that it "replaces" V'_2 in the structure (31b) of the first conjunct. Since the adjunct is not included, we can say that it has been "left behind" rather than being replaced. In (32b), *lo hizo* can be interpreted as replacing V'_1, so that the adjunct is included in the material replaced by *hacerlo*.[5]

Summarizing to this point, we have seen that *hacerlo* can replace any V′ in a structure, so that an adjunct phrase may either be replaced or "left behind." We will now see that *hacerlo* must replace a V′, never just a verb: a complement cannot be left behind. This is shown by the ungrammaticality of (33):

(33)   *Pedrito pateó la pelota y José lo hizo el jugete.
        "Pedrito kicked the ball and José did so the toy."

The intended reading of (33) is that *hacerlo* replaces only *pateó* in the first conjunct, leaving behind the complement. The ungrammaticality of (33) shows that *hacerlo* replaces only V′, not V.

Let us now apply the *hacerlo* test to examples with prepositional phrases, as in (34):

(34)   Juan habló de política de nuevo.
        "Juan spoke of politics again."

If the PP *de nuevo* is an adjunct in (34), it should be able to be left behind under *hacerlo* replacement. Likewise, if the PP *de política* is an adjunct, it should be able to be left behind. If either of these constituents is a complement, however, leaving it behind should produce ungrammaticality. The relevant examples are shown in (35)-(36):

(35)   Juan habló de política de nuevo y José lo hizo por primera vez.
        "Juan spoke of politics again and José did so for the first time."

(36)   *Juan habló de política y José lo hizo de economía.
        "Juan spoke of politics and José did so of economics."

The grammaticality of (35) shows that, since the PP *de nuevo* can be "left behind," this PP is an adjunct. The ungrammaticality of (36) shows that the

---

[5] Sentence (32b) is actually ambiguous. *Lo hizo* can be interpreted as replacing either V′ in the first conjunct.

PP *de política* must be a complement of the verb, since it cannot be "left behind" by *hacerlo* replacement. The *hacerlo* test therefore provides one type of evidence for distinguishing prepositional complements from adjuncts. The only limitation on the use of this diagnostic is that, because *hacerlo* itself is an active predicate, it cannot be used if the predicate of the first conjunct is stative:

(37)   *Juan se parece a José, y Pedrito lo hace también.
        "Juan resembles José, and Pedrito does so too."

Consequently, the status of complements versus adjuncts of statives cannot be "diagnosed" using the *hacerlo* test.

A second test that distinguishes prepositional complements from adjunct PPs is the ability of the preposition to be replaced by other prepositions. An adjunct headed by a preposition can typically be replaced by a different adjunct, headed by a different preposition:

(38)   Recibí un mensaje . . .
        "I received a message . . .
        a. de José.
           from José."
        b. para Susana.
           for Susana."
        c. por teléfono.
           by phone."
        d. en la biblioteca.
           in the library."
        e. durante la conferencia.
           during the lecture."

By contrast, the preposition that heads a PP complement is typically "fixed," and replacing the preposition produces ungrammaticality:

(39)   a. Soñé con/*de María.
           "I dreamed about (lit.: with)/*of Maria."
        b. Conté con/*en tu ayuda.
           "I counted on (lit.: with)/on your help."
        c. Insistió en/*con tu ayuda.
           "S/he insisted on/*with your help."

The prepositions in (39) cannot be replaced freely by other prepositions, which is one indicator that these prepositional phrases are complements. (The *hacerlo* test confirms these examples as complements.)

Certain predicates do allow substitution of their complement preposition, but only within a certain range. This is illustrated by the grammatical versus ungrammatical alternatives in (40):

(40)   a. Puse el bolígrafo en / sobre / detrás de / debajo de / encima del escritorio.
        "I put the pen in / on / behind / under / on top of the desk."
        b. *Puse el bolígrafo para/con el escritorio.
        "I put the pen for/with the desk."

The substitutability of prepositions in (40a) appears to be an exception to the generalization given above. However, notice that all of the grammatical prepositions in (40a) express location, while the ungrammatical preposition *con* in (40b) does not. The range of substitutions that are grammatical can be accounted for on the assumption that the Theta-role assigned by *poner* is a Locative role, and that all of the prepositions in (40a) have a Locative feature. Predicates that theta-mark a complement with a Locative role generally allow this range of substitution.

We have seen above that complement PPs can be distinguished from adjunct PPs in terms of their behavior under *hacerlo* replacement, and with respect to the range of substitutions of the preposition. These differences can be accounted for in terms of the structural difference between complements and adjuncts: only the former are sisters of the head. This difference in turn follows from theta-theory. A complement PP is a sister of the head, because it must be in this position in order to be theta-marked by the verb. An adjunct PP cannot be a sister of the head, because if it were, it would be subject to interpretation as a complement – so the position of sister to the head is uniquely a complement position. An adjunct PP therefore must be higher in the structure, where it is a sister of V', and dominated by V' (shown, for example, in (31b) above).

3.5   Complements: direct object DPs

We will now consider properties of DP complements. We saw above that two diagnostics distinguish PP complements from PP adjuncts. It is to be expected that DP complements should also pattern differently from adjuncts, and we will see below that this is in fact the case. This is expected because DP complements, like PP complements, are theta-marked by the verb, and therefore are sisters of the head. Adjuncts, however, are higher in the structure, generated as sisters of V'. However, we will also see that, in some respects, DP complements pattern differently from PP complements.

One of the diagnostics introduced above, *hacerlo* replacement, can be applied to DP complements. In fact, it was shown above in Section 3.4 that DP complements differ from adjuncts under *hacerlo* replacement (cf. (32) versus (33)). Several additional properties of direct object DPs distinguish them from adjuncts. These properties also differentiate DP complements from PP complements. Before introducing these properties, let us briefly consider why DP and PP complements might be expected to behave differently in some respects. Theta-role assignment could not be relevant, since both DPs and PPs are theta-marked by the verb. One way in which DP and PP complements differ is that DP complements are assigned Case "directly" by the verb. This Case is referred to as Objective (or Accusative) Case. A direct object DP then is a complement that is related to the verb both by Theta-role assignment by V and by Accusative Case assignment. A prepositional complement is linked to the verb by Theta-role assignment only. Consequently, DP complements should have certain properties attributable to the Case relation that are not expected for PP complements or adjuncts. These properties, which will be discussed below, include: (a) clitic "doubling" in certain cases; (b) passivization; and (c) co-occurrence with Personal *a*.

The first property that is particular to DP complements is their co-occurrence with clitics under certain conditions. DP complements differ from PP complements in this respect: PP complements do not co-occur with clitics, nor do adjuncts introduced by prepositions.[6] One context in which DP complements co-occur with a clitic is if the DP is a reflexive or reciprocal (i.e., an anaphor), or a pronominal. The clitic agrees with (or "doubles") the grammatical features of the DP as shown in (41):

(41)   a. Susana *(se)   pateó   a   sí misma.
        S.   CL-refl. kicked PA herself
        "Susana kicked herself."
        b. Susana *(lo)   pateó a   él.
        S.   CL-DO kicked PA   him
        "Susana kicked him."

In (41a) the object of the verb *patear* is the reflexive phrase *a sí misma*; in (41b), the object is the pronoun *a él*. Both sentences are ungrammatical without the clitic. Adjuncts, on the other hand, do not co-occur with a clitic, even if they contain an anaphor or pronominal. Two types of adjuncts which illustrate this are emphatic reflexives and benefactives introduced by *para* "for." First, notice that these two types of phrases are indeed adjuncts, as is shown by their behavior in the *hacerlo* construction:

(42)   EMPHATIC REFLEXIVE:
        Susana resolvió el problema por **sí misma**, y Pedro lo hizo con ayuda.
        "Susana solved the problem by **herself**, and Pedro did so with help."

---

[6] The form of Spanish clitics was summarized briefly in Chapter 1. We will not consider the derivation of clitics used in illustrations below, since this topic will be considered further in Chapter 4.

(43)   BENEFACTIVE:[7]
         Compré un coche **para Juan**, y Marta lo hizo para Pedro.
         "I bought a car **for Juan**, and Marta did so for Pedro."

The boldfaced constituents can be left behind under *hacerlo* replacement, indicating that they are not complements of the verb. Observe now that these constituents do not co-occur with a clitic:

(44)   a. Susana resolvió el problema por sí misma.
            "Susana solved the problem by herself."
         b. *Susana se resolvió el problema por sí misma.
            "Susana CL(refl.) solved the problem by herself."

(45)   a. Compré un coche para él.
            "I bought a car for him"
         b. *Le compré un coche para él.
            "CL I bought a car for him."

Nor do prepositional complements occur with a clitic double:

(46)   a. Juan (*se) habló consigo mismo.
            "Juan CL(refl.) spoke with himself."
         b. María (*le/lo) habló con él.
            "Maria CL(Acc./Dat.) spoke with him."

A second context in which DP complements co-occur with a clitic is the left dislocation construction, in which a constituent interpreted as discourse topic

---

[7] Benefactives can also be introduced by the preposition *a*, as in (i):

(i)   Le   compré   un coche a   Juan.
         CL(Dat.) bought-1st.sg. a   car   for J.
         "I bought Juan a car."

In this construction, the benefactive behaves like a complement according to several tests, including the *hacerlo* test:

(ii)   *Susana le compró un coche a José, y Pedro se lo hizo a ella.
         "Susana bought José a car, and Pedro did so for her."

Notice that the corresponding English benefactive can also behave like a complement, in that it undergoes Dative shift *(I bought a car for her / I bought her a car)*. In both languages, these "quasi-complements" can still be differentiated from complements that are theta-marked by the verb under other diagnostics, such as passivization. In neither language can the benefactive become the subject of a passive, as shown by (iii) and its gloss:

(iii)   *José fue comprado un coche.
         "José was bought a car."

For discussion of the different types of indirect objects, see Strozer (1976), Demonte (1994a).

is in pre-clausal position (see Chapter 5 for discussion). As shown in (47), Left dislocation of a DP complement is ungrammatical without a clitic double:

(47) a. La respuesta, Susana *(la)   sabe.
       the answer, S.   (CL(Acc.)) knows
       "The answer, Susana knows it."
      b. El problema, María *(lo)   resolvió.
       the problem, M.   (CL(Acc.)) solved
       "The problem, Maria solved it."
      c. La pelota, Pedrito *(la)   pateó.
       the ball,   P.   (CL(Acc.)) kicked
       "The ball, Pedrito kicked it."
      d. A   Pedrito, su mamá *(lo)   besó.
       PA P.   his mother (CL(Acc.)) kissed
       "Pedrito, his mother kissed him."

Compare the above examples with left-dislocated adjuncts in (48a–c) and the prepositional complement in (48d):

(48) a Para Juan, (*le)   compré   un coche.
       for J.   (CL(Dat.)) bought-1st.sg. a car
       "For Juan, I bought a car."
      b. El martes, (*le/lo)   compré   un coche.
       the Tuesday (CL(Dat./Acc.)) bought-1st.sg. a car
       "Tuesday, I bought a car."
      c. Con el vecino, María (*le/lo)   cantó.
       with the neighbor, M.   (CL(Dat./Acc.)) sang
       "With the neighbor, Maria sang."
      d. Con el vecino, María (*le/lo)   habló.
       with the neighbor, M.   (CL(Dat./Acc.)) spoke
       "With the neighbor, Maria spoke."

In these examples, Left Dislocation is possible, but becomes ungrammatical with the clitic.

Summarizing to this point, clitic doubling of a DP complement is required in certain contexts, but clitic-doubling of PP complements and adjuncts does not occur. This difference can be accounted for on the hypothesis that a clitic is a reflex of a Case relation between a verb and its complement. If the verb does not assign Case to a constituent, then a clitic should never "double" that constituent.

A second property of DP complements is that they can "surface" as the subject of passive clauses:

(49) a. María resolvió el problema.
       "Maria solved the problem."

   b. El problema fue resuelto (por María).
      "The problem was solved (by Maria)."

(50)   a. José invitó a María.
       "José invited Maria."
       b. María fue invitada (por José).
       "Maria was invited by José."

Neither adjuncts nor prepositional complements are grammatical as the subject of a passive:

(51)   a. Compré un coche para Juan.
       "I bought a car for Juan."
       b. *Juan fue comprado un coche.
       "Juan was bought a car."

(52)   a. Hablamos con los vecinos.
       "(We) spoke to the neighbors."
       b. *Los vecinos fueron hablados (con).
       "The neighbors were spoken (with)."

It is standardly assumed that the movement of a DP object to subject position in passive clauses is attributable to Case. The passive participle of a verb assigns a Theta-role to its complement, but cannot assign Case to it, because Case is "absorbed," i.e., taken up by the participial affix. In a structure such as (53),

(53)

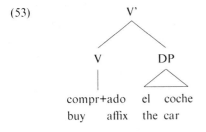

```
                    V'
                   /  \
                  /    \
                 V      DP
                 |     / \
                 |    /___\
            compr+ado  el  coche
            buy    affix the car
```

the Case feature of the verb is assigned to the affix (-ado), leaving the DP complement without Case. Because this DP must be assigned Case, it must move to a position in which it can be assigned Case by another head. As discussed in 3.3 above, one head which can assign Case is INFL, which assigns Nominative (subject Case). The DP object undergoes movement to the Specifier of IP, where it is assigned Nominative (see (54)). Consider now the fact that prepositional complements do not undergo passivization. A verb that selects a prepositional complement does not have an Accusative Case feature to assign to its sister, since it selects a PP, not a DP complement. Therefore in a structure like (53), the passive participle would not have a Case feature to assign to the participial affix. Therefore, Case is never "absorbed" by this affix, and the participle would not be a well-formed constituent.[8]

A third property of DP complements is their co-occurrence with Personal a, typically if the DP is interpreted as [+ANIMATE] and [+SPECIFIC]:[9]

(54)

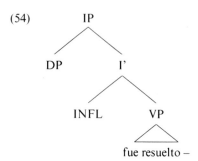

fue resuelto –

(55)   a. No veo *(a) María.
        "I do not see PA Maria."
        b. No veo (*a) el problema.
        "I do not see PA the problem."

(56)   Buscamos (a) una secretaria.
        "We are looking for PA a secretary." (a specific person)
        "We are looking for any secretary."

In (55a), the animate, specific complement requires Personal a; in (55b), the inanimate object cannot co-occur with Personal a. Example (56) is grammatical with or without Personal a, and its interpretation varies accordingly: with Personal a, the complement is interpreted as [+SPECIFIC]. As shown below, Personal a co-occurs only with direct complements of verbs. It does not occur in other contexts, such as within adjuncts:[10]

---

[8] The availability of such passives in English, on the other hand, appears to be related to the property of preposition-stranding in English, which has been suggested (Stowell 1981) to indicate that English prepositions undergo reanalysis with their governing verb. Reanalysis appears to be a device which "rescues" the absorption of Case, transmitting it to the affix.

[9] As pointed out in Chapter 1, Personal a can also occur with inanimate objects, if an inanimate object is "personified" – e.g., *llamar a la muerte* "to call death" – or if both subject and object are inanimate – e.g., *El invierno sigue al otoño* "Winter follows autumn."

[10] The occurrence of Personal a with DP complements raises several questions, including the nature of the morpheme, why it occurs only with complement DPs, and why there are restrictions on its occurrence, such as animacy and specificity. See Lois (1982) and Torrego (1998) for detailed discussion of Personal a.

(57)   a. Marta resolvió el problema por sí misma.
         "Marta solved the problem herself."
         b. *Marta resolvió el problema por a sí misma.
         "Marta solved the problem by PA herself."

Summarizing, we have seen that DP complements behave differently from adjuncts with respect to all of the diagnostics examined. Among these, certain of these properties are common to DP and PP complements; others are particular to DPs; the latter have been suggested to be related to Case. The properties discussed above are summarized in (58)–(59):

(58)   Complement (PP and DP) properties:
         a. cannot be left behind under *hacerlo* replacement;
         b. specific markers (non-replaceable prepositions, Personal *a*).

(59)   Complement DP properties:
         a. Clitic "doubling" in certain contexts;
         b. Co-occurrence with Personal *a*;
         c. Become grammatical subject of passives.

3.6   Indirect objects

We turn now to indirect objects. We will see below that these complements also have properties that distinguish them from adjuncts, and properties that distinguish them from prepositional complements and direct objects. In 3.6.1, similarities between direct and indirect objects will be presented; in 3.6.2, differences between direct and indirect objects are summarized, and in 3.6.3, differences between indirect objects and prepositional complements.

Properties of indirect objects will be illustrated below using two types of predicates: ditransitive verbs (verbs of "transfer") such as those in (60), and simple transitive verbs of "contact," such as those in (61). (The indirect object is shown in boldface):

(60)   a. María le   mandó un paquete **a Pedro**.
            M.   CL(Dat.) sent   a package to P.
            "Maria sent a package to Pedro."
         b. Susana le   enseña matemáticas **a José**.
            S.   CL(Dat.) teaches math   to J.
            "Susana teaches math to José."

(61)   a. Juan le   golpeó la nariz **a Eduardo**.
            J.   CL(Dat.) hit   the nose to E.
            "Juan hit Eduardo's nose."

b. Beatriz le   frotó   los dedos **a su hija**.
B.   CL(Dat.) rubbed the fingers to her daughter
"Beatriz rubbed her daughter's fingers."

The examples in (60) and (61) all have three DPs: (1), a subject, the Nominative Case-marked argument, which in these examples precedes the verb; (2), a direct object that is assigned Objective (Accusative) Case by the verb, as discussed above in 3.4; and (3) the boldfaced indirect object, which is typically analyzed as receiving Dative Case. Dative Case is marked morphologically by (a) the morpheme *a* preceding the DP and, frequently, (b) a Dative clitic (*le* in all of the above examples), which agrees with the indirect object in person and may agree in number.[11] The two verb classes illustrated above differ from each other with respect to the Theta-role assignment, a point to which we will return in 3.6.2.

3.6.1   Similarities between direct and indirect objects

Indirect objects behave like direct objects with respect to their behavior under *hacerlo* replacement and with respect to clitic doubling in the contexts discussed above. The examples in (62) show that an indirect object cannot be left behind under *hacerlo* replacement:

(62)   a. *María le   enseñó historia a Pedro, y   Susana (se) lo
             hizo   a José.
             M.   CL(Dat.) taught history to P.,   and S.   (CL(Dat.))
             did so to J.
             "Maria taught history to Pedro, and Susana did so to José."
         b. *María le   ató las manos a Pedro, y   Susana (se) lo
             M.   CL(Dat.) tied the hands to Pedro and Susana (CL(Dat.))
             hizo   a José.
             did so to José.
             "Maria tied Pedro's hands, and Susana did so to José."

---

[11] Dative clitics in the 3rd person do not show number agreement if a 3rd person direct object is also present:

(i)   Susana les   mandó un paquete.
        S.   CL(Dat.3rd.pl.) sent   a   package
        "Susana sent them a package."
(ii)   Susana se   lo   mandó (a ellos).
        S.   CL(Dat.3rd.) CL(Acc.3rd.sg.) sent   (to them)
        "Susana sent it to them."

In (i), Dative *les* is plural in form (compare sg. *le*), but the form *se* which occurs with sequences of IO(3rd. person) – DO(3rd. person) does not have a plural *ses* form.

Recall from 4.3 that a complement cannot be left behind under *hacerlo* replacement, because *hacerlo* replaces only V', not V, and complements are daughters of the lowest V' in the structure. The ungrammaticality of sentences in (62) shows that these indirect objects pattern like other complements and unlike adjuncts with respect to *hacerlo* replacement.

Indirect objects pattern with direct objects with respect to clitic doubling in contexts discussed previously:

(63)   a. Susana *(se)   mandó un paquete a sí misma.
        S.   (CL(refl.)) sent   a package to herself
        "Susana sent a package to herself."
        b. José *(le)   mandó un paquete a ella.
        J.   (CL(Dat.)) sent   a package to her
        "José sent her a package."

(64)   a. María *(se)   golpeó la nariz a sí misma.
        M.   (CL(refl.)) hit   the nose to herself
        "Maria hit her own nose."
        b. María *(le)   golpeó la nariz a él.
        M.   (CL(Dat.)) hit   the nose PA him
        "Maria hit his nose."

(65)   a. A Pedro, Susana *(le)   mandó un paquete.
        To P.,   S.   *(CL(Dat.)) sent   a package.
        "Susana sent a package to Pedro."
        b. A Pedro, Susana *(le)   golpeó la nariz.
        to P.,   S.   *(CL(Dat.)) hit   the nose
        "Pedro, Susana hit his nose."

Examples (63) and (64) show that reflexive and pronominal indirect objects require an appropriate form of the Dative clitic; omission of the clitic results in ungrammaticality. Likewise, a left-dislocated indirect object requires a clitic, as shown by the ungrammaticality of the sentences in (65) without the Dative clitic.[12]

---

[12] These facts are perhaps not surprising. Indirect objects typically co-occur with a Dative clitic even when the indirect object is an ordinary DP, such as a proper name, and it is often assumed (and taught) that the Dative clitic double is obligatory. However, indirect objects subdivide with respect to the obligatoriness of the clitic, as discussed in Strozer (1976). For one type of indirect object, the clitic is in fact optional:

(i)   Susana va   a mandar(le) un paquete a José.
        S.   is going to send(CL) a package to J.

Demonte (1994, 1995) studies these alternations in detail. She shows that the absence of the clitic has systematic grammatical and semantic properties, corresponding roughly to the alternation in English between direct–indirect object order and the Dative-shift construction (e.g. *Susan sent José a package*).

Summarizing, we have seen above that indirect objects behave like direct objects with respect to *hacerlo* replacement and clitic doubling. Taken by themselves, these facts lead to the hypothesis that direct and indirect objects should have the same analysis: theta-marked by the verb, and assigned Case by the verb. On this analysis, the only difference between direct and indirect objects would be described in terms of the Case that the verb assigns: direct objects are assigned Accusative, and indirect objects assigned Dative. However, we will see below that this analysis is not fully adequate, because there are respects in which indirect objects differ from direct objects, which this analysis does not predict.

3.6.2 Differences between direct and indirect objects

Indirect objects differ from direct objects in several ways. Let us begin with two diagnostics discussed above in relation to the direct object: Personal *a* and passivization.

The absence of Personal *a* with indirect objects is perhaps not surprising. Its use with indirect objects would generate sequences like (66):

(66)   *Juan le   mandó dinero **a** **a**   su hermano.
        J.   CL(Dat.) sent   money to PA his brother
        "Juan sent his brother money."

Second, indirect objects do not undergo passivization:

(67)   a. *Pedro (le) fue mandado un libro (por Juan).
           "Pedro was sent a book (by Juan)."
        b. *Pedro (le)   fue golpeado la nariz.
           P.   CL(Dat.) was hit   the nose
           "Pedro was hit the nose."

The failure of indirect objects to undergo passivization is typical of Romance, in contrast with English.[13]

A third property of indirect objects that distinguishes them from direct objects is that various types of constituents can be marked with Dative morphology and display the complement properties described above, even though they are not theta-marked by the verb. One such case is benefactive phrases, which can be expressed either by a PP introduced by *para*, as in (68a), or as an indirect object, as in (68b):[14]

---

[13] As noted in Chapter 1, there are individual exceptions, such as the verb *preguntar* "ask," which in some styles (particularly journalese) allows the indirect object to be passivized: *El presidente fue preguntado...* "The president was asked..."

[14] Several other instances of "Dativization" are discussed in Masullo (1992).

(68)   a. Susana compró un coche para sus amigos.
        "Susana bought a car for her friends."
       b. Susana les   compró un coche a sus amigos.
        S.   CL(Dat.) bought a   car   to her friends
        "Susana bought a car for her friends."

The PP in (68a) behaves like an adjunct, but the Dative form in (68b) behaves like a complement, as shown by their behavior under *hacerlo* replacement:

(69)   a. Susana compró un coche para sus amigos, y   Pedro lo hizo para
        sus hermanos.
        "S.   bought a   car   for her friends and P.   did so for
        his brothers
        "Susana bought a car for her friends and Pedro did so for his brothers."
       b. *Susana les   compró un coche a sus amigos, y   Pedro
        se lo hizo a   sus hermanos.
        S.   CL(Dat.) bought a   car   to her friends and P.(CL(Dat.))
        did so   for his brothers
        "Susana bought a car for her friends and Pedro did so for his brothers."

In (69a), the adjunct phrase introduced by *para* can be left behind under *hacerlo* replacement. The corresponding phrase in (69b), introduced by *a* and doubled by a clitic, behaves like a complement: it cannot remain behind under *hacerlo* replacement.

The adjunct behavior of benefactives indicates that they are not assigned a Theta-role by the verb. Nevertheless, a benefactive DP can be "Dativized," which means that in the course of the derivation, it can be licensed in a complement position. This accounts for the ability of these phrases to occur with a Dative clitic double, as in (68b), and for their complement behavior with respect to *hacerlo* replacement, as in (69b). Adjuncts cannot, however, surface as direct objects. Alternating with *María cantó para sus amigos* "María sang for her friends," there is no *María los cantó* meaning "María sang for them."[15]

Another type of "Dativized" indirect object that is not theta-marked by the verb is the indirect object of verbs of contact, which have been illustrated throughout the preceding discussion. These indirect objects alternate with direct objects, as shown by the phrase *sus amigos* "his friends" in (70):

[15] In constructions with semi-auxiliaries like causative verbs, Accusative Case (like Dative Case) can be assigned to a DP that is theta-marked by a following infinitive. For example:

(i)   Juan hizo escribir a   Pedro.
       J.   made write   PA P.
       "Juan made Pedro write."

(70)   a. José les   golpeó las rodillas a   sus amigos.
        J.   CL(Dat.) hit   the knees   to his friends
        "José hit his friends' knees."
        b. José golpeó a   sus amigos en las rodillas.
        J.   hit   PA his friends on the knees
        "José hit his friends on the knees."

In (70a), the phrase *sus amigos* is an indirect object, in (70b), a direct object. The "Dativization" of this phrase is perhaps described most easily in relation to the analysis of (70b). In this example, the verb *hit* is a simple transitive verb, which assigns the role "Theme" to its object, *sus amigos*, and assigns Accusative Case to that phrase. The phrase *en las rodillas* is an adjunct of location in (70b), as shown by its behavior under *hacerlo* replacement:

(71)   Juan golpeó a Eduardo en la nariz, y Pedro lo hizo en la oreja.
        "Juan hit Eduardo on the nose, and Pedro did so on the ear."

In (71), the PP can be left behind by *hacerlo* replacement, indicating that it is a sister of V′, not of V – in other words, it is higher in the structure than complements.

Now consider (70a), with the same verb, but which has both a direct object and an indirect object. This verb is not thematically ditransitive. It still assigns a single Theta-role Theme to its direct object. Here, however, the direct object is a DP that expresses a "part" of an individual, while the indirect object expresses the "whole" individual. This particular kind of part/whole relation is known as a relation of "inalienable possession." The indirect object is the inalienable possessor of the direct object body part. Because the two DPs are not separate entities, they could not have two separate thematic roles assigned by the verb. (If they did, they would be expected to refer to separate individuals, rather than a part/whole relation.) They must therefore comprise a single argument of the verb, which expresses the part/whole relation via a complement-internal theta-marking relation. As shown in (72), a role of "Possessor" is assigned by the body-part noun.

(72)

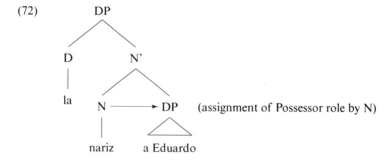

(assignment of Possessor role by N)

The DP in (72) is in turn assigned a Theta-role by the verb (see (73)).

(73)

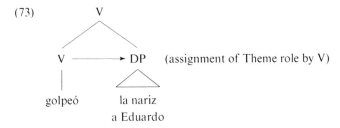

golpeó — la nariz a Eduardo — (assignment of Theme role by V)

We have seen so far that the "inalienable possessor" is not theta-marked by the verb, but by the body-part noun, within the complement DP. This possessor is "Dativized," in the sense that, in the course of the derivation, it comes to be grammatically related to the verb. It bears Dative morphology, which nouns cannot assign, and behaves like a complement of the verb in other relevant respects, as examples throughout this section have shown. The "Dativized" object is syntactically identical to the theta-marked object of ditransitive verbs.

Summarizing, we have seen above that indirect objects have properties that are not shared by direct objects. Indirect objects do not co-occur with Personal *a*, do not undergo passivization, and the Case morphology of the indirect object may be assigned to different constituents. The Dative constituent may be: (a) a theta-marked complement of the verb, as in the case of verbs of transfer; (b) an adjunct, particularly a benefactive; or (c) an argument of the direct object DP (an inalienable possessor).

3.6.3   *Theta-marking and Case assignment to indirect objects*

In this section, we will address some issues related to the analysis of indirect objects, including: (a) theta-marking of the indirect object of ditransitives, and (b) the description of Dative *a*. In previous discussion, it has been shown that complements are generated as sisters of the head of phrase. This assumption has a role in accounting for the behavior of complements under *hacerlo* replacement, and in accounting for the conditions under which Theta-role assignment occurs. Theta-marking of complements was described above as a relation between a head and its sister constituent. If a verb theta-marks two complements, direct and indirect objects, as is the case for ditransitive verbs, the simplest structure consistent with the foregoing assumptions is that the head and the two complements are all sisters, as shown in (74). The problem with this structure is that it violates a widely accepted restriction against ternary branching. The V' in (74) is ternary (with three branches descending from V').[16] If ternary branching is excluded, there must be an additional node dominating one complement or the other. One alternative is (75). This structure is consistent with binary branching, but it presents other problems. It is exceptional with respect to theta-marking, since the indirect object is not a sister of the head, and therefore cannot be assigned a Theta-role directly by the head. Furthermore, it predicts that indirect objects should behave like adjuncts, rather than complements. For example, this structure leads to the expectation that the indirect object should be able to be left behind under *hacerlo* replacement, because there is a V' lower in the structure that *hacerlo* could replace. Structure (75) is thus inadequate with respect to accounting for the properties of indirect objects.

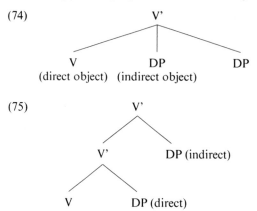

(74)

V'

V (direct object)   DP (indirect object)   DP

(75)

V'

V'   DP (indirect)

V   DP (direct)

The "paradox" of indirect object structure has been given another solution in work by Richard Larson (1988). Under Larson's proposal, a ditransitive verb actually has two "parts," or phrasal heads, each of which is in an appropriate structural relation to one of the complements. Adapting the analysis somewhat, we may take the D-structure to be as shown in (76). Here, the verb *dar* is a sister of the indirect object, which is assigned a Theta-role by the verb. There is a separate head of phrase in the structure, which is empty at D-structure. It is filled in the course of the derivation via movement of the verb, as in (77). In this higher position, the verb can assign a Theta-role to the direct object. Although the verb is not a sister of the direct object, it c-commands it (cf. 3.2), since the first branching node that dominates the verb also dominates

---

[16] Larson (1988) and Demonte (1995) present arguments (beyond the scope of the present discussion) proposing that the direct and indirect objects are not symmetrical (mutually c-commanding), as they would be if the structure in (74) were correct.

the direct object. (Notice that the indirect object is shown in (77) as a DP. An alternative, to be discussed below, is that it is a PP headed by Dative *a*.)

(76)

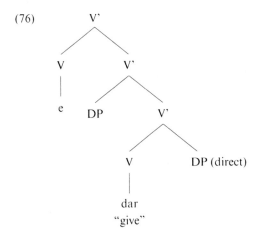

(77)

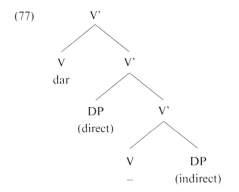

Because the conditions for theta-marking of both complements are satisfied in (77), these complements should behave differently from adjuncts, since adjuncts are not c-commanded by the verb. Both complements are predicted to be replaced by *hacerlo*, and not left behind: *hacerlo* cannot replace any of the lower V′ nodes in (78), because none of these nodes dominates the (entire) verb. Since the verb necessarily undergoes movement to the higher V position (to theta-mark its direct object), *hacerlo* can replace only this higher constituent. Therefore, *hacerlo* cannot leave behind either the direct object or the indirect.

Let us now turn to the issue of Case assignment to the indirect object, and in particular to the status of Dative *a*. The question that arises with respect to this morpheme is whether it is a true preposition or whether, like Personal *a*, it is a reflex of Case assignment by the verb. Neither of these analyses accounts straightforwardly for the properties of indirect objects discussed above.[17] Consider first the hypothesis that Dative a is a preposition, as shown in the partial structure (78b), corresponding to the VP for (78a).

(78)　　a. Juan le　　　regaló un libro a　José.
　　　　　Juan CL(Dat.) gave　a　book to José

　　　　b.

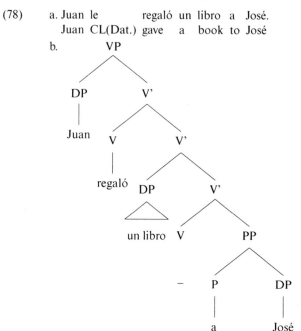

Here, the indirect object is a PP, headed by Dative a, which assigns Case to its DP complement. This analysis is compatible with several of the properties of indirect objects discussed above. If correct, it accounts for ways in which indirect objects pattern with PP complements rather than prepositions with respect to the absence of Personal a and impossibility of passivization. It also correctly predicts that Dative a does not behave like Personal a. A second difference is shown by the contrast between (79) and (80), where the adjective phrase is predicated of the object:

(79)　　Vi　a　[mi amiga enojada].
　　　　saw PA my friend angry
　　　　"I saw my friend angry."

[17] The peculiarities of Dative a have been the topic of numerous studies, and there is little consensus as to whether Dative a is a preposition or not. For detailed discussion of Datives see Strozer (1976) and Masullo (1992). An alternative analysis of theta-marking of the indirect object is presented in Zubizarreta (1987). She proposes that the Theta-role of indirect object is assigned by Dative a and by the verb. On this analysis, the verb and preposition are a complex predicate in the lexicon.

(80)   *Mandé una carta a [mi amiga enojada].
        sent   a   letter to my friend angry
        "I sent a letter to my friend angry."

The direct object in (79) accepts a secondary predicate as a modifier, the indirect object in (80) does not. Demonte (1986) shows that indirect objects pattern with PPs with respect to secondary predicates, a fact which she argues follows from their prepositional phrase structure, as distinct from that of direct objects preceded by Personal a.

There are then several types of evidence that support an analysis of Dative a as a preposition. However, this analysis requires some auxiliary hypothesis to account for the differences between indirect objects and other PP complements, including the occurrence of clitic doubling and "Dativization" phenomena. These phenomena suggest that the PP headed by Dative a comes "into construction" with the verb in terms of a grammatical relation that is independent both of Theta-role assignment and Case assignment. Note that the alternative, according to which Dative a is not a Preposition, would require auxiliary hypotheses to account for differences between Dative a and Personal a, as well as other differences between direct and indirect objects.

3.6.4   Summary

In this section, similarities and differences between indirect objects and other complements were presented. Let us summarize the main generalizations outlined in the discussion. First, we saw in 3.6.1 that indirect objects pattern generally with complements, not with adjuncts, with respect to the basic structural diagnostic of *hacerlo* replacement. Indirect objects are not, however, identical in their behavior to either prepositional or direct objects. Unlike PP complements, they require clitic doubling under the same conditions as do direct objects. However, in other respects indirect objects differ from direct objects: they disallow passivization, and Personal a differs from Dative a in crucial respects, as discussed in 3.6.3. Indirect objects present interesting issues with respect to both theta-marking and Case. Constituents that are not theta-marked (such as benefactives) can be "Dativized," and even the conditions under which "ordinary" indirect objects of ditransitive verbs are theta-marked require a more abstract analysis of the Verb Phrase than had been previously assumed. Finally, with respect to Case-marking, it was shown that Dative a is best analyzed as a preposition which assigns Case to the Dative DP. This analysis leaves as an open question why clitic doubling occurs with these objects, and why "Dativization" is as robust as it is, compared with other complements.

3.7   Complements of "unaccusative" verbs

Section 3.3 above discussed the external argument of VP: the argument that normally corresponds to the subject of the clause. According to the analysis given there, an external argument is generated in the Specifier of VP, as a sister of V' (which assigns a compositional Theta-role to the DP). The D-structure position of the external argument is shown by the DP position in (81). From this position, the external argument moves to the Specifier of IP, where it is assigned Nominative Case by INFL. Note that the external argument in (81) is structurally distinguished from complements, which are sisters of the verb (or at least c-commanded by it, as discussed in 3.6.3). This structural difference between external and internal arguments is supported by diagnostics that are sensitive to the structural relation between the argument and the head. In (82) for example, we see that the external argument can, naturally, remain behind under *hacerlo* replacement:

(81)

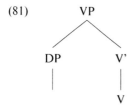

(82)   María leyó el diario, y Pedro lo hizo también.
        "Maria read the paper, and Pedro did so too."

Unlike complements, the external argument disallows bare NPs:[18]

(83)   *Niños leyeron estos libros.
        "Children read these books."

There are, however, certain verb classes whose grammatical subjects do not behave in expected ways relative to diagnostics which distinguish external from internal arguments. One of these classes is "presentational" verbs, described as such because they introduce the (existence or presence of) DP into the discourse. This includes verbs like *llegar* "arrive," *venir* "come," *aparecer* "appear," *salir* "come/go out," and negatives of them, such as *faltar* "lack," *desaparecer* "disappear."[19] As shown in (84) and (85), these verbs allow bare NP subjects, but only following the verb:

[18] An exception is coordinate constructions, as noted in Chapter 1.
[19] The verb classes whose behavior is discussed here are not particular to Spanish. Cross-linguistically, roughly the same predicates display properties that differentiate their subjects from "ordinary" subjects. For discussion, see Levin (1993), Levin and Rappaport-Hovav (1994); for Romance, see Tortora (1997) and references cited there.

(84)   a. Llegaron estudiantes.
            arrived   students.
            "Students arrived."
         b. *Estudiantes llegaron.
            "Students arrived."

(85)   a. Faltan tomates.
            lack   tomatoes
            "Tomatoes are lacking."
         b. *Tomates faltan.
            "Tomatoes are lacking."

Intransitive verbs that are not members of this class do not allow bare NP subjects:[20]

(86)   a. *Cenó gente (a las ocho).
            dined people (at eight o'clock)
            "People dined (at eight o'clock)."
         b. *Gente cenó (a las ocho). (=86a)

(87)   a. *Tosen niños.
            cough children
            "Children are coughing."
         b. *Niños tosen. (=87a)

In these respects, the subject of these predicates pattern with complements. Yet, in other respects they are superficially subjects, not objects. Like other subjects, their pronoun form is Nominative, and they agree with the verb in person and number. Unlike objects, they do not co-occur with Personal *a*, and they do not require clitic doubling. In Romance languages other than Spanish, additional diagnostics differentiate these arguments from "ordinary" external arguments. For example, in French and Italian, these predicates take a different auxiliary, one corresponding to "be" rather than "have" in the compound past tense:[21]

---

[20] It may be possible to override the prohibition on bare NPs as subjects of this verb class by placing the sentence within a discourse frame such as the one shown in (i):

    (i)   A. ¿Qué pasó?
               "What happened?"
            B. Primero, abrimos el restaurante, después, **cenó gente**, y finalmente
               cerramos como a las doce.
               "First, we opened the restaurant, then people dined, then finally we
               closed around midnight."

[21] Corresponding arguments in Italian and French pattern like complements with respect to the distribution of certain clitics. For detailed discussion, see Burzio (1986).

(88)   a. Molti studenti **hanno** telefonato.
             "Many students have telephoned."
         b. Molti studenti **sono** arrivati.
             "Many students have (lit.: were) arrived."

(89)   a. Jean **a** mangé.
             "Jean has eaten."
         b. Jean **est** arrivé.
             "Jean has (lit: was) arrived."

English also has diagnostics that distinguish presentational subjects – for example, they can occur in the *there* construction: *There arrived many students*; *There ate many students*.

Building on work by Perlmutter (1978), these predicates have been analyzed as assigning a Theta-role only to an internal argument, as shown in (90b), the D-structure corresponding to (90a).

(90)   a. Llegaron los estudiantes.

         b.

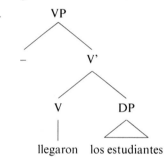

Unlike other verbs that select an internal argument however, these verbs do not assign Accusative Case to their complement – hence, their description: "unaccusative verbs." The argument must have Case, however, and in order to satisfy the Case requirement, the DP moves to the specifier of IP, where it is assigned Nominative (see (91)).

When this movement takes place, the DP has the surface properties normally associated with subjects: Nominative Case, subject–verb agreement, and other properties associated with the Specifier of IP position. At the same time, the subject is still linked to the position in which its Theta-role is assigned: the complement of V. This is the position that is responsible for the object-like properties of the DP.

Recall from above that bare NPs are grammatical only if the subject follows the predicate: *Llegaron estudiantes; *Estudiantes llegaron* "Students arrived." This contrast suggests that the bare NP is still in the complement position. The question arises, in these derivations, as to how the NP gets Case, if it does not

(91)

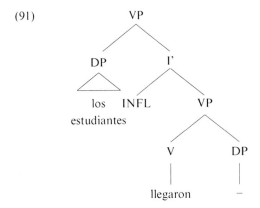

move to the Specifier of IP. One solution to this problem proposed in Burzio (1986) is that Nominative Case is "transmitted" from subject position to the NP in object position. Case transmission is made possible due to the presence of a null pronoun in subject position:

(92)　　$[_{IP}$ pro^i INFL $[_{VP}$ $[_{V'}$ llegaron estudiantes^i]]]
　　　　"There arrived students."

An alternative analysis, according to which unaccusative verbs assign a Case distinct from Accusative, is proposed in Belletti (1988). On this analysis, the verb *llegaron* in (92) assigns Partitive case to its complement.

Unfortunately, Spanish does not provide clear diagnostics that support analyzing the post-verbal subject as remaining in object position, as in (92). *Hacerlo* replacement, at first glance, seems suggestive:

(93)　　a. Los profesores llegaron y los estudiantes lo hicieron también.
　　　　　"The teachers arrived and the students did so too."
　　　　b. *Llegaron profesores y lo hicieron estudiantes también.

The contrast between (93a) and (93b) seems to show that once the DP has moved to the Specifier of IP, as in (93a) with a pre-verbal subject, the subject can be left behind under *hacerlo* replacement. In (93b), the post-verbal subject, filled by a bare NP, cannot be left behind, apparently indicating that the DP is still in complement position. However, the results of this test are clouded by the fact that (93b) may be ungrammatical for another reason: the proform *hacerlo* imposes certain semantic requirements on its subjects – essentially, an Agent reading. The unaccusative verb *llegar* does not assign an Agent role to its internal argument, but rather a Theme role. Therefore, the ungrammaticality of (93b) may be due to the mismatch between the type of argument selected by *llegar* (Theme) and the type of argument selected by *hacerlo* (Agent). Why then is (93a) grammatical? One possibility is that verbs like *llegar* have two lexical entries: an "unaccusative" entry, and a second, Agentive entry, which selects an Agent as an ordinary external argument. Since the role of Agent can only be an external role, assigned compositionally by VP, then (93a) is possible. Both conjuncts have an Agentive verb. In (93b) however, *hacerlo* would be analyzed as Agentive, but the internal argument of *llegaron* in the first conjunct could not be an Agent, since it is an internal argument, as shown by its bare determiner.

Summarizing, we have seen in this section that certain intransitive verbs have surface subjects that behave according to some diagnostics (which vary cross-linguistically) like complements – i.e., like sisters of the head. The exceptional behavior of these predicates has been accounted for by analyzing the verb as "unaccusative": a verb which selects an internal argument, but which does not assign Case to that argument. The argument undergoes movement to the Specifier of IP, where its Case requirement is satisfied by assignment of Nominative by INFL. The D-structure position of the subject is the position that is responsible for complement-like behavior of the subject.

3.8   Summary

In this chapter, we have considered certain aspects of the syntax of the Verb Phrase. We began with a review of the distribution of VP, which occurs typically as a sister of INFL, as the primary predicate of a clause. Unlike AP, VP does not occur as a secondary predicate or adjunct, unless the adjunct is itself a clause. The licensing of VP that accounts for its distribution was related to Predication, which is obligatory for clauses, and the Tense–V relation, whose nature is less well studied. Subsequent sections of the chapter examined relations between the verb and its arguments. Differences between arguments of the verb and adjuncts (or modifiers) were discussed, as were differences among various arguments. Section 3.3 discussed the derivation of external arguments, which are theta-marked in the Specifier of VP, and move to the Specifier of IP to be assigned Case. Predicates that do not theta-mark an external argument, such as *parecer* "seem," can nevertheless have a referential subject as a result of movement ("Raising") of a subject from a subordinate clause. The topic of subject position and licensing is of course more complex than was suggested here. We return In Chapters 4 and 5 to this topic. Sections 3.4–3.6 discussed properties of PP complements, direct objects and indirect objects, each of which behaves differently from adjuncts according to some diagnostics, and which also behave differently from each other, particularly with respect to their Case-relation to the verb. Finally, in Section 3.7, a separate class of predicates known as "unaccusatives" was introduced. The surface subject of these VPs does not behave like an ordinary external argument, but shares certain properties with complements. It was shown how these properties could be accounted for on the hypothesis that the surface subject is generated in complement position, but is not assigned Accusative by the "unaccusative" verb. The DP therefore moves to the Specifier of IP, and is assigned Nominative Case by INFL, or receives Case in object position – either by Case transmission, or by assignment of Partitive Case by the verb.

4

VP-related functional categories

4.1 Introduction

In Chapter 3, our discussion focused on two aspects of VP syntax: the distribution of VP, and phrase-internal structural relations between the verb and its arguments. In this chapter, we will examine several grammatical processes which participate in licensing VP constituents at S-structure. To introduce the issues that will be taken up in this chapter, let us begin by reviewing the D-structure discussed in Chapter 3 for a transitive predicate such as (1).

(1)　　a. Juan leyó el　diario.
　　　　　　J.　　read the newspaper
　　　　b.　　　　　IP

INFL　　VP

DP　　　V'

Juan　　V　　　DP

leyó　　el diario

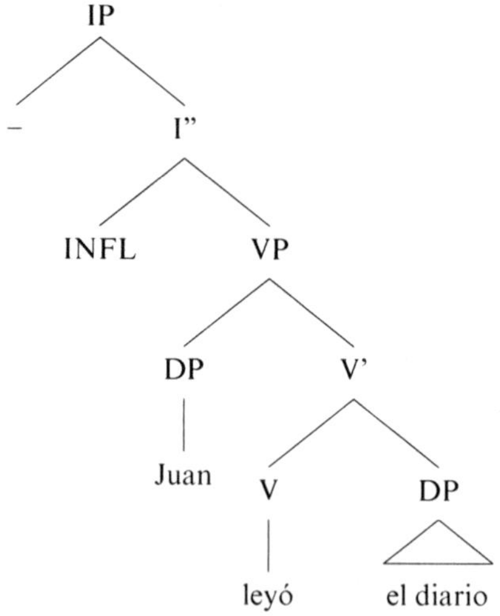

Given the similarity between the D-structure order of constituents in (1b) and the surface form of the sentence (1a), it might appear that little needs to be said about the derivation once the D-structure is formed. In fact, one might question whether IP is necessary at all: conceivably, a clause could be analyzed as consisting of nothing more than the VP itself. However, there are reasons

158

why the IP must be present. The standard approach to the VP–IP relation that has been adopted in recent generative literature rests on the distinction between "lexical" and "functional" categories discussed in Chapter 2. IP is assumed to be a functional category which has a role in licensing constituents of VP. IP is, in this sense, a functional "extension" of VP (Grimshaw 1991), much as DP is a functional extension of NP. One of the functional relations between INFL and VP has already been introduced in Chapter 3 (Section 3.3): INFL is the head which assigns (Nominative) Case to the clausal subject. Movement of DP to the Specifier of IP is necessary to satisfy this abstract Case requirement, so the derivation of (1b) includes DP movement:

(2)

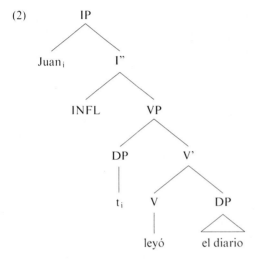

In this chapter, we will discuss three other movements which affect the licensing of VP constituents. In Sections 4.2 and 4.3, the relation between Tense features of INFL and V will be examined. In 4.2, we will see that the distribution of VP-adverbs provides evidence that V has raised to INFL at S-structure. Then in 4.3, several further aspects of V-to-INFLNFL movement are addressed. We will discuss the temporal licensing of the VP by Tense features, how this licensing operates, and what implications it has for the analysis of clauses with auxiliary verbs. We will suggest that there is a second functional category in the VP extended projection which participates in licensing of verbs: Aspect. Sections 4.4 and 4.5 will then introduce two additional constituents: clitics (4.4) and negation (4.5), which have also been analyzed in recent work as functional heads. Our discussion in this chapter leaves aside the licensing of one constituent: the subject. For the purposes of this chapter, we will assume that the subject occupies the Specifier of IP, as discussed in Chapter 3

(Section 3.3). We return in Chapter 5 to a fuller discussion of the distribution of the subject.

4.2   VP-adverbs and the verb/tense relation

In this section, we will focus on the distribution of VP-adverbs. As the discussion will show, the distribution of VP-adverbs has been argued to provide evidence which bears on the relation between V and INFL. To narrow our discussion, it will be useful to distinguish between *sentence adverbs* and *VP-adverbs*. Sentence adverbs modify (or have scope over) the entire proposition expressed by a clause. They are standardly analyzed as dependents of IP (the S node in earlier terminology). We will refer to them as IP-adverbs below. There are several semantic sub-types of IP-adverbs, a matter which we leave aside here. IP-adverbs include PPs such as *por supuesto* "of course," *sin embargo* "nevertheless," non-derived adverbs such as *quizás* "perhaps," and a number of *-mente* "-ly" adverbs such as *naturalmente* "naturally," *realmente* "really," *obviamente* "obviously." These adverbs typically correspond to adjectives which select clausal subjects. For example, *Obviamente leí el diario* "Obviously I read the newspaper" corresponds to *Es obvio que leí el diario* "It is obvious that I read the newspaper."[1] IP-adverbs can occur in the positions shown in (3):

(3)   a. Probablemente María leyó ese libro.
       "Probably Maria read that book."
    b. María probablemente leyó ese libro.
       "Maria probably read that book."
    c. (?)Maria había probablemente leído ese libro.[2]
       "Maria had probably read that book."

---

[1] Some adverbs can modify more than one type of constituent. For example, *naturalmente* "naturally" is ambiguous between sentential modification, with the reading "it is natural that x," and VP modification, with a manner interpretation (e.g., *Estos tomates maduraron naturalmente* "These tomatoes ripened naturally").

[2] The order: auxiliary–adverb–participle may vary in acceptability according to the particular auxiliary used. Separation of *haber* from a following participle is generally worse than separation of *estar* or passive *ser* from a following participle:

(i)   María estaba probablemente leyendo ese libro.
       M.   was   probably   reading that book
(ii)   El libro había sido probablemente prohibido por la censura.
       the book had been probably   banned   by the censors
(iii) *El libro había probablemente sido prohibido.
       the book had probably   been banned

Given the acceptability of (i) and (ii), one might conclude that IP-adverbs can intervene between constituents of the VP, and perhaps the status of (iii) reflects an

d. (?)María había leído probablemente ese libro.
   "Maria had read probably that book."
e. (?)María había leído ese libro probablemente.
   "Maria had read that book probably."

As shown in (3a–b), IP-adverbs occur grammatically before or after the subject, and only marginally following the auxiliary (3c), the participle (3d) and the entire VP (3e). For (3d,e), it is not clear whether IP-adverbs are fully grammatical with normal intonation contours, although pause intonation is not obligatory for adverbs in these positions. Example (3e) is grammatical with a pause between the object and the adverb, in which case it is presumably in a "clause-peripheral" (dislocated) position. We will focus here on the contrast between (3a,b) and (3c,d). Let us suppose that adverbs can adjoin to X' projections (as in (4)). Here, the adverb is adjoined either to IP or to I'. If these are the only positions in which IP-adverbs can be generated, (3a) and (3b) are accounted for, as are the ungrammaticality of (3d) and (3e). However, the order in (3c) remains as a question: there, the adverb intervenes between the auxiliary and the following participle. We will return to this derivation in (4.3), where we address the structure associated with auxiliary verbs.

(4)

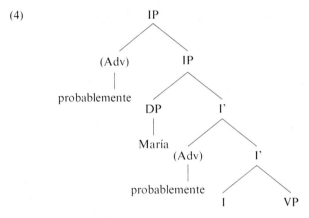

VP-adverbs are adverbs that modify the event (or state) expressed by VP, or some constituent of it. These include the adverb types illustrated in (5):[3]

idiosyncrasy of the perfective construction, as suggested in Zagona (1988). However, if auxiliaries *ser* and *estar* are analyzed as raising verbs, their complement IPs would be expected to select IP-adverbs.
[3] Just as some IP-adverbs can also modify other constituents (see note 1), some VP-adverbs listed in (5) can modify constituents other than VP. For example, the Extent adverbs can modify quantifiers and adjectives: *Leyeron [apenas tres páginas]* "They read barely three pages"; *Es [casi ciego]* "He is almost blind."

(5)   VP-Adverbs:[4]
        a. Time: ayer "yesterday," hoy "today," ahora "now," mañana "tomorrow,"
        anteayer "the day before yesterday," frecuentemente "often," antes "before,"
        aún "still/yet," todavía "still," ya "already,", etc.
        b. Place: aquí "here," allí "there," lejos "far," cerca "near," abajo "below,"
        afuera "outside," etc.
        c. Extent/degree: casi "almost," apenas "barely," meramente "merely," sólo
        "only," etc.
        d. Manner: bien "well," mal "badly," rápido "quickly," quedo "quietly,"
        fácilmente "easily," etc.
        e. Quantity: mucho "a lot," poco "little," demasiado "too much," menos
        "less," etc.

The classes shown in (5) reflect various types of modification of VP, and, as
we will see below, these types behave roughly as classes with respect to their
distribution. However, it should be noted that members of each class may
differ from one another with respect to other features. For example, *aquí*
"here" and *afuera* "outside" differ with respect to deixis; *afuera* "outside" and
lejos "far away" differ with respect to specificity. These features can affect the
distribution of particular items (cf. note 4). We will focus our discussion on
the general patterns of distribution of the classes in (5). In 4.2.1, the distribution of these adverbs relative to the subject, verb and complements is summarized. Sections 4.2.2 and 4.2.3 discuss the derivation of the occurring orders,
particularly in relation to the position of the verb at S-structure.

4.2.1   Distribution of VP-adverbs relative to S-V-O

VP-adverbs can occur in any of the positions marked by "x" in (6):[5]

---

[4] Each of these types can be sub-classified. For example, Place adverbs may be [±spe-
cific] (e.g., *aquí* "here" is [+SPECIFIC], *lejos* "far" is [-SPECIFIC]). Such features affect
the behavior of particular items within a class. For example, only [+SPECIFIC] Place
adverbs can be clause-initial:

(i)   a. Juan conoció a su amigo lejos/allá.
           "Juan met his friend far away / there."
        b. Allá Juan conoció a su amigo.
           "There Juan met his friend."
        c. ?*Lejos Juan conoció a su amigo.
           "Far away Juan met his friend."

[5] In addition to the orders given in the text, the constituent order pattern (i) is possible,
as illustrated in (ii):

(i)   Adv – V- Subject – Object
(ii)   a. Siempre dice Juan la misma cosa.
           always says J.   the same   thing

(6)   x – Subj – x – V – x – Obj -x

However, not all sub-classes can occupy all positions. Let us first consider the post-verbal positions, before and after a complement. As shown in (7), all adverbs except Extent adverbs can occupy one or both post-verbal positions:

(7)   Post-verbal adverbs
     a. Los trabajadores recibieron ayer/ya   el   sueldo.   (Time)
       The workers   received   yesterday/already their salary.
     a' Los trabajadores recibieron el sueldo ayer/ya.
     b. ?Juan conoció allá a su mejor amigo.[6]   (Place)
       J.   met   there his best   friend.
     b' Juan conoció a su mejor amigo allá.
     c. *Los estudiantes terminaron apenas el examen.   (Extent)
       The students   finished   barely the exam.
     c'.*Los estudiantes terminaron el examen apenas.[7]
     d. María leyó cuidadosamente el diario.   (Manner)
       M.   read carefully   the newspaper.
     d'. María leyó el diario cuidadosamente.
     e. Susana ama mucho a su hija.   (Quantity)
       S.   loves much   her daughter.
     e'.Susana ama a su hija mucho.

The range of adverbs which can appear in pre-verbal positions is more restricted, as shown in (8) and (9):

(8)   Subject – Adverb – V – Object
     a. Los trabajadores ya/ayer recibieron el sueldo.   (Time)
       "The workers already/yesterday received their salary."
     b. Juan allá conoció a su mejor amigo.   (Place)
       "Juan there met his best friend."
     c. Los estudiantes apenas terminaron el examen.   (Extent)
       "The students barely finished the exam."

     b. Poco hablan ellos de ese tópico.
       little speak they of that topic
     c. Allí cuenta la gente historias interesantes.
       there tell   the people stories   interesting
       "There the people tell interesting stories."

This order is taken up in Chapter 5, where variation in the position of the subject is described.

[6] The occurrence of *allá* between the verb and its complement may be possible only if the complement is dislocated – that is, with an intonation shift indicating that it has been moved from complement position.

[7] The example is ungrammatical on an Extent reading of the adverb. *Apenas* can have a manner interpretation "with great difficulty." On this reading, *apenas* can follow the complement.

d. *?María cuidadosamente leyó el diario.   (Manner)
   "Maria carefully read the paper."
e. *Susana mucho/demasiado ama a su hija.   (Quantity)
   "Susana a lot/too much loves her daughter."

(9)   Adverb – Subject – V – Object
        a. Ya/ayer los trabajadores recibieron el sueldo.   (Time)
           "Already/yesterday the workers received their salary."
        b. Allá Juan conoció a su mejor amigo.   (Place)
           "There Juan met his best friend."
        c. *Apenas los estudiantes terminaron el examen.   (Extent)
           "Barely the students finished the exam."
        d. *?Cuidadosamente María leyó el diario.   (Manner)
           "Maria carefully read the paper."
        e. *Mucho/demasiado Susana ama a su hija.   (Quantity)
           "A lot/too much Susana loves her daughter."

As shown in (8) and (9), adverbs of Manner and Quantity cannot immediately precede the finite verb, and neither these nor adverbs of Extent can appear in the pre-subject position.

4.2.2   Post-verbal adverbs

In this section, we will focus primarily on VP-adverbs which appear between the verb and its complement. VP-final adverbs represent the expected order, the position in which adjuncts of all types appear.[8] The problems raised by: [V – adverb – object] order are the same as those discussed in Chapter 2 (Section 2.8) with respect to the order: [N – adjective – complement]. The central problem is that Theta-theory predicts that complements should be closer to the head than non-complements, since the head must c-command a constituent in order to theta-mark it. That prediction is borne out by the surface order in English: the equivalent of (7d) for example, *Maria read carefully the newspaper*, is ungrammatical. However, in Spanish – like Romance generally – VP-adverbs can intervene between the verb and its complement.

There are two general ways of accounting for the derivation of [V – adv – object] order: (a) base-generation of the surface order, or (b) by movement of one or more constituents. Let us first consider how the derivation would proceed under each of these approaches. The base-generation approach assumes that the constituents in (9) are in the same configuration at D-structure and at S-structure. On this approach, the constituent: [*leyó frecuentemente el*

---

[8] Some verbs take adverbs as complements, such as *sentirse bien/mal* "to feel well/bad(ly)," *vestirse bien* "to dress well," etc. These adverbs are sisters of the verb, rather than adjuncts.

diario] would be generated with the adverb as a sister of the verb, as in (10a) or (10b).

(10)   a.

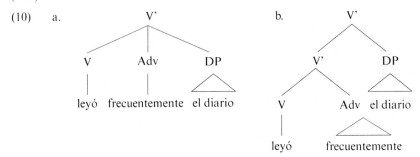

In (10a), V′ is a ternary-branching structure, so that both the adverb and the direct object are sisters of the verb. In (10b), the adverb is the sister of the verb, and the direct object is higher in the structure. This diagram observes the constraint on binary branching – the restriction that any node can have at most two branches descending from it.

A second approach to the derivation of [V – adv – object] constituent order is via movement of the subject and the verb to the left, as shown in the derivation in (11). On this approach, the adverb is generated in a position adjoined to VP (or alternatively, moved there from a VP-final position). Two other VP constituents have moved: the external argument has moved to the Spec of IP (as discussed in Chapter 3), and the verb has moved to the head of IP.

Both of the approaches outlined above derive the correct order of constituents, but they differ in several important ways. Consider first the base-generation analysis illustrated in (10a). One drawback to this analysis is that it violates the constraint on binary branching (Chapter 2, Section 2.8). A second drawback is that it obscures the structural distinction between arguments and adjuncts, as noted above. The structure (10b) on the other hand observes the constraint on binary branching, and does make a structural distinction between the complement and the adjunct. However, the distinction is the opposite of that predicted by theta-theory: in (10b), the adjunct is c-commanded by the verb, while the complement is not. The movement analysis avoids these problems, since in (11), the complement is a sister of the verb, and the adjunct is generated in a VP-adjoined position. The two approaches also make different claims as to the position of the verb at S-structure. The base-generation analysis assumes that, at S-structure, the verb is still in its D-structure position as the head of VP; the movement analysis shown in (11) analyzes the verb as occupying a position outside VP, in the head of IP.

The movement analysis (Emonds 1978) claims that, in Romance, both main verbs and auxiliary verbs move to INFL. In English, on the other hand, only

(11)   a. D-structure

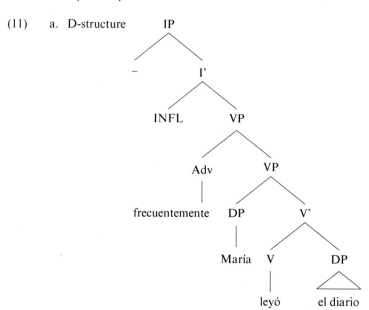

    b. S-structure

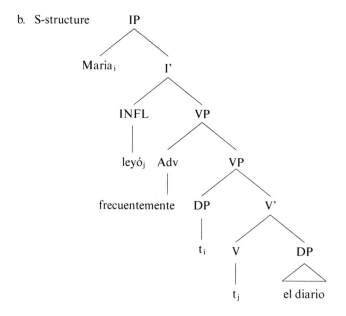

auxiliaries and main verb *be* move to INFL. One type of evidence supporting this analysis is found in the contrasts between Spanish and English with respect to question inversion. In Spanish, both main verbs and auxiliaries can move to clause-initial (pre-subject) position in questions:

(12)   a. ¿Leyó Juan el   diario?
             read J.   the newspaper
             "Did Juan read the newspaper?"
         b. ¿Está Juan leyendo el   diario?
             is   J.   reading the newspaper
             "Is Juan reading the newspaper?"
         c. ¿Había Juan leído el   diario?[9]
             had   J.   read the newspaper
             "Had Juan read the newspaper?"

In English, only auxiliaries can be inverted:

(13)   a. *Read Juan the newspaper?
         b. Is Juan reading the newspaper?
         c. Had Juan read the newspaper?

The contrast between (12a) and (13a) can be accounted for on the assumption that question inversion involves movement of INFL to pre-clause position. Unless a verb can move to INFL, it cannot undergo inversion in questions. In both English and Romance, auxiliaries move to INFL, hence the grammaticality of inverted auxiliaries in the (b) and (c) examples.

This analysis also accounts for another contrast between Spanish and English. In Spanish, VP-adverbs can follow both auxiliaries and main verbs (cf. note 2):

(14)   a. (?)Juan había frecuentemente leído el   diario.
             J.   had   often   read the newspaper
         b. Juan leyó frecuentemente el   diario.
             J.   read often   the newspaper

In English, adverbs can follow an auxiliary verb only:

(15)   a. Juan had often read the newspaper.
         b. *Juan read often the newspaper.
         c. Juan DID often read the newspaper.

Although we have not yet discussed the internal structure of VPs with auxiliaries, let us assume minimally that they originate somewhere within VP. On

---

[9] The present perfect form of the compound tense does not allow fronting of the auxiliary by itself:

(i)   a. ?*¿Ha Juan leído el diario?
             "Has Juan read the newspaper?"
         b. ¿Ha leído Juan el diario?

Suñer (1987) suggests that this contrast is due to the clitic status of the form *ha*.

this assumption, the distribution of adverbs in (14) and (15) is accounted for directly by the movement analysis. In (14), one verb, either an auxiliary or main verb, moves to INFL, where it can be followed by a VP-adjoined adverb. In (15a), an auxiliary verb has also moved to INFL, and can be followed by a VP-adjoined adverb. In (15b), the main verb cannot move to INFL, hence it cannot be followed by a VP-adjoined adverb. In (15c), the pleonastic verb *do* occupies INFL (as is supported by its ability to be inverted in questions), and can be followed by a VP-adjoined adverb.

Summarizing, we have seen that the movement approach analyzes the verb as exterior to the Verb Phrase at S-structure. The hypothesis that any verb can move to INFL in Spanish, while V-to-INFLNFL movement in English is restricted to auxiliaries, accounts for differences between the two languages with respect to verb-fronting in questions, following adverbs.

With respect to the position in which adverbs are generated, it can be assumed that all of the adverb classes that can occupy post-verbal position (all except Extent adverbs) can be generated in one of two ways: (a) in VP-final position (adjoined to V' or VP), or (b) in a VP-initial position (adjoined to V' or VP). On this analysis, there are two ways of accounting for the impossibility of Extent adverbs in these positions. One possibility is that they are generated in these same positions, but must themselves undergo movement; alternatively, they may be generated higher in the structure.

4.2.3   Pre-verbal adverbs

Recall from 4.2.1 that adverbs of Time, Place and Extent can be pre-verbal – the latter, obligatorily. Given the analysis in 4.2.1, according to which the verb occupies INFL at S-structure, it follows that these adverbs must also be VP-external at S-structure. And on the assumption that the subject occupies the Specifier of IP, the pre-verbal adverbs must occupy an IP-adjoined or I'-adjoined position.

Recall that these are the positions in which IP-adverbs appear (cf. (4)). One approach to the derivation of these adverb orders would be to assume that a VP-adverb can move from a VP-internal position, adjoining to I' or IP. If this analysis is correct, there must be a semantic restriction on this movement, since adverbs of Manner and Quantity cannot undergo it. Alternatively, it may be that the adverbs which appear in pre-verbal positions can be interpreted as a type of IP-adverb, ones which are event-oriented. This hypothesis finds some support in that an adverb like *allá* cannot be pre-verbal unless it has scope over the entire event:

(16)

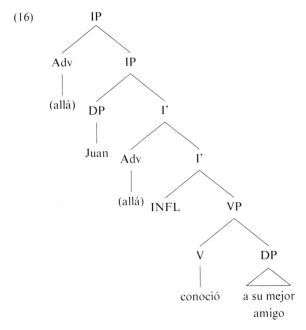

(17)   a. Juan allá conoció a su amigo.
        "Juan there met his friend."
        b. (*)Juan allá disparó la flecha.
        "Juan there shot the arrow."

In (17a), the adverb has scope over the entire event: it describes the location of the entire event, including the location of the subject. In (17b), *allá* can also have scope over the entire event, but there is also a reading on which it does not. On this reading, the adverb specifies only the location of the arrow, and only at the end of the event. The adverb does not have scope over the subject.[10]

The analysis of pre-verbal adverbs as event-oriented IP-adverbs does, however, present difficulties: on this analysis Extent adverbs would be analyzed as exclusively IP-adverbs, since they do not appear in any post-verbal

---

[10] Notice also that a pre-verbal Place adverb has scope over negation, while a post-verbal adverb is ambiguous:

(i)   a. Juan allá no conoció a su amigo. "Juan there didn't meet his friend."
       b. Juan no conoció a su amigo allá. "Juan didn't meet his friend there."

In (ia), the Place adverb is outside the scope of negation: there was an event in a location specified by *allá*, and the event was a non-meeting. In (ib), negation can have scope over the locative, with the reading: "It is not the case that Juan met his friend there."

positions. However, the fact that they cannot be clause-initial (pre-subject) remains unexplained. Also, the fact that Time adverbs can appear in all positions in VP as well as in IP, with no apparent difference in scope or restrictiveness, is not explained.

Summarizing the main points of this section, it was shown in 4.2.1 that VP-adverbs can occur in any position before or after the subject, verb and object of a transitive clause. However, not all types of adverbs appear in all of these positions. In 4.2.2, the post-verbal positions were analyzed. It was shown that the occurrence of adverbs between the verb and its object is unexpected under the assumptions that have been presented previously as to the relative positions of complements and adjuncts. However, this order is only problematic on the assumption that the verb is within VP at S-structure. The hypothesis that the verb has moved to INFL explains the order of adverbs, and explains relevant contrasts between Spanish and English. In 4.2.3, the analysis of pre-verbal adverbs was discussed. On the assumption that the verb is in INFL, these adverbs are I' or IP adjuncts – at least at S-structure, although not necessarily at D-structure. Although this analysis accounts for the pre-verbal positions for VP-adverbs, it does not provide any immediate explanation for differences in distribution of the various sub-classes of VP-adverbs.

4.3　Auxiliary verbs, tense and aspect

As noted above, the hypothesis that V moves to INFL in Spanish accounts for the order of VP-adverbs relative to the verb and its complements. Also, relevant contrasts between English and Romance follow, on the hypothesis that English main verbs (except *be*) do not move to INFL. Two aspects of this analysis have not been addressed to this point, however. First, the question arises as to what triggers V-to-INFL movement. That is, if the verb did not move, what type of principle would be violated? Second, what is the parameter that differentiates English and Romance? Finally, why do auxiliary verbs seem to be "immune" to the parameter? That is, auxiliary verbs move to INFL in both English and Romance; it is only main verbs which cannot move to INFL in English. Although these topics remain under active investigation, we will summarize below recent proposals that have been advanced to account for these phenomena. Section 4.3.1 outlines the approach to V-to-INFLNFL movement proposed in Chomsky (1993), which analyzes movement as a means of satisfying the "checking" of features associated with functional categories. This analysis accounts for parametric variation, such as the V-to-INFLNFL parameter, in terms of the "strength" of the functional feature in question. In 4.3.2, we turn to the structure of auxiliary verbs and their movement characteristics. As we will see, the feature-checking approach to verbal licensing leads to the hypothesis that there is a functional category in addition to INFL which participates in the licensing of VP: Aspect.

4.3.1   Triggering V-to-INFL movement: feature checking

Let us now consider the question of what triggers movement of a verb to INFL. To begin, let us examine more closely what the INFL head consists of. It is assumed to include features for Tense and for Agreement, as shown in (18). The TENSE features of INFL are its specification for finiteness and, if finite, for a specific tense (e.g., Past). The AGR features of INFL correspond to the person and number features of the subject, features which appear as part of the verbal inflection in finite clauses. Both of these feature sets are functionally related to VP constituents. The AGR features of INFL are related to the Case of the subject DP, as will be discussed further in 4.4.3 and in Chapter 5. The Tense features of INFL provide a temporal specification for the event denoted by the VP, as discussed in Chapter 3 (Section 3.2). INFL is thus a category which carries out functions in relation both to DP and to VP as a whole. Following Pollock (1989), much recent work has analyzed Agreement and Tense as separate heads, each dominated by a separate phrasal node. Here, the two heads will be analyzed as a unit.

(18)

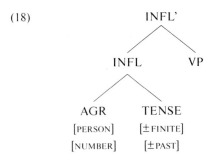

The mechanics of "linking up" INFL with DP and V have evolved along with broader developments in syntactic theory. Early analyses assumed INFL (or its predecessor, the "Aux" node) to contain the verbal affixes for Tense and Agreement. For example, the D-structure of (19a) might be as shown in (19b):

(19)   a. Ellos cantaron.
            they   sing-pa.3rd.pl.
            "They sang."
        b. [ellos [$_{INFL}$ -aron] [$_{VP}$ [$_V$ cant-]]]
            they   -pa.3rd.pl.   sing

The affix would then be merged with the verb-stem via affix-hopping (movement of the affix onto the verb stem) or via movement of the verb-stem to INFL. In recent work, following Chomsky (1993), it has been assumed that all words are fully inflected as they enter the syntax. A verb is then already inflected for Tense and Agreement features. On this approach, INFL contains abstract features, rather than the affix itself:

(20)   [ellos [$_{INFL}$ [+FINITE] [3rd.pl.NOM.] [$_{VP}$ cantaron]]
        they   sing-pa.3rd.pl.

The role of INFL is to "check" the features of V and DP, rather than to assign features to them. Feature-checking is the mechanism by which functional heads satisfy the syntactic requirements associated with their functions. For example, [+FINITE] INFL checks the [+FINITE] feature of the verb. If the features match, this licenses INFL relative to its function of temporally specifying VP. If features do not match, or if features remain unchecked, the derivation cannot produce a syntactically well-formed sentence. INFL must therefore attract to it categories which have the right features to match its own functional features. The categories which INFL must attract include DP, related to its Case function, and V, which it specifies temporally. Thus, a more detailed analysis of INFL would include these categorial features: a set of D-features, which "attracts" a DP, and a set of V-features, which attracts a verb:

(21)   AGR: TENSE:
        [PERSON]   [±FINITE]
        [NUMBER]   [±PAST]
        [CASE]
           D   V

In the course of a derivation, the V-features of TENSE can be checked once a verb moves to INFL, leaving a "trace" (t) in its original position, as shown in (22).

(22)

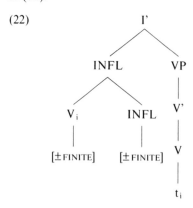

Example (22) shows one of the configurations in which feature checking can occur: between a functional head and an X^0 adjoined to it. Feature checking can also occur between a functional head and an XP in its specifier position. An example of this latter relation is the DP–INFL relation which checks Case and other D-features of the subject. In (23), the D-features of INFL are checked, if the Specifier of IP contains a DP whose features match the D-features of INFL.

(23)

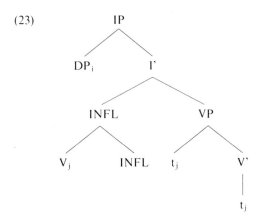

The approach described above predicts that the derivation of every clause (in every language) involves movement of a DP to the Specifier of IP, so that the D-features of INFL are checked, and movement of a verb to TENSE, satisfying feature-checking of the temporal specification of the verb. Thus, all languages have the structure shown in (23) at some stage of their derivation. However, we saw in 4.2.1 that there is a parametric difference between English and Spanish with respect to V-to-INFL movement. Here, we will consider briefly one formulation of the parameter which distinguishes the two languages. Chomsky (1993) proposed that parametric variation in S-structure representations is due exclusively to language-particular differences in the properties of functional categories, and characterizes these differences in terms of feature "strength." In the case of V-to-INFL movement, the parameter resides in the strength of the V-feature of INFL: in English, the V-feature of INFL is "weak," so that verbs do not move to INFL until late in the derivation, in the covert syntax between S-structure and logical form. In Spanish and other Romance languages, the V-feature of Tense is "strong," and a verb must be attracted to Tense by S-structure. This formulation of the parameter accounts for the contrast between English and Romance with respect to the position of main verbs in finite clauses. However, it does not provide a straightforward account of English auxiliaries: if the

V-feature of INFL is weak in English, no verb is expected to occupy INFL at S-structure. It was shown above, however, that English auxiliaries do occupy INFL, based on the distribution of VP-adverbs with English auxiliaries, and their movement to clause-initial position in questions. In effect, auxiliaries seem to be "immune" to the English/Romance V-to-INFL parameter, a point to which we return once we have considered the derivation of auxiliaries in more detail.

4.3.2   Auxiliary verbs

There are three issues that arise with respect to the derivation of clauses containing sequences such as (24):

(24)   Susana [ha   estado estudiando].
        S.   has been   studying

One question is, how are the auxiliary verbs structurally related to other VP constituents, particularly to the following verb? A second question is, how are the inflectional features of each verb in the sequence licensed? A characteristic of auxiliary verbs like those in (24) – the aspectual auxiliaries – is that the form of the following participle is rigid: it is necessary therefore to account for the grammaticality of (24), versus the ungrammaticality of *Susana ha estudiando "Susana has studying." Finally, what features of auxiliaries differentiate them from "main verbs," such that their differences with respect to V-to-INFL movement are accounted for?

With respect to the first issue, the structural relation between the auxiliary and the following participle, there have been two general approaches in the generative literature. Early work within X'-theory analyzed auxiliary verbs (other than the copula) as Specifiers or Adjuncts of VP. For a sentence such as (24), the auxiliaries would be generated as in (25) or (26). These approaches to auxiliary verb structure take note of the fact that the main verb, which heads the entire VP, is the constituent which is selectionally dominant. The main verb, not the auxiliary, is the theta-marking head, and other adjuncts must be selectionally compatible with features of the main verb. These analyses also have in common a structural characterization of auxiliaries: unlike the main verb (estudiando "studying"), the auxiliaries are not dominated by a separate VP. Auxiliaries are structurally "minor" categories, lacking full phrasal structure. This way of describing the dependence of auxiliaries on a main predicate is inadequate, though, because auxiliaries do have their own phrasal structure. They can introduce their own adjuncts, and make available more specifier positions than are present in clauses without auxiliaries. This is illustrated by the distribution of elements such as *no*, and the "floated" quantifier *todos*. Consider first the contrast in (27):

(25)

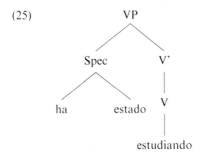

(26)

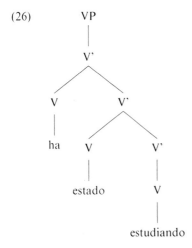

(27) a. Juan no estaba NO   estudiando.
   J.   not was   NOT studying
   "Juan wasn't NOT studying."
b. *Juan no NO   estudiaba.
   J.   not NOT studied
   "Juan didn't not study."

Typically, only a single instance of *no* "not" is possible in a given clause, as shown by the status of (27b). A second negative is possible, with strong stress, but only if an auxiliary is present, as in (27a). This contrast suggests that *no* may be generated as a Specifier of VP. On this hypothesis, (27b) would be ungrammatical because there is only one VP, so only one Specifier position in which *no* could be generated. In (27a), there are two VPs, hence two Specifier positions in which *no* can be generated.

   Likewise, the "floated" quantifier *todos* (cf. Chapter 2, Section 2.6) can co-occur with a second quantifier, but only in the presence of an auxiliary:

(28)   a. Mis amigos estaban siempre todos estudiando lingüística.
            my friends were   always all   studying   linguistics
            "My friends were always all studying linguistics."
         b. *Mis amigos estudiaban siempre todos lingüística.
            my friends studied   always all   linguistics (=28a)

If an auxiliary is present, as in (28a), both constituents are grammatical, an indication that a second VP is present. In the derivation of (28a), a quantifier occupies the specifier of each of the two VPs. The quantifiers appear to be adjacent, as a result of movement of the auxiliary to INFL. In (28b), there is no auxiliary verb, hence no second VP, so only one VP specifier position is available. These contrasts indicate that auxiliary VPs are full phrases, despite their absence of argument structure.

The second approach to auxiliaries analyzes them as being in a head–complement relation with the following constituent (see (29)).

(29)

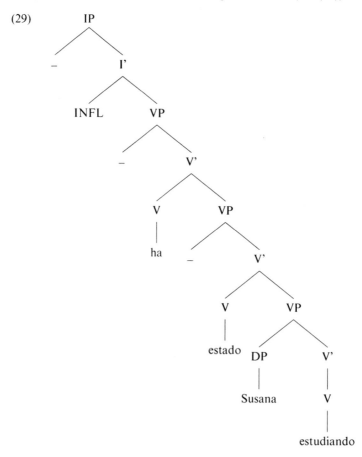

This analysis overcomes the limitations of the analyses described above. The "core VP," headed by the main verb, together with its arguments, is the lowest VP constituent in the structure. This VP is the complement of the VP headed by *estar*, which in turn is the complement of the VP headed by *ha*. Each VP has an independent Specifier, so multiple negation and quantifiers are possible, as in (27a) and (28a). The derivation involves movement of the subject DP through the Specifier positions of each VP to the Specifier of IP. The highest verb, *ha*, will move to INFL.

One possible drawback to the structure in (29) is that it does not explain the morphology of the participle following the auxiliary. The traditional transformational account of participial morphology is based on affix-hopping. However, given the assumptions outlined in 4.3.1 above, an affix-hopping analysis is no longer viable, if words enter a derivation fully inflected. Assuming a feature-checking approach to the licensing of verbal morphology as discussed in 4.3.1, the complement must be a more complex constituent. On this approach, the participial morphology would be associated with the checking of features for another functional head. We return to this point below.

Summarizing to this point, we have seen above that auxiliary verbs head their own VP, and the participle is the head of a phrase which is structurally the complement of the auxiliary. However, the hypothesis that the complement category is a VP is problematic, in that it fails to account for the licensing of the participle's morphology. Let us then assume that the structural relations shown in (29) are correct, but that the auxiliary's complement may be some category other than VP.

This brings us to the second issue raised at the beginning of this section: how is the morphology of the participle licensed? To see how this might be accomplished, let us recall how verbal morphology is licensed in simple clauses: the verb is attracted to INFL by the V-feature of Tense, and feature agreement with respect to features such as [+FINITE], [±PAST] allows the features of the verb and INFL to be checked, licensing both of these heads. What appears to be needed for participles is an additional INFL-like node, which checks features of the participle. Suppose this node is INFL, as shown in (30):

(30)   [. . . INFL [auxiliary [INFL [participle . . .]]]]

Given a D-structure like (30), the participle would move to the lower INFL, checking participle features, and the auxiliary would move to the higher INFL, likewise checking its features. If the structure in (30) is correct, it provides an immediate explanation for the licensing of the participle, and does so in a way that also explains why IP-adverbs can follow auxiliaries: because the complement of the auxiliary is IP. However, there are both empirical and conceptual difficulties with the notion that auxiliaries select an IP complement. If the clause were an IP, its INFL node should be specified for [±FINITE], and the participle should then conform to the syntax of [±FINITE] verbs. This prediction fails, however, with respect to such properties as independent negation and clitic placement. Compare the raising verb + infinitive in (31) with the auxiliary + participle sequences in (32):[11]

(31)   a. Juan parece [no saber   la respuesta].
        J.   seems not to know the answer
        b. Juan parece [saberlo].
        J.   seems to know-CL(DO)
        "Juan seems to know it."
        c. *Juan parece [lo saber].
        J. seems CL(DO) to know (=31b)

(32)   a. *Juan ha [no estudiado ese capítulo].
        J.   has not studied   that chapter
        b. *Juan ha [estudiádolo].
        J.   has studied+CL(DO)
        "Juan has studied it."
        c. *Juan ha [lo   estudiado]
        J.   has CL(DO) studied
        "Juan has studied it."

In the clausal (IP) complement of *parecer* "seem" in (31), the IP has standard infinitival properties: it can be negated, and clitics associated with the infinitive must be enclitics (follow the verb), as shown by the contrast between (31b) and (31c). The participle construction in (32a) is ungrammatical with independent negation and with clitics, whether enclitic, as in (32b), or proclitic, as in (32c). The impossibility of independent negation and clitics associated with the participle in (32) suggests that the participle is not specified either as [+FINITE] or [-FINITE], and is therefore not likely to be an IP.

The problems noted above for the INFL hypothesis correlate with a conceptual problem with respect to the temporal interpretation of participles: it implies that participles have a value for finiteness, which is problematic with respect to its temporal construal. We will give a brief overview of the nature

---

[11] The data in (32) with auxiliary *haber* "have" also apply to progressive *estar*, with one exception. Unlike perfect participles, progressive participles do admit enclitics:

(i)   Juan está [estudiándolo].
       J.   is   studying+CL(Acc.)
       "Juan is studying it."

This fact suggests that progressive *estar* might be analyzed as a raising verb of the restructuring class.

of the problem, arguing that the morphology of the participle is not Tense-related, but Aspect-related.

The [±FINITE] feature of INFL specifies the location of an event on the "time-line." A [+FINITE] event is interpreted as past, present or future in relation to another time, typically the "utterance time" of the sentence. A [-FINITE] event is not specified for a temporal location. However, this partition does not apply well to aspectual + participle constructions. In particular, the participle is not interpreted as either finite or non-finite, but is interpreted as an "aspect" of a more complex set of states. To illustrate, compare the (a) and (b) examples in (33) and (34):

(33)   a. Juan vive en Madrid.
         J.   lives in Madrid
         b. Juan ha vivido en Madrid.
         J.   has lived in Madrid

(34)   a. Juan escribe una novela.
         J.   writes a   novel
         "Juan is writing a novel."
         b. Juan ha escrito una novela.
         J.   has written a   novel

In the (a) examples with a simple present tense, the event is interpreted as "present" or cotemporaneous with the utterance-time of the sentence. In the (b) examples, although the clause is still present tense, the participle is not systematically ordered relative to the utterance-time. Example (33b) is actually ambiguous as to whether Juan lives in Madrid at utterance-time or not; (34b) is unambiguous: the event of writing a novel precedes utterance time. Comparison of (33a) and (33b) suggests that what the auxiliary + participle morphology does is split the event into a set of states: the state of Juan's living in Madrid and a state of Juan at the present time; these can be thought of as "aspects" of the event, which in (33b) may or may not be cotemporaneous. In (34b), the two states are: Juan's writing a novel, and Juan at the present time. In this case, the two states are not cotemporaneous: the writing precedes the state of Juan at the present time. Based on this generalization, it is reasonable to suppose that the function associated with participial morphology is a function which translates an event into a part, or "subevent," of a complex event. This generalization extends to progressives:

(35)   a. Juan vive en Madrid.
         J.   lives in Madrid
         b. Juan está viviendo en Madrid
         J.   is   living   in Madrid

In (35a), the clause describes a single state of Juan: his living in Madrid; in (35b), the clause describes two states of Juan: Juan living (at place x), and

Juan's living in Madrid. Progressive morphology can be described here as locating the second state as a subpart of the first.

If the preceding description of participles is accurate, then the aspectual auxiliaries can be analyzed as subcategorizing an Aspect Phrase (AspP) which contains functional features corresponding to perfective and progressive aspect (e.g. [±PERF], [±PROG]).[12] The participle itself, which heads VP at D-structure, can be analyzed as undergoing feature checking by an Aspect head, in a manner analogous to the INFL–V relation, as shown in (36). To derive the S-structure of (36), the auxiliary $había$ moves to INFL, and the participle $estu$-

(36)   a. Susana había estudiado.
        S.   had   studied

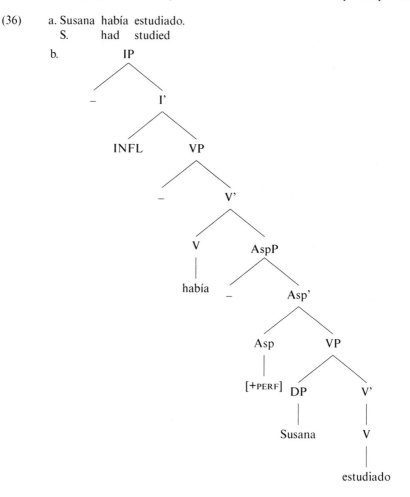

b.

_____

[12] Lema (1991) analyzes the auxiliary itself as an Aspectual head. This analysis obviates the need for a feature [+AUXILIARY], which is adopted in Belletti (1990).

diado moves to the head of the AspP, where its morphological features are checked. The subject moves through Specifier positions up to the Specifier of IP, where D-features are checked. On this analysis, IP-adverbs like *probable- mente* would be analyzed as adjuncts of IP or of AspP: the heads which license V-features. This analysis reduces the distribution of VP to two positions, both shown in (36): as sister of INFL, and as a sister of Asp. In Chapter 3 (Section 3.2), it was noted that the canonical position in which VP occurs is as a sister of INFL, and the primary exception to this generalization is that VP can be a sister of an auxiliary verb. On the analysis shown in (30), VP is uniformly gen- erated as a complement of a functional category which checks the morphol- ogy of the head.

Finally, let us return to the issue of the V-to-INFL parameter. Recall from 4.3.1 that the analysis of the parameter in terms of the strength of the V- feature of INFL accounts for the difference in surface constituency of main verbs in Spanish versus English. Unexpectedly, however, English auxiliaries move to INFL in overt syntax, just as do Spanish auxiliaries. The "immunity" of English auxiliaries to the "INFL-parameter" is difficult to reconcile with the assumption that the strength of the V-feature of INFL is responsible for the contrast between English and Romance main verbs. If, however, there is an additional functional category, AspP, which intervenes between INFL and main verbs, then it is possible that the parameter lies in the strength of the V- feature of this head. To see how this might be executed, suppose the sequence of heads is as in (37):

(37)   INFL – (V) – Aspect – V

Suppose now that the V-feature of INFL is strong in both languages, so V is attracted to INFL at S-structure. If an auxiliary is present, it moves, in both Spanish and English. What if no auxiliary is present? In this case, if Aspect is absent, main verbs should move to INFL in both languages. However, suppose that Aspect is always present, sometimes with "minus" values for its features – just as INFL is present, even with minus values for its [FINITE] feature.[13] Then the sequence of heads is as in (38):

(38)   INFL – Aspect – V

---

[13] The possibility that AspP is always present raises a question as to the distribution of multiple negation and quantifiers discussed previously (cf. (27), (28)). These were excluded from structures which contain only one verb, based on the claim that there is no second specifier position in which to generate a second element. If AspP is always present, the question that must be resolved is whether or not it allows inde- pendent specifiers.

In this structure, a main verb must first move through Aspect before it can move to INFL. If this structure is correct, it is possible to account for the contrast between auxiliaries and main verbs in terms of the strength of the V-feature of Aspect. Suppose that, in Spanish, Aspect has a strong V-feature. A main verb will move to Aspect, checking its V-feature, then move to INFL, checking the V-feature of Tense. In English, the V-feature of Aspect is weak. Main verbs cannot move to Aspect in the overt syntax, and therefore cannot move to INFL. However, in English, INFL has a strong V-feature: this feature must be checked before S-structure, but it cannot be checked by movement of a main verb. It can only be checked by a modal or pleonastic *do* – elements which are standardly assumed to be generated in INFL.[14]

On the analysis outlined above, auxiliary verbs are "immune" to the parameter which differentiates English and Romance because they, unlike main verbs, can be inserted in the structure higher than Aspect. This leads to the question of what function the Aspect head carries out in relation to VP such that it must be present in the functional structure above VP – regardless of whether the verb has participle morphology or not. A possible answer to this question is available on an analysis of Aspect as having the same type of internal structure as is assumed for INFL. Recall that INFL has both V-related features and D-related features, the latter associated with the checking of subject features, including Case, person and number. It may be that Aspect is structured in the same way, and that its D-features are associated with the object position, rather than the subject position. Tense and Aspect are then the heads which license the grammatical subject and object respectively. We will return to this point below as we examine the derivation of object clitics. For the present discussion, the relevant point is that auxiliaries can be viewed as verbs which lack both an internal argument, and (perhaps therefore) intrinsic aspectual features. Unless they are inflected for aspect, they do not require an Aspect head to dominate their VP. Besides perfective *haber* "have," items that might be analyzed as auxiliary verbs include progressive *estar*, passive *ser*, and the copulas, *ser* and *estar*. Perfective *haber* and progressive *estar* are standardly analyzed as "aspectual" auxiliaries, for reasons discussed above. The remaining items are non-aspectual, and there is no clear semantic generalization that covers them, or that unifies them with aspectual auxiliaries. In fact, these verbs differ from "main verbs" only in a negative sense: they do not select arguments, and therefore never constitute the primary (semantic) pred-

---

[14] A remaining problem is the main verb *be*. This verb moves to INFL, but cannot be assumed to be generated above Aspect, because it can co-occur with aspectuals.

icate of a clause.[15] However, because these verbs all behave alike with respect to such phenomena as V-to-INFL movement in English, it has often been assumed that they, together with the modals (and pleonastic *do* in English), comprise a subcategory of verbs distinguished by the feature [+AUXILIARY]. If this feature exists as a subcategory of verb, then it is possible that English INFL could be analyzed as attracting the feature [+AUXILIARY], rather than the feature [+V]. As noted in Lema (1991), however, this feature does not seem to play any significant cross-linguistic role in the theory of functional categories.

Summarizing, Section 4.3.1 outlined the feature-checking analysis of V-to-INFL movement. On this analysis, lexical items are inserted in syntactic derivations fully inflected. The inflectional features of a lexical category – in this case the verb – enter into a checking relation with the features of a functional head – in this case, INFL. Thus, V-to-INFL movement is triggered by the requirement that inflectional features be checked. Cross-linguistic variation with respect to the presence or absence of overt movement is accounted for in terms of the "strength" of the functional features which must be checked. Only strong features are checked prior to S-structure. The contrast between Spanish and English with respect to V-to-INFL movement was accounted for in terms of the strength of the V-feature of INFL. On this account, the movement of auxiliary verbs to INFL remains unexplained. In 4.3.2, the derivation of clauses with auxiliaries was discussed. It was argued that the structural relation between an auxiliary and the following participial phrase is a head–complement relation, and that the following participial phrase cannot be simply a VP. It must also contain a functional category which checks participial features. It was suggested that this functional category is not INFL, but Aspect Phrase. This hypothesis accounts for the form and interpretation of the participial phrase, and the distribution of IP-adverbs. Finally, if AspP is present in all clauses, not only those with auxiliaries, the relative strength of the V-feature of Aspect may be responsible for the contrasting behavior of English auxiliaries and main verbs.

[15] There is one exception to this generalization, following Sánchez and Camacho (1995). They argue that one sub-type of copular *ser*, "equative" *ser* (e.g. *Juan es el hombre de azul* "Juan is the man in blue"), subcategorizes an argument DP.

4.4   Clitics

In this section, we will examine the derivation of clauses with clitics. One of the central issues for the derivation of clitics concerns their relation to the arguments of the verb. In (39) for example,

(39)   a. María compró ese coche.
           "Maria bought that car."
        b. María lo   compró.
           M.   CL-DO bought
           "María bought it."

the transitive verb *comprar* "buy" occurs with a DP complement, as expected, in (a), but in (b) the complement position is not lexically filled. Instead, the verb is preceded by a clitic. One question raised by this alternation is: how is the transitivity of the verb satisfied in (39b)? It seems clear, in informal terms, that the clitic corresponds in some way to the missing direct object, an intuition which is supported by the fact that (39b) is ungrammatical without the clitic. In precisely what formal way the clitic is associated with the object of the verb has been a topic of long-standing debate among generative grammarians. In 4.4.1 and 4.4.2 we will summarize two traditional approaches to the derivation of clitics. One is the movement approach, which assumes that the clitic originates in the canonical object position, and undergoes movement to its surface position associated with the verb. The second is the "base-generation" analysis, which assumes that clitics originate in a clitic position associated with the verb. For each of these approaches, we will consider their advantages and drawbacks, and, in the course of the discussion, we will consider properties of clitics which have motivated these approaches. In 4.4.3, we will discuss recent proposals of a third type, based on the hypothesis that clitics are functional categories.

4.4.1   The movement approach to clitics

Recall that the central question raised by the alternation in (39) is how to account for the contrast between the distribution of full phrase complements, as in (39a), and cliticized complements, as in (39b). The distribution of full-phrase complements is as expected. Assuming that Spanish is a head-initial language, a verb theta-marks a DP complement to its right: The derivation of (40) involves movement of V-to-INFL, as discussed in 4.2 and 4.3, and the complement DP surfaces to the right of the verb. One aspect of this derivation has not been discussed yet: the complement DP must also satisfy the requirement for Case. In Chapters 2 and 3, object Case was described as assigned by the verb. On this analysis, the object DP is fully licensed in its D-structure position, and its surface order is accounted for. However, under the feature-checking theory outlined above, it is expected that Case features are checked by a functional category. We will set this issue aside, and return to it in 4.4.3. For the moment, let us assume that, whatever the mechanics of object Case feature checking, it does not impinge on the relative ordering of the verb and its phrasal complement. What about the derivation of (39b)? Its surface form has no overt DP in complement position, yet the verb is interpreted as transitive, and the clitic has person and number features which correspond to the interpreted complement: 3rd person singular. One approach to the derivation of (39b) has been to assume that its D-structure is just like (40), except that the complement DP is a clitic pronoun (see (41)). The S-structure of (41) involves movement of the clitic to the left of the verb. Early accounts of clitic movement (Emonds 1975; Quicoli 1976) generally attribute the need for movement to the fact that the clitic is an unstressed morpheme which must attach to another constituent.[16] There have been several proposals regarding the "landing site" of clitic movement (i.e., the position to which the clitic moves). The traditional (and most prevalent) analysis assumes that the clitic attaches to the verb when it undergoes movement (see (42)).

(40)

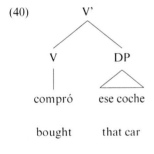

(41)

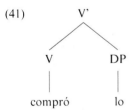

[16] The clitic status of *lo* is shown by the fact that it cannot be phonologically separated from a verb. For example, in answer to the question *¿Qué compraste?* "What did you buy?", the answer *Lo* "It" is impossible. (Compare: *¿Qué compraste?*, "What did you buy?" *Eso.* "That.")

(42)

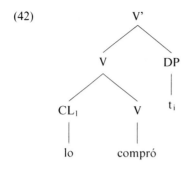

Adjunction of the clitic to the verb is motivated on grounds that the verb is the clitic "host," i.e., the constituent on which the clitic is phonologically dependent. On this analysis, (42) represents an intermediate stage in the derivation. Once the clitic adjoins to V, the complex verb would then move to INFL. An alternative version of the movement hypothesis (Kayne 1989) analyzes the landing site of clitic movement as INFL. On this analysis, the verb first moves to INFL, then the clitic adjoins to the V+INFL complex (see (43)). The advantages of the movement analysis are straightforward: first, it analyzes complements as having a uniform D-structure, as shown by the similarity between (40) and (41). Second, the movement analysis attributes clitic movement to a property which is well motivated, the status of the clitic as a clitic. Movement of the clitic in the syntax allows the clitic morpheme to be structurally adjacent to its host. The contrast between the S-structure position of full phrases and of clitics is therefore explained. A third advantage of the movement analysis is that it provides a natural account of the fact that clitics can appear in construction with a verb other than the theta-marking head:

(43)

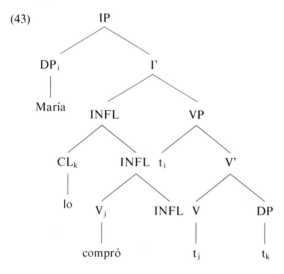

(44)   a. María lo   había comprado.
          M.   CL(DO) had   bought
          "Maria had bought it."
         b. María lo   está comprando.
          M.   CL(DO) is   buying
          "Maria is buying it."

(45)   María lo   quiere comprar.
          M.   CL(DO) wants to buy
          "Maria wants to buy it."

In (44), the clitic appears in construction with an auxiliary. In (45), it appears in construction with a main verb (*quiere*), not the verb with which the clitic is thematically associated (*comprar*). That *lo* is interpreted as a complement of *comprar* is confirmed by the contrast between (45) and (46):

(46)   a. *María lo   había comprado un libro.
          "Maria CL(DO) had   bought   a book."
         b. *María lo   quería comprar un libro.
          "Maria CL(DO) wanted to buy   a book."

In (46), the non-finite verb selects its own complement, *un libro*, and the clitic cannot be added. This shows that in (44) and (45), which are parallel in other respects, the clitic is interpreted as the complement of the non-finite verb. It follows that when a clitic appears in construction with a verb other than the theta-marking head, there must be an empty category related to the clitic lower in the structure. This empty category is provided automatically under the movement analysis, because movement always leaves a "trace" or empty category in the position vacated by the moved constituent.

One problem for the movement analysis is the phenomenon of clitic "doubling," illustrated in (47), for direct objects, and (48), for indirect objects:

(47)   a. María se   vio a   sí misma.
          M.   CL(DO.refl.) saw PA herself
          "Maria saw herself."
         b. María lo   vio a   él.
          M.   CL(DO) saw PA him
          "Maria saw him."

(48)   a. Pedro se   envió una carta a   sí mismo.
          P.   CL(IO.refl.) sent a   letter to himself
          "Pedro sent a letter to himself."
         b. Pedro le   envió una carta a   ella/María.
          P.   CL(IO) sent   a   letter to her/M.
          "Pedrol sent a letter to her/Maria."

Direct and indirect object clitics co-occur with full-phrase reflexives and pronominals; indirect object clitics (and direct objects, in some dialects) co-occur also with ordinary referential arguments. Clitic doubling is problematic for the movement analysis, because if the clitic originates in the theta-marked position, there is no obvious source for the full phrase. One solution to this problem (Hurtado 1989b) is the hypothesis that the full phrase is generated as an adjunct, which is linked indirectly to the clitic. Another solution, to be discussed further below in 4.4.3, is to generate the [clitic + phrase] as a complex constituent.[17]

An additional problem for the movement analysis is that certain clitics do not alternate with full phrases:

(49)　　a. Los niños　　se　　comieron los dulces.　　(Aspectual *se*)
　　　　　　the children CL ate　　　　the sweets
　　　　　　"The children ate up the sweets."
　　　　　b. El　barco se　hundió.　　(Middle *se*)
　　　　　　the boat　CL sank
　　　　　　"The boat sank."
　　　　　c. Juan se　　　　parece　a　Pedro.　　(Inherent Reflexive *se*)
　　　　　　J.　　CL(refl.) resemble PA P.
　　　　　　"Juan resembles Pedro."

The aspectual clitic *se* in (49a) emphasizes the completedness of the event. "Middle" *se* in (49b), on the gloss given, is standardly analyzed as a derivational morpheme which marks the deletion of the Agent Theta-role from the verb's argument structure (Saltarelli 1994). The clitic in (49c) is an "Inherent Reflexive." It does not correspond to an argument of the verb, and cannot co-occur with a full phrase (Luján 1976). Because these clitics do not correspond to arguments, there is no obvious full phrase source for them. The fact that they appear at S-structure in the same positions as argumental clitics implies that not all clitics which appear in clitic positions have arrived there by movement.

Summarizing, one approach to the derivation of clitics is by movement from DP positions. This approach allows a uniform D-structure position for complements, since both full phrases and clitics are assumed to originate in complement positions. It can also provide a natural account for the S-structure distribution of clitics, on the assumption that clitics move in order to be able to attach to a host, a requirement which follows from their clitic status. The movement analysis also accounts naturally for the appearance of clitics in construction with verbs other than the theta-marking head, since all instances of clitic placement are derived by movement. This analysis, however, does not easily accommodate the phenomenon of clitic doubling, and does not extend to clitics other than those that are argument-related.

---

[17] For a critique of these solutions to clitic doubling, see Suñer (1988) and Franco (1993).

4.4.2 The base-generation approach

The second approach to clitics is the base-generation approach. As its name implies, this approach claims that clitics do not move from full-phrase argument positions, but are base-generated as a constituent of a complex verb (Rivas 1977; Strozer 1976; Jaeggli 1982; Borer 1984). On this analysis, full-phrase complements are generated exactly as described in 4.4.1: a DP to the right of the verb is the theta-marked argument, but if the complement is a clitic, the argument requirements of the verb are satisfied in a different manner. The precise properties attributed to the clitic, and to the clitic + verb complex, vary in different studies. One approach is illustrated by the structure (50b).

(50) a. María lo   compró.
      M.   CL(DO) bought
      "Maria bought it."

b.

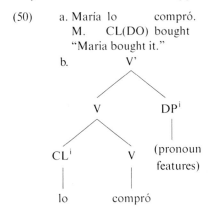

On this approach, the DP that is a sister of the complex verb is the argument position; it is theta-marked by the verb, exactly as in non-clitic, full-phrase complement constructions. The clitic is formally linked to the DP by an agreement process, shown in (50b) as co-indexing.[18] The clitic then agrees with DP in person and number.

The crucial difference between clitic and non-clitic complements is the manner in which the verb assigns its Case. Normally, the verb assigns Case to DP; but if a clitic is present, the clitic is assigned object Case, because it overtly represents the grammatical features of the argument.

The primary advantage of this approach over the movement analysis is that it provides a natural account for the phenomenon of clitic doubling. Because the clitic is not generated in argument position, the DP position can either be occupied by a covert pronoun or by a full phrase. When a full phrase is present, the DP can receive Case by two mechanisms. On one view, the agreement relation causes the Case feature assigned to the clitic to be "shared" by the clitic

---

[18] Notice that the co-indexing in (50b) is a superscript, which is distinct from the subscript notation that links a moved constituent with its trace.

and the DP. Another hypothesis is that clitic doubling is possible only if an additional Case assigner is present, such as a preposition, like Dative a, and Personal a. A second advantage to this approach is that it captures a generalization concerning the distribution of covert pronouns. In null subject languages, covert subject pronouns are grammatical, a fact which is standardly attributed to the richness of subject–verb agreement morphology, which allows the person and number features of the covert pronoun to be identified. The analysis of clitics outlined above extends this generalization to objects: the agreement between the clitic and DP allows the person and number features of the covert object pronoun to be recovered. Likewise, both subject and object DPs can be overt, which follows from the sharing of Case/Agreement features. Furthermore, this approach is compatible with the existence of clitics which do not correspond to arguments. [CLITIC + V] compounds can be formed in the lexicon, either as a result of derivational lexical processes such as middle formation, or by free insertion of clitics like aspectuals or inherent reflexives. Because these clitics do not correspond to arguments, they need not be licensed by Case/Agreement in the same way as argument DPs.

The primary drawback to the base-generation approach is that it predicts that clitics cannot undergo movement at all. This is so because the [CLITIC + V] constituent is analyzed as a compound verb, and, as such, is expected to behave like a single lexical item. Parts of the verb, like other compounds, are therefore predicted not to move apart from each other once they are inserted in a derivation. This is problematic for the base-generation hypothesis because at S-structure, clitics do not necessarily appear in construction with the verb with which they are selectionally related, as illustrated in (44)–(45) above.

Summarizing, the base-generation approach analyzes the clitic as inserted in the syntax as a component of a compound verb, not in the argument position theta-marked by the verb. This analysis provides a natural account of clitic doubling, and of covert pronominals. However, the base-generation analysis illustrated here predicts incorrectly that clitics should not move away from the verb to whose argument they are grammatically related, since parts of compound lexical items cannot otherwise undergo independent movement.

4.4.3   Clitics as functional heads

We have seen above that both of the traditional approaches to the generation of clitics capture certain of their core properties, but each has significant empirical drawbacks as well. In this section, we will briefly examine how the evolving role of functional categories in the grammar may shed light on the apparent paradox presented by the movement versus base-generation problem presented by clitics.

One line of research in this area develops the hypothesis that clitics are NP-related functional items (Uriagereka 1992; Belletti 1995). This hypothesis is conceptually related to the movement analysis, according to which clitics originate in argument positions. Recall that one drawback to the movement analysis is that it cannot easily accommodate clitic doubling, because it generates the clitic as an object pronoun, as shown in (41), repeated below. If the DP in (41) is a pronominal, the phrase has no internal structure, since, normally, pronominals do not co-occur with determiners, quantifiers, or other modifiers. The clitic should then constitute the entire argument. Suppose, however, the clitic is not a pronominal, but is instead a head of DP, as in (51). On this analysis, the problem of clitic doubling is easily resolved, because the determiner, unlike pronominals, does co-occur with additional material internal to its complement NP.[19]

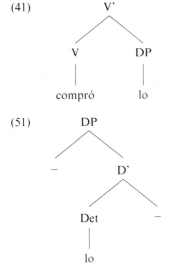

(41)

(51)

A second line of research that is conceptually related to the base-generation approach is the hypothesis that clitics are base-generated, not as a part of the verb, but as a head of a functional category that is VP-related. Thus far, we have discussed two such categories: INFL and Aspect head. It was suggested in 4.3 that the Aspect head is present in all clauses, and contains features for [±PROGRESSIVE], [±PERFECTIVE]. To see how clitics may be associated with these

---

[19] There are several possible approaches to the internal structure of the NP containing the full phrase double of the clitic. One possibility is to suppose that the clitic determiner subcategorizes a PP; another possibility is that the full phrase is a DP, with structure analogous to "determiner doubles" such as (i) (cf. Chapter 2, Section 2.5):

(i)   el   hombre ese
        the man   THAT
        "that man"

projections, recall from 4.3.1 that INFL is analyzed as containing two sets of features: Tense features and Agreement features, as shown in (21), repeated below.

(21)   AGR   TENSE
        [PERSON]   [±FINITE]
        [NUMBER]   [±PAST]
        [CASE]
          D   V

These features enter into checking relations with two VP constituents: with the verb, and with the subject DP. This AGR portion of INFL has been called "Agreement-subject" or "Agr-s." It has been argued that subject clitics are in fact generated in this AGR portion of INFL. It has been assumed as well that there is an object-related AGR head which checks Case and other features of the object, and that object clitics are generated in this head (Franco 1993). Let us suppose that Agreement-object (Agr-o) is associated with the function of the Aspect Phrase:

(52)   AGR-object   Aspect
        [PERSON]   [±PROGRESSIVE]
        [NUMBER]   [±PERFECT]
        [GENDER]
        [CASE]
          D   V

This complex is functionally related to the verb and its object in a manner analogous to the INFL–VP relation. That is, Aspect has a V-feature, which triggers movement of V-to-Aspect for V-feature checking, and the direct object is also attracted to the Specifier of the AGR-o phrase for D-feature checking. This is illustrated in (53) (for simplicity, we omit the subject and the IP portion of the structure):

(53)   a. compró ese coche
           "bought that car"

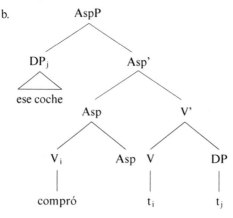

In (53b), the verb has moved to the Aspect head, whose V-feature is checked. The verb will undergo further movement higher in the structure, eventually reaching INFL, as discussed previously. The DP has moved from its theta-position to the Specifier of Aspect Phrase, checking the D-features of Agr-o, in a manner structurally analogous to the movement of a subject to the Specifier of Agr-s associated with Tense.

In a clause with an object clitic, the clitic is assumed to instantiate the Agr-o head. Notice that the features of Agr-o include a gender feature. This feature is independently motivated, since passive participles show gender agreement. The Agr-o complex now contains the feature array displayed by object clitics, and may be the D-structure position in which object clitics are generated. Relevant portions of the structure for (54a) are shown in (54b). In (54b), the clitic is generated as the Agr-o head of Aspect. Its features are checked by movement of DP to the Specifier of Aspect Phrase. The DP in (54) is a covert pronoun, but, under dialect-specific conditions, could also be an overt phrase, in clitic-double constructions.

(54)   a. lo compró

b.

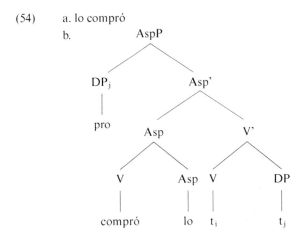

This analysis, like the base-generation analysis, generally approaches clitics as V-related, rather than D-related, in the sense that they are generated in a VP-related functional head. Like the traditional base-generation analysis described above, clitics are related to the argument via an agreement relation. Here, that relation is a Specifier–head relation, and the clitic is a realization of the Case-checking function in the VP extended projection. An advantage of this analysis is that it explains why Spanish pronominal clitics occur in clauses but not in other categories, such as within Noun Phrases. Since DP does not have Tense and Aspect, any Agr Phrases which occur within other categories do not have the same checking functions as these. Unlike the traditional base-generation analysis discussed in 4.4.1, the analysis in (54) does not generate the clitic as part of a compound verb. This approach potentially overcomes the principal drawback to the base-generation analysis, since the Aspect head can, in principle, move separately from the verb.

Two final observations are in order with respect to the functional analysis of clitics. First, notice that the analysis of clitics illustrated in (54) is also compatible with the Determiner analysis of clitics illustrated in (51). That is, the clitic could be analyzed as the constituent which moves to an abstract Agr-o constituent in Aspect, satisfying the D-feature checking of that head. On this analysis, movement of the clitic would be accounted for on the basis of D-feature checking. Second, neither of the analyses outlined here provides an obvious explanation for movement of clitics to INFL, where they precede a finite verb. However, the analysis in (54) would suggest that an account in terms of the relation between Tense and Aspect might be explored.

Summarizing the main points of this section, two traditional approaches to the analysis of clitics were introduced: the movement analysis, which analyzes clitics as originating in the position of full phrases; and the base-generation analysis, which analyzes clitics as generated as a constituent of a compound verb. Each of these analyses captures some properties of clitics, but each has limitations. In 4.4.3, it was shown how an analysis of clitics as functional heads, either D-related or V-related, potentially overcomes the most severe limitations of earlier analyses.

4.5   Negation

We turn now to clausal negation. In this section, we will discuss recent approaches to negation and Negative Concord, based on the hypothesis that negation is a functional category in the VP/IP projection. We will begin in 4.5.1 with a discussion of simple negation and the "Neg Phrase" hypothesis. In 4.5.2, we consider the phenomenon of Negative Concord, and how the analysis of Negation as a functional category has been applied to its analysis.

4.5.1   Clausal negation with no "not"

The morpheme *no* "not" appears in designated S-structure positions. As shown in (55), it precedes the first verb in the clause, whether auxiliary or main verb, and whether finite or non-finite:

(55)   a. Juan **no** leyó el   diario.
         J.   not read the newspaper
         "Juan did not read the newspaper."

b. Juan **no** había leído el diario.
    J.   not had   read the newspaper
    "Juan had not read the newspaper."
c. *Juan había **no** leído el diario.
    J.   had   not read the newspaper
d. Juan quería [**no** leer   el diario].
    J.   wanted [not to read the newspaper]
e. Juan quería [**no** estar leyendo el diario].
    J.   wanted not to be reading the newspaper
f. *Juan quería [estar **no** leyendo el diario].[20]
    J.   wanted to be not reading the newspaper

In (55a) and (55b), *no* precedes the finite verb; it cannot follow an auxiliary, as shown in (55c). *No* also precedes the first infinitive, whether it is an auxiliary or main verb. A second generalization concerning the distribution of *no* is that it must be adjacent to the verb. Only clitics can intervene between *no* and the verb; other constituents cannot:

(56)   a. *No Juan leyó el diario.
           not J.   read the newspaper
           "Juan didn't read the newspaper."
       b. *Juan no ayer   leyó el diario.
           J.   not yesterday read the newspaper
           "Juan didn't read the newspaper yesterday."
       c. Juan no lo   leyó.
           J.   not CL(Acc). read
           "Juan didn't read it."

The uniform distribution of *no* in clauses has led to the assumption that it is generated in a position higher than INFL, since finite verbs occupy INFL at S-structure. Laka (1990) argues that Spanish *no* is generated as the head of a functional category "Sigma Phrase," which alternates with the emphatic affirmative *sí* "yes." Following much recent research, I will refer to this category as "Neg Phrase." Let us see what the D-structure of a sentence like (55a) would be, assuming that Neg is higher than INFL. As a first approximation, consider (57), where we omit the Aspect Phrase, for ease of presentation. To derive the S-structure, the finite verb moves to INFL, deriving the order: *No leyó Juan el diario.* This order is grammatical, with the subject following the

---

[20] Example (55f) is possible if understood as containing constituent negation rather than clausal negation. This reading is brought out by adding a continuation such as the one in (i):

(i)   Juan quería estar no leyendo el diario, sino descansando.
       "Juan wanted to be not reading the newspaper, but resting."

verb. To derive a pre-verbal subject, the external argument moves to the Specifier of IP. Notice, however, that in (57) the Specifier of IP is lower than the Neg Phrase. Movement of the subject would incorrectly derive: *No Juan leyó el diario. This problem is resolved by the "Split INFL" hypothesis (Pollock 1989), which, as noted briefly in Section 4.3.1, analyzes as separate heads the Agreement and Tense features of INFL. Following Belletti (1990), the Agr-s phrase is assumed standardly to precede Tense. Once these heads are separate, Neg can be between them:

(57)

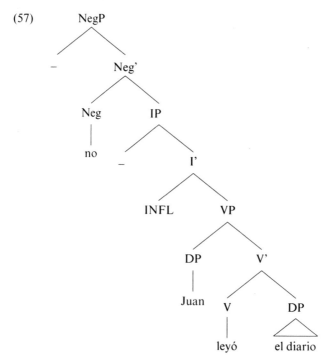

(58)   Agr-s – Neg – Tense

Assuming that the finite verb moves to Tense, the correct order of Negation relative to the verb is derived. A pre-verbal subject will also be the first constituent, since the subject DP will move to the Specifier of the Agr-s phrase, thereby preceding negation. Adverbs must also be prohibited from adjoining to the right of Negation – in other words, adverbs must adjoin to the Agr-s phrase, not to Tense Phrase.

   Two comments on this approach to negation are in order. First, the hypothesis that the negative morpheme is base-generated in the Neg Phrase leads to the assumption that the position of the Neg Phrase in universal grammar can be parametrized. In English, negative not follows INFL:

(59)   a. John has not read the newspaper.
          b. *John read not the newspaper.
          c. John did not read the newspaper.

Assuming that English auxiliaries move to INFL at S-structure, but main verbs do not, the order in (59) suggests that the Neg Phrase is below INFL, and perhaps below auxiliaries:

(60)   English: Agr-s – Tense – Neg

A second issue concerns the position of Agr-s and of subjects generally, which will be taken up in Chapters 5 and 6. The status of Agr-s (and likewise, Agr-o) as a separate phrasal head (as shown in (58)) has been questioned in some recent studies. Furthermore, assuming that it is a separate head, its position relative to Tense has been debated. If the Split INFL hypothesis should be shown incorrect in future research, then an alternative mechanism is needed to capture the position of pre-verbal subjects.

4.5.2   Negative Concord

The term "Negative Concord" concerns the interpretation of negation in the presence of a class of items referred to as "n-words," such as *nadie* "nobody/anybody," *nunca*, "nothing/anything," *nada* "nothing/anything," etc., and NPs introduced by *ningún* "no," as in *ningún libro* "no book." As indicated by the glosses, these items are only sometimes negative in meaning. This is illustrated for *nadie* in (61):

(61)   a. Nadie vino.
             "Nobody came."
          b. No vino nadie.
             not came anybody
             "Nobody came."

In (61a), pre-verbal *nadie* is interpreted as a negative, glossed as "nobody." In (61b), *nadie* co-occurs with *no*, but these are construed as a single negative. Example (61b) does not mean "nobody didn't come" (i.e., "everybody came"); it is identical to (61a) in meaning. Informally speaking, the two constituents function together as a discontinuous negative under certain conditions. The conditions for Negative Concord are, first, that either *no* or an *n*-word must be pre-verbal, as shown in (62):

(62)   a. Nadie dijo nada.
             nobody said anything
          b. Juan no dijo nada.
             J.   not said anything
             "Juan didn't say anything."

c. *Juan dijo nada.
   J.   said anything

In (62a), an *n*-word is pre-verbal, and, in (60b), *no* is pre-verbal. Example (60c) is ungrammatical without a pre-verbal negative. Second, only one negative constituent can be pre-verbal, as shown in (63):

(63)   a. No vino nadie.
           not came anybody
           "Nobody came."
        b. *Nadie   no   vino.
           Nobody didn't come.
        c. *Nadie   nada   dijo.
           nobody anything said

Negative Concord has been analyzed in terms of a Specifier–head licensing relation between the *n*-word and the head of Neg Phrase (Haegeman and Zanuttini 1991; Uribe-Etxebarría 1994). This can be cast in terms of the feature-checking approach to functional categories described in 4.3.1. Assume, for example, that the Neg Phrase contains an abstract feature for [+NEG]:

(64)

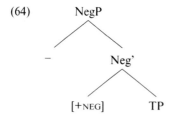

This feature must attract a constituent specified for [+NEG], and feature checking is the mechanism for grammatically licensing clausal negation. The assumption that this feature is strong accounts for the fact that one negative constituent must be pre-verbal. It must attract either *no* or an *n*-word, the items which have Neg features to check. To derive (62a), *nadie* moves to the Specifier of NegP, and checks the strong feature of the abstract functional head, as in (65).

(65)

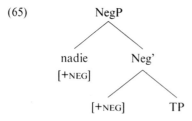

To derive (62b), *no* is inserted (not moved from a lower position), and it then checks the feature of the abstract head. Alternatively, *no* might be analyzed as a phrase, which, like *n*-words, is in the Specifier of NegP. These alternatives are shown in (66). In (66a) *no* is a head. It is required in order to check a feature of the abstract [+NEG] head of NegP. In (66b), *no* is analyzed as a phrase. On either analysis, both the pre-verbal distribution of *no*, and the uniqueness of the pre-verbal negative constituent are accounted for. The impossibility of multiple negatives in pre-verbal position is accounted for on the assumption that constituents only move to check features, and cannot move otherwise. Once a negative constituent has checked the strong feature of Neg, no other constituent can move to NegP before S-structure. The distribution of Negative constituents is thus analogous to interrogatives, an insight captured in Haegeman & Zanuttini's proposal. Another fact which must be accounted for is that, while *n*-words can be post-verbal, *no* cannot. The functional analysis of *no* accounts for this by base-generating *no* as the head of Neg Phrase. This is also accounted for on a feature-checking approach, on the assumption that *no* is base-generated in Neg Phrase in one of the positions shown in (66).

(66)

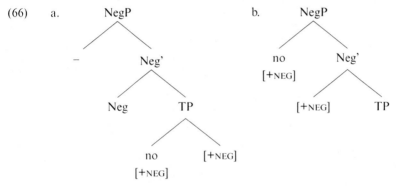

Although the functional analysis of Neg Phrase may account for the distribution of negative constituents at S-structure, there are several details of negation that require further analysis. One issue concerns the parameter that distinguishes Negative-Concord and non-Negative-Concord languages. If it is assumed that the licensing of *n*-words operates uniformly across languages, it remains to be explained why Spanish *n*-words like *nadie* and *nada* can be genuine negatives when pre-verbal, but not separate negatives when post-verbal.[21] Also, Bosque (1980) notes that *n*-words can be licensed in certain contexts which lack an overt negative. This is shown by the contrast in (67):

[21] The Negative-Concord parameter has been attributed to lexical properties of *n*-words. However, what these properties are precisely has been debated extensively. For discussion, see Suñer (1995) and Bosque (1980).

(67)   a. María canta mejor que ninguno de nosotros.
          M.   sings better than any   of us
          b. *María canta tan bien como ninguno de nosotros.
          M.   sings as well as   any   of us

In (67a), the negative constituent is contained within a comparative clause with an ellipted predicate; it cannot be assumed to be licensed internal to that clause, as is shown by (67b), which is ungrammatical for many speakers.

Summarizing, we have seen in 4.5.1 that a functional analysis of negation accounts for the distribution of negative *no*, assuming that it is generated in a Neg Phrase, which is higher in clause structure than the S-structure position of the verb. This requires a Split INFL analysis, with Neg Phrase intervening between Agr-s and Tense. In 4.5.2, we saw that the distribution of *n*-words is accounted for, on the assumption that the Neg head has a strong feature which attracts a negative constituent to it before S-structure.

4.6   Summary

This chapter has examined several aspects of the syntax of the VP in relation to the functional categories which license VP constituents. The distribution of VP-adverbs was examined in Section 4.2. The order of the verb in relation to adverbs shows that verbs move out of VP to INFL in the derivation to S-structure. Section 4.3 introduced the feature-checking approach to V-movement, and examined the structure associated with auxiliary verbs, and movement of auxiliaries. That section proposed that the functional heads which attract V include INFL (specifically the Tense features of INFL) and Aspect. The Aspect head was suggested to be necessary to license participle morphology in clauses with aspectual auxiliaries, and was suggested to be present in all clauses, just as INFL is. This hypothesis provides one way of accounting for parametric variation with respect to movement of main verbs. Section 4.4 discussed the derivation of clitics. The two traditional analyses of clitics, movement and base-generation, each account for certain properties of clitics, but do not provide natural explanations for others. Recent approaches to clitics have analyzed them as functional categories, either in NP-related or VP-related functional projections. On both of these approaches, the Aspect/Agr-o head may play a central role, either as the position in which clitics are generated, or the position to which they move. These analyses can relate the movement of clitics to the D-feature checking of objects, although movement of clitics to INFL is not naturally accounted for. Nevertheless, each of these approaches provides a more adequate description of the syntax of clitics than was possible under early formulations. Section 4.5 discussed negation. Analysis of negation as a functional category in IP was shown to account for the distribution of negative *no* and for basic properties of *n*-words.

5

Subjects, topics and declarative constituent order

5.1 Introduction

In this chapter, we will take up the issue of the order of the clausal subject relative to the verb and objects in declaratives. In Chapter 1 it was noted that Spanish declaratives are generally grammatical with either pre-verbal or post-verbal subjects:

(1)   a. **María** compró un coche.   (S-V-O)
          M.   bought a   car
       b. Compró **María** un coche.   (V-S-O)[1]
       c. Compró un coche **María**.   (V-O-S)

Stated informally, the central question to be addressed here is: what properties of Spanish are responsible for this "flexibility" in constituent order, as compared with a language like English, where subject order is "fixed"? This question has been investigated actively from the earliest stages of the principles and parameters framework. Below, we will discuss some of the central issues that bear on this problem, and consider informally the main lines of investigation that have been explored within the principles and parameters framework.

In previous chapters, the analysis of the clausal subject has been touched on only briefly. It was noted in Chapters 3 and 4 that the subject is generated VP-internally, and is assumed to move to the Specifier of IP to satisfy its Case requirement. Nominative Case is assigned, or "checked" (cf. Chapter 4, Section 4.3.1), by the head of IP, INFL:

---

[1] It was noted in Chapter 1 that at least for some speakers, V-S-O order for sentences like (1b) is not as fully acceptable as S-V-O or V-O-S. However, V-S-O becomes acceptable if the subject is non-agentive, as in sentences like: *Sufrió el paciente dolores terribles* "The patient suffered terrible pains." Since V-S-O order is available for at least some predicates, it will be assumed here to be grammatical.

202

(2) $[_{IP}$ DP$_i$ INFL $[_{VP}$ t$_i$ $[_{V'}$ V . . .]]]
        NOM < – Case

The movement shown in (2) derives the S-V-O order that is observed in declaratives in English. This particular type of movement has been referred to as "A-movement" – that is, movement to an "argument position," as discussed in Chapter 3. The main question that will be addressed below is whether the same form of movement occurs in Spanish. A related issue is, how are the alternative orders in (1b) and (1c) generated? Finally, we will consider the relationship between the "flexibility" of subject order and the grammaticality of covert subjects.

We begin the discussion in Section 5.2 with an introduction to basic issues related to the licensing of the subject in a language like Spanish, in which the subject displays freer constituent order than in "fixed" subject order languages. As the discussion will show, evolving assumptions about movement make it difficult to account for the licensing of Spanish subjects in a way parallel to fixed-order languages. We conclude that Spanish does not have the same type of A-movement that derives S-V-O order in English. We will then explore some of the alternative ideas that have been proposed regarding what determines the position of the subject. Beginning in 5.3, we consider the traditional notion that constituent order is sensitive to the "discourse informational content" of constituents. That is, notions such as "old versus new information," "Theme-Rheme," or Topic-Comment analysis of sentences have been claimed to affect the order of constituents in declaratives. Section 5.3 will introduce two of these notions, "Focus" and "Topic," which appear to be significant for characterizing constituent order. We will then go on to review two approaches to the derivation of pre-verbal constituents as affected by Topic-hood. Section 5.4 explores the hypothesis that features related to discourse information content are grammaticalized as functional features of the clause in Spanish, and, consequently, they may trigger movement of certain constituents to pre-verbal positions. Section 5.5 considers Topic constituents called "dislocated" Topics, of which there are two types with distinct syntactic properties. Both of these types of dislocated constituents have been argued to be adjuncts, rather than specifiers, and not derived by movement. Finally in Section 5.6, we turn to the issue of the relationship between "flexible" subject order and null subjects. We begin with a description of the "Null Subject Parameter" (Rizzi 1982; Jaeggli 1982) as formulated within the "Government and Binding" framework. We then consider some alternative formulations of the parameter.

5.2.   The problem of "free" subject order

As noted above, the main question that we consider here is how the clausal subject is licensed in Spanish, and, in particular, why it is possible for subjects to appear either pre-verbally or post-verbally in declaratives. In this section, we will discuss why the "optionality" of pre-verbal subjects is not easily accounted for. The main issue is that, as the principles and parameters framework has evolved, the operation of "move alpha" has become more constrained. Initially, movement was considered to be entirely optional: particular movement might or might not occur. As long as no principle came to be violated in the structure derived by the movement, both results were expected in principle to be fine. More recently, many authors (following Chomsky (1993)) have assumed that movement is to be avoided if it is not necessary. This is so because it seems that grammars are constrained by principles "economy." Because movement adds complexity to a derivation, it has been assumed in much recent research that movement cannot occur unless it must, to avoid violating some principle. As a result, the theory leads to the view that optional movement does not actually occur.

In this section, we will see how this evolving view of movement affects the analysis of subjects. We begin the discussion in 5.2.1 with a review of assumptions that have been introduced already in Chapter 4 concerning the role of functional categories in triggering movement. Then in 5.2.2, we apply these assumptions to the analysis of the clausal subject, under the additional assumption that movement is impossible unless it is triggered by a feature of a functional category. As we will see, the framework as outlined to this point does not provide a satisfactory analysis for the flexibility of order of the subject.

5.2.1   Review of the role of functional categories

In Chapter 4 (Section 4.3.1), several assumptions were introduced regarding how functional categories contribute to the licensing of constituents in a derivation. We will review these assumptions here, focusing on the following three characteristics of functional categories such as INFL:

(3)   Characteristics of Functional Categories
       a. "Check" features such as Case, rather than assign features;
       b. "Attract" a category with the appropriate feature to check;
       c. Parametric variation: features are either "strong" or "weak."

Let us again illustrate these in relation to the features of INFL. Recall that INFL contains features for Tense and Agreement, as shown in (4). Both of these feature sets are functionally related to VP constituents: AGR features of INFL are related to the subject DP. The Tense features of INFL are functionally related to the verb. In Chapter 4 we focused on the verbal features of Tense, and their relation to movement of V-to-INFL. Recall that the notion of INFL as a functional category provided an alternative to the process of Affix-hopping. That is, instead of having a verb stem "hook up" with its affix in the syntax, as in (5),

(4)

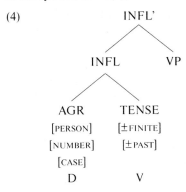

INFL'

INFL   VP

AGR   TENSE
[PERSON]   [±FINITE]
[NUMBER]   [±PAST]
[CASE]
D   V

(5)   [ellos [$_{INFL}$ –aron] [$_{VP}$ [$_V$ cant-]]]
        they   -pa.3rd.pl.   sing

we assume instead that a verb is already inflected before it enters the derivation. On this approach, INFL does not "assign" the Past affix to the verb. Instead, INFL contains abstract features rather than the affix itself:

(6)   [ellos [$_{INFL}$ [+FINITE] [3rd.pl.NOM.] [$_{VP}$ cantaron]]]
        they   sang

Assuming an analysis like (6) rather than (5), the role of INFL is to "check" that the appropriate features are present on the verb. This "checking" can occur only in a local environment, and the result is that the verb must move close enough to the features of INFL for checking to take place. In this sense, INFL indirectly "attracts" the verb. Once V-to-INFL takes place, feature checking takes place. For our purposes, we can think of checking as a kind of feature agreement, although the technical aspects of checking are more involved than is described here.

So far, we have reviewed the notion that functional categories like INFL contain abstract features which must match, or be checked against, the features of an appropriate element in the derivation. We also saw that, in order for feature checking to take place, it can be necessary for a constituent that is too far away from INFL to move, so that it is close enough for this to happen. In this sense, the functional category "attracts" a category to it.

The last point to consider is how parameters occur. Recall from the discussion of the previous chapter that language-particular variation in feature checking is due to the "strength" of the features of functional categories. In the case of V-to-INFL movement, the parameter resides in the strength of the verbal features of INFL: in Spanish, this feature is "strong," which means that it must be checked early in the derivation – in effect, before the point that we have referred to as S-structure. In English, this feature is "weak," which means that it cannot be checked early in the derivation. In fact, it cannot occur until after the S-structure representation is determined, so that it is a "covert" movement. The parametric difference in word order can be illustrated as follows. From a common "deep structure," shown schematically in (7a), we have the two superficial orders, (7b) and (7c):

(7)   a. $[_{IP}$ INFL $[_{VP}$ SUBJECT $[_{V'}$ V OBJECT]]]
        b. $[_{IP} [_{INFL}$ V$_i$ + INFL] $[_{VP}$ SUBJECT $[_{V'}$ t$_i$ OBJECT]]]   (overt movement)
        c. $[_{IP}$ INFL $[_{VP}$ SUBJECT $[_{V'}$ V OBJECT]]]   (no overt movement)

In (7b), the verb has moved to INFL as an overt process, due to the "strong" verbal feature of INFL. In (7c), the verb has not moved to INFL, since the verbal feature of INFL is "weak." The verb in (7c) would move covertly, in the Logical Form component of the syntax. Notice that, if no other processes affected the derivation in (7), the two languages in question would have different basic word order. The language illustrated in (7b), which has a strong verbal feature in INFL would have: V-S-O order as its basic order. The language illustrated in (7c), which has a weak verbal feature in INFL, would have S-V-O order as its basic declarative order. However, these derivations represent only part of the picture. The INFL features that are related to the subject have not been specified for strength. Below, we will consider this component of INFL in relation to the question of subject order.

5.2.2 *Movement of the subject to the specifier of IP*

Let us now consider how the mechanisms described above affect the subject constituent. We saw above that there is a relationship of feature checking between INFL and two related lexical categories: the verb, and the subject. We showed how the strength of the verbal feature determines whether or not the verb moves to INFL (at least, as an overt process). We turn now to the corresponding features of INFL that are related to the subject. The subject-related features of INFL include the agreement features (person, number) and the Case feature. This set of features will be considered as a group, and, for convenience, we will refer to them as "noun-features" or "N-features," just as the features of Tense are verb-features.[2]

Just as the verb features of INFL are specified as either "strong" or "weak," so are the N-features of INFL. There are two possible outcomes for the subject, according to the strength of INFL's N-features. These are shown by the schematic derivations in (8). The verb is shown as moving overtly to INFL, as was discussed for Spanish in Chapter 4 (Section 4.3):

(8)   a. $[_{IP}$ INFL $[_{VP}$ SUBJECT $[_{V'}$ V OBJECT]]]
        b. $[_{IP} [_{INFL}$ V_i + INFL] $[_{VP}$ SUBJECT $[_{V'}$ t_i OBJECT]]]
        c. $[_{IP}$ SUBJECT$_j$ [INFL V_i + INFL] $[_{VP}$ t_j $[_{V'}$ t_i OBJECT]]]

Beginning with an initial structure (8a), the verb moves to INFL, and the strong verb features of INFL can be checked. The N-features might be either strong or weak. Example (8b) depicts a language in which the N-features are weak, and the subject does not move, at least as an overt movement. Example (8c) depicts a language in which N-features are strong, and the subject moves to the Specifier of IP.

Consider now why neither of the options in (8b) or (8c) is adequate for Spanish. If the N-features of INFL are analyzed as "strong," it would be expected that movement of a subject (as a movement in the overt syntax) would be obligatory, since this is the characteristic of "strong" features: they must undergo feature checking before the point at which surface word order is fixed. On the other hand, if the N-features of INFL were "weak," then movement of the subject should be impossible, since weak features do not require checking before surface word order is fixed. Both of these options lead to an expected "fixed" order, which is problematic for Spanish. That is, the mechanisms described cannot account for the grammaticality of the various orders that are possible for the subject:

(9)   a. **María** compró un coche.   (S-V-O)
           M.   bought a   car
        b. Compró **María** un coche.   (V-S-O)
        c. Compró un coche **María**.   (V-O-S)

If the N-features of INFL were strong, then both (9b) and (9c) should leave the strong N-feature of INFL unchecked prior to S-structure. If the N-features of INFL were weak, then (9a) should be impossible. Notice that there are two ways of deriving a surface order for (9a), both of which are inconsistent with

---

[2] A more technically precise way of referring to these features is as "D-features," since the category that bears them is a DP, not an NP.

the feature strength of INFL features for Spanish. One way would be to do no movement, leaving the verb as the head of VP, and the subject in the Specifier of VP. This would be impossible, since as we discussed in Chapter 4, the verb features of INFL are "strong" in Spanish. On the other hand, (9a) could be derived by analyzing both the verb features and the N-features of INFL as "strong." On this analysis, the surface structure would have the verb in INFL, and the subject NP in the Specifier of IP. This revives the problem of N-features. If they are strong, the grammaticality of (9b) and (9c) are unexpected.

5.2.3   Summary

As we have seen here, the approach to constituent order that is based on feature strength, taken together with the view that movement is impossible unless it is absolutely necessary, seems inadequate to handle situations such as the one illustrated here, in cases like (9). Here, we have a constituent whose order is "free" in declaratives, while in other languages it is fixed.

This apparent paradox has led to two lines of investigation within the principles and parameters framework, which will be considered below. One possibility is that there are additional functional categories in the clause, and features other than the N-features of INFL can be responsible for triggering movement of constituents. In particular, it has been suggested that a functional category that is active in Spanish is one that is related to the discourse function of constituents. We discuss this concept in 5.3, then in 5.4 consider how it may illuminate properties of the subject. A second possibility that has been explored is that, since movement is so tightly constrained, it is possible that alternations like those in (9) point to a derivation that does not have movement. This possibility is considered in 5.5.

5.3   Discourse roles: Focus and Topic

Several traditions in the grammatical literature have discussed the "information load" borne by different constituents of a sentence. Terms such as "old and new information," "theme and rheme," "topic and comment" have been used to describe the contribution of various sentence constituents to the flow of information within the discourse. In this section two central concepts related to information structure will be introduced: Focus, and Topic. We begin with the notion of Focus, in 5.3.1, then, in 5.3.2, we will consider one subcase of non-Focal material, that of Topic.

5.3.1   Focus

The discourse context within which a sentence is framed determines the "discourse role" for sentence constituents. For example, in the exchange in (10), the (a) sentence provides a discourse context for the answers in (b)–(d):

(10)   a. ¿A quién vio José?
            "Who did José see?"
        b. José vio a Pedro.
            "José saw Pedro."
        c. Vio a Pedro.
            "(He) saw Pedro."
        d. A Pedro.
            "Pedro."

The question in (10a) asks for information about the individual whom José saw. The answers in (b)–(d) provide this information. In the answers, the only constituent which provides "new" information is the direct object, *Pedro*. The subject and verb are "given" or "previously known" by virtue of the context in (10a). Comrie (1989) refers to the "new information" as the Focus of the sentence, and all other constituents as "Non-Focus." Zubizarreta (1998) takes the relevant division to derive from the discourse notion of presupposition. What the speaker and hearer assume to be true at the time that the sentence is uttered is "presupposed"; elements of a sentence which are not presupposed are the Focus of a sentence. Zubizarreta represents this distinction in terms of the feature $[\pm F]$. As is illustrated by the question and answer pairs in (11)-(13), any constituent, or the entire sentence, may be the Focus. The Focus constituent in the (b) sentences is bracketed:

(11)   a. ¿Adónde fue José?
            "Where did José go?"
        b. José fue [$_{FOCUS}$ a casa].
            "José went [home]."
(12)   a. ¿Qué hizo José?
            "What did José do?"
        b. José [$_{FOCUS}$ fue a casa].
            "José [went home]."
(13)   a. ¿Qué pasó?
            "What happened?"
        b. [$_{FOCUS}$ José fue a casa.]
            "[José went home.]"

In (11) and (12), the question in (a) determines what is presupposed (hence, Non-Focal) in the answer. In (13), the question provides no presupposition (or only that something happened); likewise, in discourse-initial contexts, an entire sentence may be a Focus.

Summarizing, sentences are assumed to contain some [+FOCUS] material, and may also contain [-FOCUS] material, although this is not always the case, as in examples like (13b). The question arises as to how the grammar identifies focal material in a sentence, and how the partition between Focal and Non-Focal material is marked. Addressing the second point first, in Spanish, the partition between Focal and Non-Focal material is not explicitly marked, as is shown by the fact that the (b) sentences in (13) may be identical, although they differ in their Focus bracketing. Although there is no explicit division between [+FOCUS] and [-FOCUS] constituents, there is nevertheless a systematic association between [+FOCUS] and intonation, and between these and word order, as argued in Zubizarreta (1998). To illustrate the relationship between Focus and intonation, note first that the normal position for the intonation peak (Nuclear Stress) in non-emphatic declaratives is the rightmost[3] stressed syllable of the predicate:

(14)   a. José fue a CAsa.
          "José went HOME."
         b. Su hermano comió una manZAna.
          "His brother ate an apple."
         c. María baiLÓ.
          "Maria danced."

This primary stress cannot fall on a [-FOCUS] constituent.[4] This is shown by the impossibility of (14a), repeated below, as an answer to (15):

(15)   ¿Quién fue a casa?
          "Who went home?"

(14a)   *José fue a CAsa.
          "José went HOME."

The question in (15) establishes *fue a casa* as presupposed, or [-FOCUS]. This material will then also be [-FOCUS] in the answer, (14a). The only [+FOCUS] constituent of (14a) is its subject:

(16) $[_{[+F]}$ José $[_{[-F]}$ fue a casa]]

---

[3] Zubizarreta (1998) argues that the crucial context is hierarchical: the most deeply embedded constituent is stressed.

[4] This generalization is termed the Focus Prosody Correspondence Principle. See Zubizarreta (1998:38) and references cited.

Primary stress then falls on a [-FOCUS] constituent, *casa*. For (14a) to become a possible answer to (15), either its intonation or its word order can be altered, as shown in (17): [5]

(17)   a. JoSÉ fue a casa.   (emphatic stress on José)
         b. Fue a casa JosÉ.   (Nuclear Stress on José)

In (17a), word order remains the same, but intonation changes: an emphatic stress, rather than Nuclear Stress, is assigned to the [+FOCUS] constituent. In (17b), intonation remains the same, but the order of subject and predicate is reversed, so that the [+FOCUS] subject is in position to be assigned Nuclear Stress.[6]

Summarizing, we have seen above that a sentence may consist of both [+FOCUS] ("new," or non-presupposed) and [-FOCUS] ("old" or presupposed) constituents. The "scope" of [+FOCUS] may vary for a given sentence according to the context in which the sentence is uttered, as illustrated in (11)–(13). Although word order is not exclusively determined by Focus, the two are systematically related. Non-emphatic (Nuclear) stress falls on the rightmost (hierarchically lowest) word stress in a clause, and this stress must coincide with [+FOCUS]. The "alignment" of stress with [+FOCUS] may produce variation in either stress or word order.

5.3.2   Topic

The notion of TOPIC, like Focus, is determined relative to a discourse context. Comrie (1989) describes Topic as the constituent that expresses what the sentence is "about." For example, given the context (18),

(18)   ¿Qué pasó con José?
         "What happened to José?",

the reply will be a sentence whose Topic is *José*:

(19)   a. [$_{TOPIC}$ José] se fue.
            "José went away."
         b. Eligieron presidente a [$_{TOPIC}$ José].
            "They elected José president."

---

[5] Example (17a) may be more natural than (17b), at least for some speakers. In this respect, it appears to pattern with V-O-S (with true transitive predicates). See note 10.

[6] Zubizarreta (1998) proposes that the reordering of subject and predicate like that in shown in (17b) is triggered by the [F] status of the predicate. The movement is termed "p-movement."

The notion of "aboutness" that is generally taken to underlie the concept of Topic is based on the presuppositions of speaker and hearer. In the dialogue beginning in (18), it is presupposed that something happened to José; the phrase $[_{DP}$ *José*] thus is presuppositional, and in the context of the question (18), is the natural discourse Topic of answers in (19). In contexts other than information questions, where a Topic is not determined, one possibility is that a sentence will not have a Topic determined by previous discourse. The paradigm case is discourse-initial sentences ("out of the blue" statements) and sentences answering questions like "What's new?"; such sentences have no Topic. In other circumstances, where there is a previous discourse with presuppositional background, a Topic may be newly introduced. These "newly set" Topics may be preceded by such phrases as: *en cuanto a* "as for," *hablando de* "speaking of," etc. These phrases are sometimes referred to as Left Dislocations or "hanging Topics," and have some properties that are not shared by all Topic constituents.

Topic constituents, whether newly set or not, can be syntactically "dislocated." For example, (20) is an alternative to (19b):

(20)   (Hablando de) José, lo eligieron presidente.
        "(Speaking of) José, (they) elected him president."

In (20), the constituent (*Hablando de*) *José* is followed by a juncture and, optionally, by a pause.[7] Dislocated constituents are unambiguously interpreted as Topics. This is shown by the fact that left-dislocated constituents must be specific in interpretation, which follows from the status of Topics as a subcase of non-focal, or presupposed, material.[8] Compare the (a) and (b) examples below:

(21)   a. Algunos estudiantes leyeron ese capítulo, pero no sé cuáles.
           "Some students read that chapter, but I don't know which (ones)."
        b. ? *Algunos estudiantes, leyeron ese capítulo, pero no sé cuáles.
           "Some students, (they) read that chapter, but I don't know which ones."

---

[7] Dislocated Topics can also appear to the right of the clause:

    (i)   Lo   eligieron presidente, a   José.
           CL(DO) elected   president, PA J.
           "They elected him president, José."

Right-dislocated Topics differ from left-dislocated ones in some respects. For example, the Topic in (i) cannot be preceded by *hablando de* "speaking of."

[8] Zubizarreta (1989) follows Reinhart (1982) in defining "aboutness" relative to the notion *context set* (Stalnaker 1978), the set of propositions that the speaker takes to be true at a given point in the discourse.

(22)   a. Ningún estudiante leyó ese capítulo.
         "No student read that chapter."
         b. ?*Ningún estudiante, leyó ese capítulo.
         "No student, (s/he) read that chapter."

The (a) examples show that non-specific pre-verbal subjects are grammatical. In the (b) examples, however, where the subject is set off by comma intonation and is obligatorily interpreted as Topic, the non-specific Topic is ungrammatical.

Summarizing, a Topic characterizes what a sentence is "about." Topics are selected from among the elements which are presupposed at a given point in a discourse. In the context of information questions, the Topic of the answer is narrowly identified; in other contexts, the speaker may choose one (or more) such elements. Topics may be identified by appearing in a clause-peripheral position, intonationally separated from their "comment." We turn now to the derivation of constituent order in declaratives, considering in particular how the Topic status of constituents may be analyzed as affecting order.

5.4   [Topic] Movement to the specifier of IP

In this section we consider the derivation of pre-verbal subjects as an instance of movement of a "Topic" constituent to the Specifier of IP. This approach claims, in essence, that a pre-verbal subject moves to the Specifier of IP not specifically in order to participate in checking of N-features of INFL, but in order to check a feature related to its discourse role. The empirical generalization that this analysis captures is that, as a result of movement, declaratives may have the order: XP–Predicate, where XP is a Topic – whether a subject, or a non-subject. Examples of non-subject topics are illustrated in (23) (from Zubizarreta 1998):

(23)   a. Todos los días compra Juan el   diario.
            every   day buys   J. the paper
            "Juan buys the newspaper every day."
         b. El   primer día de escuela deberá acompañar cada madre a   su
            hijo.
            the first   day of school should accompany each mother PA her
            child
            "Each mother must accompany her child the first day of school."
         c. Ayer   presentó María su renuncia.
            yesterday handed-in Maria her resignation
            "Yesterday Maria handed in her resignation."

d. En este bar escribió Max su primera novela.
in this bar wrote Max his first novel
"In this bar, Max wrote his first novel."

Below, section 5.4.1.discusses the derivation of sentences like (23); then 5.4.2 will compare this type of movement with other cases of movement. On the assumption that [TOPIC] is a functional feature, 5.4.3 considers whether it occupies INFL or a higher head.

5.4.1   [Topic] Movement

Koopman and Sportiche (1991) proposed that one source of parametric variation across languages is the manner in which Nominative Case is assigned. In English-type languages, INFL assigns Case only to the Specifier of IP; in Spanish-Italian-type languages, INFL assigns Case to a DP to its right, in its VP-internal position, as shown in (24). Here, INFL assigns Case to DP in the Specifier of VP. On this analysis, the Specifier of IP is not an "A-position." Following on Koopman and Sportiche's work, other authors have noted that the Specifier of IP is then available as a landing site for "A-bar" movements. Goodall (1991) proposed that IP can be the landing site for Wh-constituents, a matter to which we return in Chapter 6 (Section 6.2).

(24)   Nominative Case assignment in Spanish/Italian

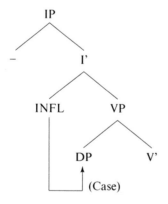

It has also been proposed that IP can function as a "Topic Phrase" – that is, that the Specifier of IP can be the landing site for Topic constituents.[9] The idea of IP as a Topic Phrase is that movement of a constituent to the Specifier of IP may be triggered by a [TOPIC] feature in INFL, rather than

[9] For different versions of this approach, see Mallén (1992), Zubizarreta (1998).

by the N-features discussed in 5.2.2. This implies that either the subject or another constituent *must* move to the Specifier of IP, if this feature is "strong." Ignoring N-features for the moment, other features of INFL would be as shown in (25):

(25) $[_{IP}$ XP $[_{INFL}$ [+TOPIC] V-features] $[_{VP}$ DP V . . .]]
         [+TOPIC]

If the subject constituent is the Topic, then the subject will of course be pre-verbal, as shown in (26):

(26)   Topic is the subject:
         $[_{IP}$ María$_i$ $[_{INFL}$ [+TOPIC] compró$_j$] $[_{VP}$ t$_i$ t$_j$ el coche]]
         [+TOPIC]

Where a constituent other than the subject is the Topic, the subject remains in its base position:

(27)   Topic is an adverb/PP:
         $[_{IP}$ Ayer $[_{INFL}$ [+TOPIC] compró$_j$] $[_{VP}$ María t$_j$ el coche]]
         [+TOPIC]

In (27), movement of the adverb to the Specifier of IP satisfies checking of the Topic feature of INFL; the subject need not move, and therefore is not expected to move. These two derivations then account for S-V-O order in declaratives and also for the XP-V-S-O pattern that was illustrated in (23) above.

It is possible in principle to extend the approach outlined above to generate clauses in which the subject is a VP-final constituent. In such clauses, if the predicate is presupposed, it is a potential candidate for Topic constituent, as in (28b), derived as in (29):

(28)   a. ¿Quién compró el   coche?
            who   bought the car?
         b. Compró el coche $[_{Focus}$ María].

(29)   Topic is predicate (Agr-o/Aspect Phrase):
         $[_{IP}$ [compró el coche] $_i$ $[_{INFL}$ [+TOPIC] V-features] $[_{VP}$ María t$_i$]]
         [+TOPIC]

The order in (29) is derived by movement of the [+TOPIC] predicate – either the VP itself or its functional projection, Aspect Phrase (Chapter 4, Section 4.3). A possible objection to this approach is that it does not allow V-to-INFL movement. This is problematic since, as discussed above in 5.2, the verbal features of INFL are "strong." If the verb did not move, presumably this would violate the requirement that the strong verbal feature be checked at the point in the derivation that corresponds to S-structure. This does not seem to be unsolvable, however, since the verbal features of INFL could perhaps be checked, since the verb is the head of VP, and VP is the Specifier of IP. The Specifier–head relation is a typical configuration in which feature checking (like feature assignment under government) is possible. In Chapter 6, we will mention another means of generating V-O-S orders, via movement referred to as "Scrambling."[10]

Finally, let us return to the issue of checking of the N-features of INFL. Suppose a Topic constituent other than the subject occupies the Specifier of IP, as in (27) or (29). This position cannot then also be filled by the subject. The question then is how are the N-features of INFL checked? One possibility is that the N-features of the subject undergo head movement (to INFL), rather than phrasal movement (to the Specifier of IP). That is, on the assumption that N-features are weak, they might be supposed to adjoin to INFL – to the head of IP – rather than moving as a phrase to the Specifier of IP. A second possibility, which is compatible with the assumption that N-features are strong, is that some property of the subject agreement features of the verb allow it to check both V-features and N-features of INFL. A third alternative is that the [TOPIC] feature which triggers preposing is not a feature of IP, but of a higher functional category, as shown in (30):

(30)   [XP F° [$_{IP}$ Subject [INFL VP]]]
         [TOPIC]

On this hypothesis, the N-features of the subject can be checked in the standard way in the Specifier of IP.

Summarizing, on the hypothesis that [TOPIC] is grammaticalized as a functional feature, it is expected that a broader range of constituents can move to the Specifier of IP than is possible in languages which lack this feature. This expectation is borne out, as shown by the grammaticality of XP-V-S-O order. The variety of constituents that can be Topics accounts in principle for the variety of positions in which the subject surfaces.

---

[10] Zubizarreta (1998) argues that leftward movement of [V–O] as a constituent is possible in Italian, but not in Spanish. She proposes that V–O–S order is derivable via leftward adjunction (or "scrambling") of the object, once V has moved to INFL:

(i)   a. [$_{IP}$ INFL [$_{VP}$ Subj [V Obj]]]
         b. [$_{IP}$ V+INFL [$_{VP}$ Subj [t$_v$ Obj]]]
         c. [$_{IP}$ V+INFL [$_{VP}$ Obj$_i$ [$_{VP}$ Subj t$_v$ t$_i$]]]

The steps in the derivation shown in (i) are: V-to-INFL, in (ib); and adjunction of the Object in (ic). Ordoñez (1997) proposes this movement (see Chapter 6, Section 6.4), but argues also for leftward movement of [V–O] as a constituent under certain conditions.

5.4.2   The [Topic] feature

We saw above that the hypothesis that [TOPIC] is a functional feature accounts for general patterns of constituent order in declaratives which contain Topics. Here, we mention questions that arise under an analysis of [TOPIC] as a functional feature of the clause. One issue concerns whether [TOPIC] behaves in a way that is expected for functional features. On the assumptions that have been outlined here, it would be expected that every IP which bears a [TOPIC] feature should show obligatory preposing of exactly one Topic constituent. The movement of one such phrase should be obligatory, since, if there were none, the [TOPIC] feature would remain unchecked. The movement should occur only once, since after checking of the [TOPIC] feature of INFL took place, any further movement of Topic constituents should be unnecessary, and therefore impossible.

Topics diverge from this expectation in that clauses may have more than one Topic, as illustrated in the embedded clauses in (31):

(31)   a. Me   dijeron que Caterina, en verano, no se   pone   esos
           zapatos.
           CL(IO) said   that C.,   in summer,   she won't put on those
           shoes.
           "They told me that Caterina, in the summer, she won't put those shoes
           on."
        b. José prometió que en agosto,   para   descansar, iremos   a la
           playa.
           J.   promised that in August, (in order) to rest,   we'll go to the
           beach.

Sequences of Topics are not expected to be possible, since once the feature is checked by movement of one constituent, no further movement should be possible. There is another construction with which [TOPIC] constituents can be compared, which are restricted to one movement per clause. This is movement of Contrastive Focus ("CF" or "Focus") constituents. In the following examples, the CF constituents are shown in capitals:

(32)   a. En VERANO no se pone esos zapatos.
           "(It is) in summer that (she) won't put those shoes on."
        b. Esos ZAPATOS no se pone en verano.
           those shoes (she) won't put on in the summer
           "It is those shoes that she won't put on in summer."
        c. *Esos ZAPATOS en VERANO no se pone.
           "It is those shoes in summer that she won't put on."

Examples (32a) and (32b) are derived by preposing, triggered by a [FOCUS] feature; in (32c), we see that preposing of more than one such constituent produces ungrammaticality. This is likewise true of interrogatives, as will be discussed in Chapter 6, and in general of constructions in which there is movement of a constituent to a non-argument position (Chapter 2, Sections 2.2–2.3). Insofar as Topic-preposing differs from this pattern, it diverges from expectations.

The Contrastive Focus construction illustrated in (32) displays order and intonation which differ from ordinary declaratives. Since declaratives with Topic constituents do not have the same characteristics, it is likely that Topic preposing is not derived by the same type of process. This conclusion is reinforced by an additional characteristic of Topic preposing that diverges from other constructions involving movement to a non-argument (or "A-bar") position. Topics allow (or require) a clitic double, while other such movements disallow it. Again, the contrast is illustrated relative to [FOCUS] constituents:

(33)   a. Esos ZAPATOS no se (*los) pone en verano.
        "It is those shoes (she) won't put (*them) on in the summer."
        b. Esos zapatos, no se *(los) pone en verano.
        "Those shoes, (she) won't put *(them) on in the summer."

The movement of Focus constituents illustrates properties that are typical of movement to A-bar positions. Although movement to these positions is not discussed until Chapter 6, it is useful to note here that Topics do not share these properties, and are therefore likely to be derived by other mechanisms. Notice also that, if Topic movement were parallel to other cases of movement triggered by a functional feature, we would expect the constituent order: XP–VP, where the constituent preceding the verb has a definable discourse role. Assuming that the verb moves to INFL, the verb should then mark a partition between Topic/non-Topic, etc.[11] This leaves two generalizations unexplained. One is that sentences can have the verb as the initial constituent, which suggests that a Topic is not obligatory. Also, when a phrase moves to pre-verbal position, we cannot predict its discourse function. A pre-verbal subject may be a Topic, but it need not be. Thus, the hypothesis of [TOPIC] feature checking does not account satisfactorily for the order and interpretation of subjects.

Summarizing, we have seen that the analysis of [TOPIC] as a functional category of the clause captures certain properties of declarative word order. However, this type of approach seems to predict that Topic constituents are

---

[11] This pattern may in fact be more general than it appears. Insofar as there may be other processes which affect constituent order, these may obscure the generalization in question. One such process that is motivated in Zubizarreta (1998) is p-movement: a local reordering which allows Nuclear Stress to align with Focus material. See Section 5.3.1.

unique, and that they should behave in a way similar to Focus constituents. In Section 5.5 below we will discuss an analysis of pre-verbal constituents that does not rely on movement or feature checking. We return then to the question of whether that analysis obviates the need for movement of the type discussed above.

5.4.3   Topics and neg constituents

We turn now to one final issue with respect to the movement analysis of Topic constituents: their order relative to negative constituents. As the data in (34) show, a pre-verbal subject must precede negative *no* "not" and *n*-words like *nunca* "never":

(34)   a. *No Juan cantó eso.
              not J.   sang   that.
              "Juan didn't sing that."
         b. Juan no cantó eso.
         c. *Nunca Juan cantó eso.
              never J.   sang   that
              "Juan never sang that."
         d. Juan nunca cantó eso.

Recall from Chapter 4 that a Neg Phrase has been proposed for Spanish which is structurally higher than IP. If the Neg Phrase analysis is correct, then it appears that Topic constituents must move to the Specifier of a Phrase higher than IP, as in (35); otherwise, they should follow NegP, as in (36).

(35) $[_{FP}$ Topic F^o $[_{NegP}$ Neg^o $[_{IP}$ Verb . . .]]]
(36) $[_{NegP}$ Neg^o $[_{IP}$ Topic Verb . . .]]

5.4.4   Summary

To summarize, one approach to the derivation of pre-verbal phrases, including subjects, is to assume that a feature other than N-features of the subject attracts a constituent to the Specifier of IP. It has been suggested in various studies that information structure is relevant for constituent order. In this section we have considered the hypothesis that a feature of this type, a [TOPIC] feature, is a functional feature of clauses, and, as such, can trigger movement of a subject or other constituent to the Specifier of IP. This hypothesis provides a natural account for the occurrence of constituents other than the subject in pre-verbal position, as well as for the "flexibility" of subject order relative to the verb and objects. This approach is not without certain problems, however. In particular, a theory-internal question arises as to whether [TOPIC] is appropriately analyzed as a functional feature, given that Topic constituents are not unique. The question also arises as to the source of differences between the movement that attracts Topics and other A-bar movements. Finally, it was noted that, if there are functional projections above IP in clause structure, then Topics must move to those upper projections, given the relative order of Topics and other pre-verbal constituents such as Negation. In 5.5.3 below, we discuss an alternative proposal for deriving pre-verbal subjects (and other constituents) which resolves some of these issues.

5.5   Dislocated topics

It was noted in Section 5.3 above that Topic constituents may be "dislocated," in which case they appear in clause-peripheral positions, as in (20), repeated below.

(20)   (Hablando de) José, lo eligieron presidente.
        "(Speaking of) José, (they) elected him president."

Such constituents are intonationally marked by a juncture and, optionally, by a pause. Cinque (1990) has argued that there are two sub-classes of dislocated Topics, with distinct syntactic properties. In 5.5.1 below, the properties of these two sub-classes will be discussed, and, in 5.5.2, we discuss their derivation, which has been argued to be by base-generation in dislocated position, rather than by movement from the clause-internal position in which the Topic is interpreted. In 5.5.3, we consider the hypothesis that this base-generated adjunct analysis of Topics may subsume non-dislocated Topics. That is, on this view, pre-verbal subjects and other pre-verbal Topic constituents have been proposed to be syntactically dislocated constituents in general, whether or not they are intonationally marked as dislocated.

5.5.1   Two types of dislocated topics

Dislocated Topics in Spanish, like Italian (Cinque 1990), are of two types: "Left Dislocations (LD)," and "Clitic Left Dislocations (CLLD)." Their properties are summarized in (37) and (38) respectively:

(37)   Left Dislocations (LD):
        a. the dislocated constituent must be an NP (DP)
        b. the coreferential element may be an overt phrase, pronoun or epithet
        c. appear in root clauses only
        d. dislocated constituent may be preceded by "topicalizing expressions"

e. dislocated constituent need not display grammatical and selectional "connectivity" with the coreferential element

f. dislocation is non-recursive

g. insensitive to syntactic islands

(38)   Clitic Left Dislocations (CLLD):

a. the dislocated constituent is not restricted to NP (DP)

b. the coreferential element cannot be an overt category

c. may appear in both root and embedded clauses

d. the dislocated constituent cannot be preceded by "topicalizing expressions"

e. dislocated constituent must display grammatical and selectional "connectivity" with the coreferential element

f. dislocation is recursive

g. sensitive to strong islands only

These properties are illustrated below; unless otherwise noted, examples are from Olarrea (1996).

The LD and CLLD constructions differ with respect to the category of the dislocated constituent. In the LD construction in (39) and (40), only a DP is grammatical, while in CLLD in (41), other phrases are possible:

(39)   a. Juan, no me acuerdo   de él.   (LD)
        J.,   not CL remember of him
        "Juan, I don't remember him."

        b. *De Juan, no me acuerdo   de él.
           of J.,   not CL remember of him
           "Of Juan, I don't remember him."

(40)   a. Juan, lo   vimos a él   en la fiesta.   (LD)
        J.   CL(DO) saw   PA him at the party
        "Juan, we saw him at the party."

        b. *A Juan, lo vimos a él en la fiesta. (=40a)

(41)   a. De Juan, no me acuerdo.   (CLLD: cf. (39b))
           of J.,   not CL remember
           "Of Juan, I don't remember."

        b. A   Juan, lo   vimos en la fiesta. (=41a)   (CLLD: cf. (40b))
           PA Juan, CL(DO) saw   at the party
           "Juan, we saw him at the party."

In (39) and (40), a DP is dislocated. These become ungrammatical if the dislocated DP is preceded by preposition or Personal a. In (41), however, the dislocated constituent can be PP or a DP preceded by Personal a. These differences correlate with a second property: in (39) and (40), the dislocated phrase is associated with an overt coreferential phrase, while in (41), the coreferential phrase is not overt. The only potentially overt constituent is a clitic – and this is possible only if the dislocated constituent allows for a clitic. In (41a), the dislocated constituent corresponds to a PP complement of the verb, for which there is no corresponding clitic in Spanish; in (41b), the dislocated constituent corresponds to the direct object of the verb, and the corresponding clitic is present – and required. As noted in (37b), the coreferential phrase may be an overt phrase of various types: non-pronominal, pronominal or an epithet:

(42)   a. El baloncesto, ese deporte le   encanta a tu   hijo.
                                                            (overt phrase)
             the basketball that sport   CL(IO) enchants PA your child
             "Basketball, that sport is loved by your son."
         b. Miles Davis, él sí   que me   fascina (tonic pronoun)
             M.   D.   he yes that CL(IO) fascinates
             "Miles Davis, he is indeed fascinating to me."
         c. (En cuanto a) Pedro, parece que el   desgraciado se lleva
             con
             as for   P.,   seems that the bastard   CL gets along
             with
             todo el mundo, inclusivo con el   enemigo. (Zubizarreta 1998)
             everyone   including with the enemy
             "As for Pedro, it seems that the bastard gets along with everyone,
             including with his enemy."

The CLLD coreferential phrase cannot be overt; it must be an empty category, although this category may require a clitic:

(43)   a. En Juan, no es posible confiar (*en él).
             In J.,   not is possible trust   in him
             "Juan, it is impossible to trust."
         b. A María, no la   ví   nunca (*a ese chica) tan enfadada.
             PA M.   not CL(DO) saw never PA that girl   so irritated
             "Maria, I have never seen (*that girl) so irritated."

The LD occurs in root clauses only, while the CLLD may be in root and embedded clauses:

(44)   a. Sin embargo,   Bernardo, estoy segura que nadie   confía
             en ese idiota.
             on the other hand B.   (I) am sure   that nobody had
             confidence
             in that idiot
             "On the other hand, I am sure that, as for Bernard, nobody had
             confidence in that idiot."
         b. *Sin embargo,   estoy segura que Bernardo, nadie   confía
                 en ese idiota. (=44a)
             on the other hand (I) am sure   that B.,   nobody had
             confidence in that idiot.

Only the LD construction can be preceded by "topicalizing expressions":

(45)   a. En cuanto a Antxon, él no va a terminar su tesis.
       "As for Antxon, he will not finish his thesis."
      b. *Te he   dicho que en   cuanto a   Antxon, lo   vi   ayer.
        (I) have told you that, as   for Antxon, CL(DO) saw yesterday
       "I told you that, as for Antxon, I saw him yesterday. "

In (45a), the LD in the root clause may be preceded by a topicalizing expression; in (45b), the embedded CLLD cannot appear with such an expression.

The examples in (46)–(48) illustrate the three final characteristics of LD: in (46), the "connectivity" between the dislocated phrase and its coreferential phrase; in (47), the non-recursion of LD; in (48), the insensitivity of LD to syntactic islands:

(46)   a. Nosotros, nadie   nos   ha visto.
       we(Nom.) nobody CL(DO) has seen
       "We, nobody has seen us."
      b. El ordenador, yo odio esas máquinas infernales.
       "The computer, I hate those infernal machines."

(47)   a. En cuanto al dictador y al pueblo, éste lo repudia a aquél .
                                           (Contreras 1978)
       "As for the dictator and the people, the latter hates the former"
      b. *Juan, el libro, él no lo ha comprado.
       "Juan, the book, he hasn't bought it."

(48)   a. Hablando de Freaks, un amigo que ha visto esa película me
       ha   dicho que es magnífica.
       speaking   of Freaks, a   friend that has seen that movie   CL(IO)
       has said   that is great
       "Speaking of Freaks, a friend that saw that movie said that it was great."
      b. (En cuanto a) el Sr. Gonzales, que María lo haya invitado sorprendió a
       todo el mundo. (Zubizarreta 1998:188)
       "As for Mr. Gonzales, that María invited him surprised everyone."

The "connectivity" referred to with respect to (46) concerns the absence of necessary agreement between the dislocated phrase and its coreferential position within the clause with respect to features such as category, Case, and number/gender agreement. In (46a), the dislocated phrase differs from its coreferential phrase with respect to Case; in (46b), the dislocated phrase is masculine singular, while its coreferential phrase is feminine plural. In (47), the non-recursiveness of LD is illustrated. In (47a), there are two LD constituents, but these are constituents of a single conjoined Topic; in (47b), where the two are not conjoined, the resulting sentence is ungrammatical. In (48), the examples illustrate that LD is not sensitive to islands: in both examples, the coreferential phrase is contained within a "strong" island – in (48a) a relative clause, in (48b) a sentential subject.

CLLD differs in each of these respects, as shown in (49)–(51):

(49)   a. *Nosotros, no nos   han dicho nada.
            we   not CL(DO) have said anything
            "We, they didn't say anything to us."
         b. *El ordenador, las   odio.
            the computer   CL(DO3rd.f.pl.) hate
            "The computer[masc.], I hate them[fem.]."

(50)   a. Ese libro   a Pedro no se   lo   dio nadie.
            that book, to P.,   not CL(IO) CL(DO) gave nobody
            "That book, to Pedro, nobody gave it to him."
         b. A María esa película no le   interesa.
            to M.,   that movie, not CL(IO) interests
            "To Maria, that movie, it doesn't interest her."

(51)   a. ??A María alguien   que le   dio un regalo no me
            saludó en la   fiesta.
            to M.   someone that CL(IO) gave a   gift   not CL(DO)
            greeted at the party
            "Maria, someone who gave her a gift didn't greet me at the party."
         b. A esos espías no sé   cómo se   puede saber quién los
            traicionó.
            PA those spies not know how one can   know who   CL(DO)
            betrayed
            "Those spies, I don't know how one can know who betrayed them."

In (49), the CLLD construction, unlike LD in (46) above, disallows "disagreement" between the dislocated phrase and the position to which it is related. In (50), we see that CLLD does allow multiple constituents, unlike the LD construction. And finally, examples like (51a) illustrate that CLLD is sensitive to *"strong" islands* – constituents out of which extraction is generally impossible; while (51b) shows that CLLD is not sensitive to a "weak" Wh-island.

Summarizing, we have seen above that Spanish displays the same two subcases of dislocated Topic constituents that Cinque identified in Italian: the LD (Left Dislocation) construction, and the CLLD (Clitic Left Dislocation) construction. The divergent properties of the two are summarized in (37)–(38) above.

5.5.2   Derivation of dislocated topics

Let us now consider how the dislocated constituents in the LD and CLLD constructions are generated. The dislocated Topic in the LD construction has been analyzed as base-generated in a Topic phrase (Rivero 1980; Hernanz and Brucart 1987):

(52) $[_{TopP}$ [(En cuanto a) Juan] TOP° [lo   vimos (a él) en la fiesta]]
                as for   J.   CL(DO) saw   PA him at the party
        "Juan, we saw him at the party."

On the assumption that there is no direct grammatical link between the Topic constituent and the following clause, several of the properties of LD follow: the fact that the coreferential element may be overt, the absence of grammatical and selectional "matching" between the Topic and the coferential phrase, and the insensitivity of the relation to syntactic islands.[12] The non-recursivity of the LD phrase would also follow if the Topic phrase enters into a checking relation with a [TOPIC] feature of the head. In other words, the LD Topic is in a Specifier position.

The CLLD Topic has been analyzed as a clausal adjunct. Let us illustrate first with a Topic corresponding to a direct object, as in (53a), with the derived structure in (53b):

(53)   a. Juan lo   vimos en la fiesta.
            J.   CL(DO) saw   at the party
            "Juan, we saw him at the party."
        b. $[_{IP}$ Juan$_i$ $[_{IP}$ – – $[_{INFL}$ lo vimos $[_{VP}$ pro$_j$ t$_v$ pro$_i$ en la fiesta]]]]

The Topic, *Juan*, is an IP adjunct. Within the clause, the coreferential phrase is an "ordinary" pronominal: that is, a covert pronoun, *pro*, which is licensed – identified – by the clitic.

Cinque (1990) has argued that the interpretive relationship between the adjunct and the covert pronoun is established via an A-bar *chain* – a set of positions which together provide a complete expression: *Juan$_i$, pro$_i$.* The chain is an A-bar chain if its highest position is in an A-bar position. Normally, chains are constructed when movement takes place. The coindexing between the moved constituent and its trace forms a chain. Here, Cinque is proposing that a chain can be formed even in the absence of movement. The chain accounts for the movement-like properties of CLLD. This includes the empty category as the foot of the chain, the sensitivity of the construction to strong islands, and the "connectivity." At the same time, these chains do not display the typical characteristics of A-bar chains that are derived by movement. One difference is the absence of a clitic-double for A-bar movement, illustrated by Wh-movement in (54):

---

[12] The occurrence of LD Topics in root clauses only may be related to their function as the discourse-topic as discussed in 5.3: that is, this Topic is the Topic of a sentence, not of a clause.

(54)   a. ¿Qué zapatos compró Susana?
        "What shoes did Susana buy?"
        b. ¿Qué zapatos *los   compró Susana?[13]
        what shoes   CL(DO) bought S.
        "What shoes did Susana buy them?"

The impossibility of the clitic in (54), compared with its obligatoriness in (53), suggests that the former does not involve movement of the direct object.[14]

A second difference between CLLD and typical cases of A-bar movement is that the latter is restricted to one preposed constituent per clause. CLLD, as noted above, is recursive:

(55)   a. *¿A quién qué libro le regalaste?
        "To whom what book did you give?"
        b. ¿A quién le regalaste qué libro?
        "To whom did you give what book?"

(56)   A Pedro, ese libro, se   lo   regalé.
        to P.,   that book, CL(IO) CL(DO) gave
        "To Pedro, that book, I gave it to him."

The preposing of only one constituent per clause is expected if the movement is necessary for checking of a functional feature. The recursion of CLLD Topics then suggests that these are not in Specifier positions, and not derived by movement, but are adjuncts.

A third property of dislocated Topics which differentiates them from typical cases of A-bar movement is that dislocated Topics do not trigger "subject–verb inversion." They are compatible with pre-verbal subjects:

(57)   Estos zapatos, Susana los compró.
        "Those shoes, Susana bought them."

(58)   a. *¿Qué zapatos Susana compró?
        "Which shoes Susana bought?"

---

[13] The contrast shown in the text does not extend to cases where the clitic is needed for independent reasons, such as if the interrogative constituent is a Dative which is obligatorily doubled, as in ¿A quién le avisaste? "Whom did you notify?"

[14] The contrast between (53) and (54) may be explained on the assumption that the empty category left by A-bar movement is a "variable," which, like referential expressions, requires Case. Assuming that clitics "absorb" Case, as discussed in Chapter 4 (Section 4.4), the empty category in (54b) would fail to be identifiable as variable, since it lacks Case. Then (53) is derivable only by means other than movement, since no variable could be licensed. The object position can be analyzed either as a trace of the moved clitic or as a covert pronoun.

b. *ESOS zapatos Susana compró.
"THOSE shoes Susana bought."

The impossibility of pre-verbal subjects in sentences like (58) appears to be a phenomenon similar to subject–verb inversion (movement of V+INFL to COMP). However, it has been argued that this account cannot be maintained in Spanish, a point to which we return in Chapter 6. However the contrast between (57) and (58) is accounted for, the informal generalization seems clear: CLLD dislocated Topics are compatible with a pre-verbal subject, while the A-bar movement illustrated in (58) is not.

Summarizing, neither LD nor CLLD exhibit properties of standard cases of A-bar movement. LD may be analyzed as generation of a Topic constituent in the specifier of a Topic Phrase. CLLD Topics have been argued to be clausal adjuncts, linked to a clause-internal covert pronominal via an A-bar chain. The Topic-pronoun chain is subject to conditions similar to those derived by movement, accounting for similarities between CLLD and movement. However, the empty category is a pronominal, and the Topic has not in fact been moved from a clause-internal position – thus accounting for differences between CLLD Topics and cases of A-bar movement.

5.5.3   Pre-verbal subjects as CLLD adjuncts

It has been argued that the CLLD analysis discussed above may be extended to account for pre-verbal subjects.[15] The claim underlying this proposal is that pre-verbal subjects display the properties of the CLLD construction, not of constituents which have undergone movement. On this analysis, the pre-verbal subject in (59a) would be derived as in (59b):

(59)   a. María compró el coche.
        "Maria bought the car."
        b. $[_{IP}$ María$_i$ $[_{IP}$ pro$_j$ $[_{INFL}$ compró$_j$ $]$ $[_{VP}$ t$_j$ t$_i$ el coche]]]

Here an overt DP, María, is adjoined to IP. IP does not contain a trace of the Topic, but rather a covert pronoun, pro, generated in the standard VP-internal subject position. This pronoun is the grammatical subject. It moves to the Specifier of IP where it checks N-features of INFL. The Topic must be licensed as having some relation to the clause. It is associated with the subject via an A-bar chain, and is then interpreted as the antecedent of pro.

The same type of analysis can be extended to a pre-verbal adverbial:

---

[15] For further discussion see Contreras (1991), Olarrea (1996) and references cited.

(60) Adverb/PP-Topic:
   a. Ayer   compró María ese coche.
   yesterday bought M.   that car
   $[_{IP}$ Ayer $[_{IP}$ pro$_j$ $[_{INFL}$ compró$_j$] $[_{VP}$ María t$_j$ ese coche] t$_j$]]]
   b. Ayer   María compró ese coche.
   yesterday M.   bought that car
   $[_{IP}$ Ayer $[_{IP}$ María pro$_j$ $[_{IP}$ $[_{INFL}$ compró$_j$] $[_{VP\ tj}$ ese coche] t$_j$]]]]

In (60a), the adverb is the only Topic; in (60b), both the adverb and the subject
are Topics. This approach claims that the Specifier of IP is a "dedicated" DP
position; however, weak N-features leave subjects in post-verbal position. The
only circumstance under which a subject DP that is interpreted as Topic will
be pre-verbal is via CLLD. Olarrea (1996) argues that the limited violations of
"connectivity" displayed by pre-verbal subjects support a CLLD analysis. In
particular, the possibility of Topic–verb "disagreement" with respect to
[PERSON] in (61) suggests that the Topic is not a Specifier of IP:

(61)   Los estudiantes tenemos   un alto concepto de nosotros mismos.
    the students   have-1st.pl. a high opinion of us-   selves
    "Students, (we) have a high opinion of ourselves."

In (61), person disagreement is permitted, but only where the plural may
include the 1st or 2nd person indicated by verbal inflection. That the verbal
inflection agrees with a *pro* subject is supported by the form of the anaphor,
which agrees with *pro*, not with the Topic.

Finally, let us compare the CLLD analysis with the movement analysis discussed in Section 5.4 above. The CLLD analysis overcomes the problems that
are inherent in the movement analysis. Because pre-verbal constituents are
generated as adjuncts, their pre-verbal position does not have to be explained
in relation to a functional feature. It is therefore to be expected that such constituents are optional, and need not be unique. Second, the non-movement
properties of Topic constituents are accounted for, since the Topic is associated with a null pronominal, rather than a trace. However, there is one generalization that is not naturally accounted for under the CLLD analysis (as
an exclusive account of how pre-verbal constituents are derived). That is, the
unmarked order of constituents in "neutral" contexts – contexts in which no
information is shared or presupposed – is S-V-O. In other words, in clauses
with no Topic, a pre-verbal subject appears before the verb, not after it. If the
CLLD analysis were extended to cover these declaratives, it would lose its
account of the fact that complements are pre-verbal only if they have a Topic
interpretation. These sentences would be accounted for under the movement
analysis discussed in 5.4. Assuming that the [TOPIC] feature is present

whether there is a Topic ([+TOPIC]) or not ([-TOPIC]), the derivation of neutral sentences might also call for movement of a [-TOPIC] constituent to satisfy the checking of the [TOPIC] feature. Because this movement would also accomplish checking of N-features of INFL, it is arguably more economical to move the subject constituent than to move a non-subject. The preference for an initial subject in neutral contexts might thereby be accounted for.

5.5.4   Summary

In this section, we have examined the properties and derivation of dislocated Topics in Spanish. In 5.5.1, we saw that there are two sub-classes of dislocated Topics: Left Dislocations (LD) and Clitic Left Dislocations (CLLD). In 5.5.2, the derivation of these two sub-classes was discussed. The LD construction was analyzed as generated in the Specifier of a Topic Phrase in root clauses. The CLLD construction was analyzed as being generated by adjunction to the clause. As the discussion showed, CLLD shares certain properties with cases of movement, although it is not derived by movement of the Topic. This is evident, given the cluster of differences between CLLD and standard cases of A-bar movement. Finally, 5.5.3 discussed an extension of the CLLD analysis, according to which pre-verbal subjects in Spanish can be generated as clausal adjuncts, interpreted via an A-bar chain in the same manner as other CLLD constituents. This analysis is consistent with the "reserving" of the Specifier of IP as a DP position, which comes to be occupied by a subject only at the end of a derivation, once covert movement has taken place, on the assumption that N-features are weak. Comparing this analysis with the movement analysis of pre-verbal subjects, we considered whether the CLLD approach obviates the need for a movement analysis of the type discussed in Section 5.4. One context in which movement may still be needed is sentences which have no Topic, but which have S-V-O as unmarked order.

5.6   Subject order and the NS parameter

The final topic that we will address in connection with declarative constituent order is the relationship between the freedom of position of the clausal subject and the grammaticality of null subjects. Early generative analyses hypothesized that these phenomena are related: free subject "inversion," or VP-final subjects, arise from the same property of grammar as do null subjects, and this generalization was formalized as the Null Subject Parameter (henceforth, "NS parameter"). This section will present a brief sketch of early formulations of the NS parameter framed within "Government and Binding" theory, then consider those generalizations under some more recent assumptions.

5.6.1   The NS parameter in government and binding

In early (rule-based) versions of transformational grammar (e.g., Chomsky 1965), it was assumed that phrase structure rules like (62a) generate subjects in clause-initial position at D-structure:

(62)   a. $S \rightarrow NP - (Aux) - VP$
        b. $VP \rightarrow V - NP$

By rule (62a), a subject NP precedes the predicate, which may be expanded as in (62b). These rules generate [S [V O]] order (and constituency) directly at D-structure. Within the principles and parameters framework, the D-structure position of the subject is determined by theta-theory. In the "Government and Binding" theory of Chomsky (1981), it is assumed that an external argument can be assigned a Theta-role in the Specifier of IP (which corresponds to the "S" node in (62)). Applying that theory to Spanish, the D-structure of (63a) would be as shown in (63b).

(63)   a. María compró un coche.
        "Maria bought a car."
        b.

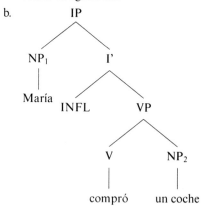

The subject NP is assigned a Theta-role by VP. Let us refer to this as the "VP-external subject hypothesis." The subject NP in (63b) is assigned Case by

INFL. Case is assigned by certain heads of phrase to an NP that is "governed" by the head. We need not define "government" here, but will rely on an informal description. A head of phrase such as INFL governs nodes that are within its maximal projection (IP), such as its specifier and its complement – although INFL governs "into" those phrases in a very restricted way. For example, INFL governs its complement, VP, in (63b), but does not govern the direct object, since the direct object has a more proximate governor: the verb.

The VP-internal subject hypothesis, discussed in Chapter 3 (Section 3.3), posits the Specifier of VP as the position in which an external argument of the verb is theta-marked. On that hypothesis, the D-structure of (63a) is as shown in (64).

(64)

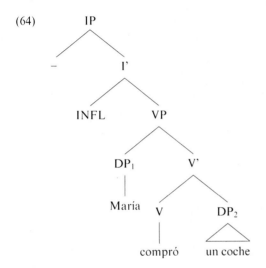

The D-structure in (64) must give rise to NP-movement, because DP_1 cannot be assigned Case in the Specifier of VP. The transitive verb *compró* does not assign Nominative Case; it assigns Objective (or Accusative) Case only to its complement. Consequently, DP_1 must move to a position where it is governed by a head which can assign Case to it. DP_1 moves to the Specifier of IP, where it is governed by INFL, and assigned Nominative Case. The S-structure for (64) is then (65). The derivations in (63) and (64)–(65) differ in their representation of the D-structure (theta) position of the subject. Both analyses derive an S-structure subject in the Specifier of IP. On both analyses, the Specifier of IP is the position in which Case is assigned by INFL, which governs the subject.

(65)

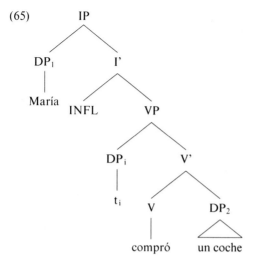

Turning now to NS languages, a correspondence has been noted between the grammaticality of null subject pronouns and the relative "richness" of agreement in languages like Spanish and Italian, compared with languages like French and English; the latter have relatively impoverished subject person and number agreement morphology in their verbal paradigms. The implementation of this observation varies in different studies but, as we will see, two generalizations are common to several approaches:

(66)   Properties of "rich" agreement
        a. Rich agreement allows the content of null pronouns to be identified;
        b. Rich agreement affects government of the subject – which affects Case.

Jaeggli (1982) and Rizzi (1982) proposed formulations of the NS parameter based on the assumption, standard at that time, that subjects are generated in the Specifier of IP. Rizzi argued that the richness of agreement in NS languages underlies a cluster of syntactic properties, including null subjects and free inversion of the subject. Rizzi attributed these properties to the clitic-like, pronominal character of the AGR features of INFL. Due to the clitic pronoun-like properties of INFL, he proposed that it could "absorb" Case. Stated informally the absorption of Case by AGR allows a null pronoun to appear in the Specifier of IP, as in (67). The phonetically empty pronoun in the Specifier of IP is a legitimate "empty category" because its content is identified by the rich agreement features of INFL. Also, the agreement relation between the NP and the clitic-like AGR, shown in (67) as co-indexing, links the covert pronoun to an overt lexical item.

(67)

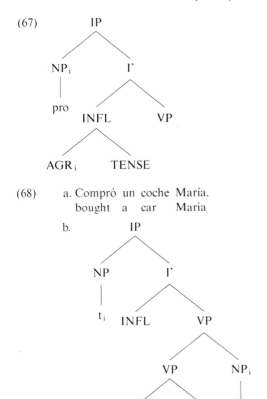

(68) a. Compró un coche María.
         bought a   car   Maria

Rizzi further argued that the structure in (67) is responsible for the occurrence of subject postposing in NS languages. To derive (68a), the subject is moved rightward, adjoining to VP, as shown in (68b). The derivation in (68b) is incomplete, however, and would produce an ill-formed derivation if no further processes apply. The NP trace in the Specifier of IP is not legitimate, because it is does not have an antecedent that is higher in the structure.[16] The

---

[16] The relation between an NP-trace and its antecedent is analogous to the relation between an overt reflexive or reciprocal phrase (an Anaphor) and its antecedent. Both traces and anaphors must be c-commanded by their antecedent. A node a c-commands node b if and only if the first branching node which dominates a also dominates b. In (69), the NP-trace in the Specifier of IP is not c-commanded by its "antecedent" – the VP-adjoined NP. The first branching node which dominates the moved NP is VP, and this node does not also dominate the trace.

second step in the process is the replacement of the trace by a covert pleonastic pronoun, as shown in (69). The structure in (69) is well formed, since pronouns, unlike traces, do not require an antecedent. The postposed NP is well formed with respect to Case theory, because it is linked indirectly to the clitic-like AGR, which bears Case.

(69)

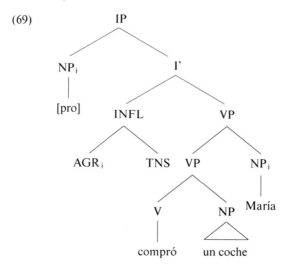

Notice that only languages which have clitic-like AGR can have null pronouns, and only these languages can therefore "rescue" a structure like (68) by insertion of a null pronoun. In English, a derivation like (68b) will always turn out to be ungrammatical because, since AGR is too "weak" to bear Case, a null pronoun could not be inserted to rescue the derivation. There are other constructions which are also accounted for on the basis of the grammaticality of (69) (cf. Chapter 1, Section 1.2.8). Once this structure is generated, further processes can apply to the post-verbal subject, such as Wh-movement. Rizzi argues that, in this position, the subject is governed by the verb, rather than INFL. Because of this, the postposed subject behaves like a complement with respect to its extraction patterns, not like a pre-verbal subject.[17]

---

[17] This can be illustrated by the contrast between English and Spanish with respect to overt complementizers in interrogatives. In English, extraction of an object, but not a subject, is compatible with an overt complementizer:

(i)   a. Who did you say that John saw?
       b. *Who(m) did you say that saw John?

In Spanish and Italian, both subject and object can be extracted over an overt complementizer:

Jaeggli (1982) argued that AGR in NS languages moves in the syntax via affix-hopping, and is attached to the verb at S-structure. The post-verbal subject such as (68a) above is governed by the verb+AGR:

(70) $[_{IP}$ PRO $[_{INFL} -]$ $[_{VP}$ $[_{V'}$ compró+AGR un coche] María]]

Summarizing to this point, the two analyses described above derive NS properties from the morphological and syntactic properties of the AGR node of INFL. In Rizzi's analysis, AGR is clitic-like, which allows it to bear Case, which in turn makes null pronouns possible, and in turn participates in licensing derivations with subject postposing. Postposed subjects are governed by the verb, and therefore behave differently from pre-verbal subjects in interrogatives and other related constructions. Jaeggli's analysis claims that post-verbal subjects are governed by V+AGR, once affix-hopping has applied.

There is one theory-internal problem with the analyses described above, which is resolved with the advent of the VP-internal subject hypothesis. The problem concerns the use of lowering rules: subject postposing and affix-hopping. Both of these rules move a constituent lower into the structure, and to the right – the opposite of other NP movements in these languages, such as object-to-subject movement in passives. The framework within which these analyses were formulated assumed that both rightward and leftward movements are freely available. Movement itself was assumed to be unconstrained; the derivation was excluded only if the resulting structure violated a general principle of grammar. More recent theories have proposed restrictions on movement which have the effect of restricting or eliminating postposing movements. As discussed in Section 5.5 above, recent research has suggested that movement of phrases is possible only to the Specifier of functional categories, and only when required to satisfy feature checking. General principles of economy have the effect of prohibiting movement that is not necessary. Rightward movement would then only be expected in languages

(ii)   a. ¿A   quién   dijiste   que   Juan   vio?
           PA whom   said   that   J.   saw
           "Who did you say that Juan saw?"
        b. ¿Quién dijiste que vio a   Juan?
           who   said   that saw PA J.
           "Who did you say that saw Juan?"

The contrast between (ib) and (iib) is argued by Rizzi to be due to the grammaticality of subject postposing. Once the subject is postposed, it is governed by the verb, and its extraction properties pattern with complements. For details of the relation between the overt COMP and extraction, see Rizzi (1982).

that have functional categories with rightward Specifier positions. Kayne (1994) argues that there are no rightward movements at all in UG. Given these more restrictive views of movement, and evolving views of the conditions under which movement is possible, the subject "lowering" analysis is less tenable.

The issue of "lowering" is resolved under the VP-internal subject hypothesis. Since the subject is generated within VP, it is not lowered when postposed. Consider first the derivation of a clause with a null subject such as (71a), which derives from the D-structure (71b). As in the previous analyses, the rich agreement features are the source of the grammaticality of (71b) with a null subject. As mentioned above, Koopman and Sportiche (1991) propose that one source of parametric variation across languages is the manner in which Nominative Case is assigned. In English-type languages, INFL assigns Case only to the Specifier of IP; this is associated with its "non-lexical" ("non-rich") properties. In Spanish-Italian-type languages, INFL assigns Case to a DP to its right, such as the covert pronoun in (71b), due to its (rich) "lexical" properties. The derivation of (71b) involves Nominative Case assignment to the null pronoun in its D-structure position.

(71)   a. Compró un coche.
        "(He/she) bought a car."

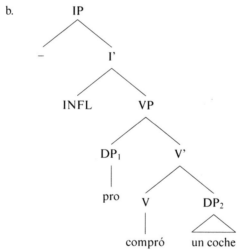

Subject postposing involves adjunction to the right, as in (72). The same "lexical" property of INFL which determines that it assigns Case to its right in (71) and (72) also determines its ability to license a phonologically null pronoun (71), and the trace of the postposed NP in (72). The complement-like behavior of postposed subjects is also captured.

(72)   a. Compró un coche María.

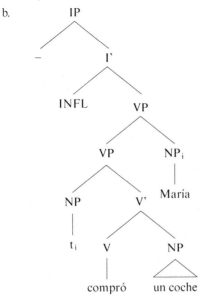

Summarizing, we have reviewed several approaches to the NS parameter under assumptions that were current within early forms of the principles and parameters framework, commonly referred to as the "Government and Binding" framework. Those analyses have two general features in common. First, post-verbal subjects are derived by an optional movement rule. This rule would move a subject from its D-structure position (either the Specifier of IP, under earlier assumptions, or the Specifier of VP, under later assumptions), adjoining it to the right of VP. Second, NS properties are attributed to the "lexical" properties of the AGR features of INFL. AGR licenses null pronouns (either due to the absorption of Case by AGR, or due to a parameter in how INFL assigns Case).

5.6.2   Richness of AGR and strength

We saw in 5.6.1 that early analyses of the NS parameter attributed the properties of NS languages to the "lexical" properties of AGR. As discussed in 5.5, under more recent assumptions about conditions under which movement occurs, it appears that the contrast between Spanish and English may be captured in terms of the strength of the N-features of AGR in INFL. In English, these features are strong, so pre-verbal subjects are obligatory; in Spanish, these features are weak, and pre-verbal subjects are not obligatory. Instead, subjects occur in a pre-INFL position as a consequence of their Topichood.

The question arises as to whether the strong/weak distinction discussed in 5.5, if correct, accounts for the possibility of null subjects.[18] We will not attempt to answer this question here, but will point out that there is a potential description of AGR in Spanish that is compatible with strong N-features of AGR. Belletti (1990), in discussing contrasts between French and Italian, suggests, following Roberts (1990), that differences between the two languages with respect to V-to-INFL movement may be accounted for in terms of the structure of the verb – in particular, the structure of its subject agreement morphology. She suggests that agreement can either be a sub-lexical (X^{-1}) morpheme in languages like French, or a zero-level morpheme in Italian. Under the more recent assumptions discussed above and in Chapter 4, according to which lexical items enter the syntax fully formed, the contrast would be as shown in (73).

(73)

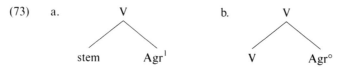

Let us suppose that (73a) represents the French/English structure of Agreement on the verb, and (73b) the Spanish/Italian structure. In sentences like (74),

(74)   a. Maria [$_{INFL}$ has [$_{VP}$ sung]].
        b. María [$_{INFL}$ ha [$_{VP}$ cantado]].
        "Maria has sung."

INFL is occupied by an inflected auxiliary in both languages, but the structure of that head differs, as shown in (73). Now suppose (contrary to what was assumed in 5.5) the N-features of INFL are strong in both English and Spanish (and Italian).

Since features can be checked either by a phrase in the Specifier of IP, or by head adjunction, the fronted verb can check features if it is structured as in (73b), since AGR is a head; but not if the verb is structured as in (73a). In this case, the sublexical AGR is syntactically inert, since it is sublexical. In general, sublexical material is "invisible" for syntactic processes. Therefore, in English,

[18] Since parameters are suggested to derive from features of functional categories, the presence or absence of a null pronoun in a language is not straightforwardly relatable to constituent order. It has been assumed standardly in generative research that empty categories (like *pro*) do not differ in fundamental ways from overt counterparts, a point which makes the systematicity of null subject pronouns perhaps difficult to relate to constituent order. For arguments that covert pronouns in fact have different interpretive properties from overt pronouns, see Montalbetti (1986).

the strong N-features of INFL can only be checked by DP movement to the Specifier of IP. In Spanish, the agreement features of the verb check N-features. IP therefore need not have a phrase in its Specifier position. A pre-verbal subject moves to the Specifier of Topic Phrase, according to the value of Topic features.

5.7   Summary

In this chapter, we have considered the derivation of the clausal subject in Spanish, with emphasis on accounting for the surface order of the subject. In 5.2, we saw that optional movement is not considered to be possible in more recent versions of the principles and parameters framework. Since movement is motivated to check features of functional heads, and economy considerations preclude unnecessary movement, it is expected that movement of the subject constituent to the Specifier of IP for checking of N-features of INFL should either be obligatory or impossible, but not optional. The question arises as to whether there are other functional features that may come into play in determining the position of the subject. In Section 5.3, one candidate for such a feature was introduced, based on the notions of Topic and Focus. In 5.4, we considered the hypothesis that a Topic feature can attract a subject or other constituent to the Specifier of IP. This hypothesis provides a natural account for the occurrence of constituents other than the subject in pre-verbal position, as well as for the "flexibility" of subject order relative to the verb and objects. However, this hypothesis incorrectly predicts that every clause will have exactly one Topic – a prediction that is not borne out. In Section 5.5, we considered an alternative analysis of pre-verbal subjects, according to which they may be generated as clausal adjuncts. On this analysis, pre-verbal subjects would be subsumed under Clitic Left Dislocation structures, which share certain properties with A-bar chains, although movement is not involved. This analysis does not require the postulation of a functional feature related to Topic status of adjuncts, simplifying the system of functional features. The movement analysis may still be needed, however, to account for the occurrence of pre-verbal subjects in neutral contexts – where there is no Topic in the sentence.

In 5.6, we considered the properties of verbal agreement, and the relationship between subject position and the NS parameter. Early analyses of the NS parameter attributed a cluster of properties, including null subject pronouns and the inversion of subjects, to lexical properties of subject agreement. We then considered this generalization in terms of more recent assumptions as to the nature of syntactic parameters as deriving from variations in feature strength. Although the derivation of subjects in Spanish is compatible with an analysis of AGR (N-features) as weak, we suggested that there is an alternative available, which can treat these features as strong, and checked by a verb in INFL.

6

A'-movement and X⁰ movement through COMP

6.1 Introduction

In this chapter, we will examine several constructions whose derivations are standardly assumed to involve movement to CP, the highest projection of clausal structure. As the discussion will show, the claim that operator-like phrases such as interrogatives move overtly to CP in Spanish has been debated in recent literature. In 6.2, we discuss Wh-movement, beginning with a summary of core properties, and then turning to issues of structure – particularly landing sites – as discussed in recent work. Section 6.3 discusses Contrastive Focus Phrases, which have been argued to be derived by A'-movement also. We again review properties of the construction and then the derivation, with emphasis on the landing site. Section 6.4 briefly summarizes several other phenomena that have been analyzed as involving A'-movements, although these constructions lack an overt operator-like element, or in some cases any overt movement. This section begins with "Scrambling" as discussed in Ordóñez (1997), then introduces three constructions that have been argued to be derived via movement of a null operator: parasitic gaps, complex adjectivals, and null indefinite objects. Section 6.5 discusses X⁰ movement to (and through) the head of CP.

6.2 Wh-movement

Traditionally, the "rule" of Wh-movement is assumed to subsume the movement of interrogative phrases in direct and indirect questions, as well as the movement of relative pronouns in relative clauses. Here, the properties of Wh-movement will be illustrated for interrogatives only. For discussion of relative clauses, see Plann (1980), Suñer (1984), Rivero (1990) and Brucart (1994). In this section, we will describe several characteristics of Wh-questions. In 6.2.1, two basic properties of Wh-questions are introduced: the obligatory movement of a Wh-phrase, and the obligatory "inversion" of a verb. We will see how, under certain assumptions, these properties follow from the Wh-Criterion of Rizzi (1996). Two assumptions that underlie this analysis are first, that "inversion" involves head movement to COMP, and, second, that Wh-movement involves movement of a Wh-phrase to the Specifier of CP. In Sections 6.2.2 and 6.2.3, we will see why these assumptions have been questioned in recent research. Addressing "inversion" first, 6.2.2 shows, following Suñer (1994), that the verb is lower in the clause, and that an additional form of licensing must be assumed in order to account for inversion effects. In 6.2.3, we consider evidence that calls into question the assumption that Wh-phrases occupy the Specifier of CP. The position of Wh-phrases has been the subject of numerous studies, and our discussion will outline the solutions to the "landing site" problem. As several authors have argued, another construction (Focus Movement) may provide evidence that bears on the choice among these alternatives. We then turn to this matter in 6.3.

6.2.1   Wh-movement and the Wh-criterion

Two central properties of Wh-movement are, first, that a single Wh-constituent appears in clause-initial position, and, second, that the position of the verb is restricted in certain ways. The clause-initial position of Wh-phrases is illustrated in (2):

(1)   Juan leyó ese libro.
        J.   read that book

(2)   a. ¿Qué libro leyó Juan?   (Direct Question)
           which book read J.
           "Which book did Juan read?"
        b. María no sabe [qué   libro leyó Juan]. (Indirect Question)
           M.   not know which book read J.
           "Maria doesn't know which book Juan read."

In the direct question (2a) and the indirect question (2b), the Wh-phrase *qué libro* "which book" appears in a clause-initial position, not in canonical object position following the verb, as in (1). Movement is necessary for the sentence to have an ordinary interrogative reading. This is illustrated by the contrast between (2a), where the Wh-phrase has moved, and "echo-questions" like (3b):

(3)   a. Speaker A:
           María leyó el diario.
           "Maria read the paper."

b. Speaker B:
    (*)¿María leyó qué?
    M.   read what
    "Maria read what?"

The sequence in (3b) is only possible in a context like (3a), where it "echoes" the previous sentence. It could not be used in a neutral context to ask a question about what María read.

Restrictions on the position of the verb are similar (though not identical) to the effects of Subject–Auxiliary Inversion in English. Examples like (4) and (5) (from Torrego 1984) show that a subject constituent cannot generally appear between the Wh-phrase and the verb:

(4)   a. ¿Qué querían esos dos? (Torrego 1984:103)
       "What did those two want?"
    b. *¿Qué esos dos querían?

(5)   a. ¿Con quién vendrá   Juan hoy?
       with whom will come J.   today
       "With whom will Juan come today?"
    b. *¿Con quién Juan vendrá hoy?

The "inversion" of the verb relative to the subject has sometimes been analyzed as movement to a position outside IP, typically to $C°$. We will see below that extending this analysis to Spanish is problematic in several respects. Before we look at further data, however, let us consider how the obligatory movement of the Wh-phrase and V-fronting have been accounted for.

Rizzi (1996) argues that the order of Wh-phrases and verbs in questions follows from the Wh-Criterion:

(6)   The Wh-Criterion
    a. A Wh-operator must be in a Spec–head configuration with $X°_{[+Wh]}$.
    b. An $X°_{[+Wh]}$ must be in a Spec–head configuration with a Wh-operator.
                                    (Rizzi 1996:64)

It is standardly assumed that a [+WH] feature (or Q feature) appears on a clause, designating it as having a question interpretation. The Wh-Criterion ensures that when this feature is present in a clause, a Wh-operator (a Wh-phrase) will occur in the Specifier of the [+WH] head, licensing both the operator and the [+WH] head. Rizzi discusses the possibility of variation in where the [+WH] feature occurs in the clause, a point to which we return below. For the moment, let us assume that the relevant head is COMP. Rizzi notes that the structure required to satisfy the Wh-Criterion is (7). In languages with overt Wh-movement, the Wh-criterion applies at S-structure, accounting for the appearance of a Wh-phrase in a clause-initial position. (In more recent terms, the [+w H] feature of C^o would be analyzed as strong. See Chapter 5, Section 5.2.) The conditions of the Wh-Criterion are met if a [+w H] phrase is in Spec of CP, and a [+w H] head is in C^o.

(7)

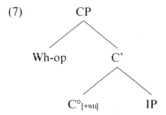

The position of the verb in interrogatives may also follow from the Wh-Criterion. To satisfy the Wh-Criterion, C^o must have a [+w H] feature. Rizzi proposes that in main clauses (non-lexically selected clauses), the [+w H] feature originates in INFL, and moves to COMP via INFL-to-C movement. The English asymmetry between embedded clauses and main clauses with respect to inversion is suggested to follow from differences in where the [+w H] feature is generated. In a complement clause, [+w H] is a feature of the embedded C^o. Movement of INFL-to-C is thus unnecessary.

Summarizing to this point, the obligatory movement of a Wh-phrase to CP is necessary to satisfy the WH-criterion. The phenomenon of inversion in root (or main) clauses is also accounted for, on the assumption that [+w H] is generated on INFL in main clauses, and on C^o in complement clauses. Rizzi notes, however, that Italian and Spanish do not exhibit this same asymmetry between main and embedded clauses:[1]

(8)   a. No sabía qué   querían esos   dos.
            not knew what wanted those two
            "I didn't know what those two wanted."
         b *No sabía qué esos dos querían.
            "I didn't know what those two wanted."

He suggests that inversion in embedded clauses like (8) may follow from cross-linguistic differences in where [+w H] is generated. In a language such as English, presumably [+w H] is generated on C^o, so the Wh-Criterion can be satisfied in embedded clauses without movement of INFL-to-C. In Italian however (and Spanish), the impossibility of pre-verbal subjects in questions suggests that the [+w H] feature may be generated on INFL, rather than C^o. Then movement of INFL-to-C^o would be necessary to satisfy the s-selection requirements of the matrix verb.

---

[1] Rizzi attributes the same pattern of inversion in embedded clauses to Romanian and Catalan as well as Spanish and Italian.

Summarizing, the Wh-Criterion accounts for the obligatoriness of Wh-movement: a Wh-phrase must move to the Specifier of a category whose head is specified as [+WH]. The Wh-Criterion may also explain verb inversion. Where the [+WH] feature is generated in INFL, INFL must move to C° to satisfy the Wh-Criterion as well.

6.2.2   Argumental agreement licensing

The preceding discussion presupposes that the landing site for Wh-movement and inversion is CP. This assumption has been questioned, however, both for Wh-phrases and for verb inversion. Here we consider the derived position of the verb. Suñer (1994) argues that the verb is not in C°, but is lower in the clause, in INFL. Evidence supporting this analysis is found in the order of pre-verbal adverbs relative to the verb:

(9)   a. ¿A   quién   jamás   ofenderías   tú   con tus   acciones?
                                                                    (Suñer 1994:345)
      PA whom   never   offend-cond.   you   with your actions
      "Who(m) would you never offend with your actions?"

      b. ¿Qué   idioma   todavía   estudia   Pepita   en su   tiempo libre?
         which language   still   studies   P.   in her time   free
         "Which language does Pepita still study in her free time?"

In these examples, an adverb can intervene between the Wh-phrase in the Specifier of CP and the verb. It is generally assumed that adverbs adjoin to XPs (phrases), not to an X′ such as the C′ in (9). (Corresponding sentences in English are ungrammatical: *Which language still does Pepita study?) The adverbs must therefore be adjoined to IP, and the verb must not be in C°.

A second argument against movement of V to C° derives from the fact that certain Wh-phrases are compatible with a pre-verbal subject. This is illustrated in examples like (10) from Torrego (1984:106):

(10)   a. ¿En qué medida la constitución ha contribuido a eso?
          "In what way has the constitution contributed to that?"
       b. ¿Por qué Juan quiere salir antes que los demás?
          "Why does Juan want to leave before the others?"

If the pre-verbal subject occupies the Specifier of IP (or is an IP adjunct, as discussed in Chapter 5 (Section 5.5)) it must be that the verb has not moved higher than INFL. If the verb can remain in INFL in interrogatives like (10) without violating the Wh-criterion, then presumably this is also possible in other interrogatives.

Suñer (1994) has proposed a licensing relation between the verb and its arguments to account for cases like (10). She shows that the generalization underlying the contrast between cases like (10), which allow a pre-verbal subject, and cases like (4), (5) and (8), which do not, concerns the status of the interrogative phrase as an argument of the verb. Non-argument interrogative phrases are compatible with pre-verbal subjects.[2] The following generalization then must be accounted for:

(11)   a. *Argument Wh-phrase – subject – Verb . . .
        b. Non-argument Wh-phrase – subject – Verb . . .

Suñer proposes that this dichotomy follows from an additional form of licensing that links the verb and its arguments:

(12)   Argumental Agreement Licensing
        a. Argumental Wh-phrases must be licensed through symmetric Arg-agreement between α (=SpecC) and β (=C).
        b. β Arg-agrees with γ (=V) only if β and γ are Arg-marked and no other Arg-marked element is closer to γ.

Because the Verb is in INFL in Spanish, (12a) can be satisfied only if C° agrees in features with INFL.

(13) $[_{CP}$ Wh $[$ C° $[_{IP}$ [V+INFL] ...]]]

In (13), the Wh-phrase must agree with C° to satisfy (12a). However, since C° lacks features, agreement is satisfied indirectly via (12b). The Wh-phrase agrees with V. If another argument of the verb occupies the Specifier of IP, then (12b) is not satisfied:

(14) $[_{CP}$ Wh $[$ C° $[_{IP}$ **DP** [V+INFL] ...]]]

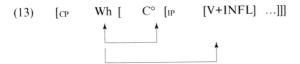

In (14), a DP subject occupies the Specifier of IP. This phrase is an argument that is closer to V than the Wh-phrase. Therefore, the agreement relation between the Wh-phrase and V is blocked, and the Wh-phrase is not licensed as an argument. If the Wh-phrase were a non-argument, (12) would not be relevant, and a pre-verbal subject would be grammatical, as in (10).

Summarizing, Suñer's analysis accounts for the contrast between argument and non-argument Wh-phrases with respect to the possibility of pre-verbal subjects. Argumental Agreement Licensing claims that pre-verbal subjects are

---

2 Some authors, such as Goodall (1991), have challenged this descriptive generalization, by showing that adjuncts like *cuándo* "when," and *dónde* "where," are incompatible with pre-verbal subjects.

ungrammatical in certain questions because they block a relation between the Specifier of CP and INFL. Thus, although the verb is lower in the structure, "inversion" effects similar to INFL-to-C movement are observed. An INFL-to-C analysis cannot be correct, however, given the distribution of pre-verbal adverbs in Wh-questions, and the limited availability of pre-verbal subjects.

6.2.3 Embedded questions and the landing site for Wh-movement

In embedded questions, a Wh-phrase may appear to the right of an overt complementizer (Rivero 1978, 1980; Plann 1982) :

(15) a. Te preguntan que para qué quieres   el préstamo.
      you ask(3rd.pl.) that for what want(2nd.sg.) the loan
      "They ask you what do you want the loan for."
   b. Murmuró   que con quién podía   ir.
      murmured(3rd.sg.) that with whom could(3rd.sg.) go
      "He asked, by murmuring, who could he go with."

This possibility is restricted to indirect questions under verbs of saying. Plann (1982) notes that the presence of the overt complementizer under these verbs correlates with an interpretation of the sentence as a reported question. If no complementizer is overt, the sentence is generally interpreted as a reported assertion.

In view of cases like (15), the position of clause-initial Wh-phrases has been suggested to be lower than the Specifier of CP. There have been several proposals as to what the derived position for Wh-phrases is. One approach has been to examine whether the structure of CP is more elaborate or articulated than is typically assumed. Rivero (1978) argued, for example – on independent – grounds, that CP must be recursive. The Wh-phrase could then be assumed to occupy a lower Specifier of CP:[3]

(16)   . . . [$_{CP}$ [$_{C}$° que [$_{CP}$ para quién C . . .]]]
                that   for   whom

A second alternative, proposed in Goodall (1991), is that the Specifier of IP may be a landing site for Wh-movement:

(17)   . . . [$_{CP}$ [$_{C}$° que [$_{IP}$ para quién V+INFL . . .]]]
                that   for   whom

The proposed structure (17) is consistent with the evidence discussed above concerning the derived position of the verb, as Goodall also argues.

---

[3] The notion that CP (then S-bar) may be recursive is introduced in Chomsky (1977). For elaboration of this hypothesis see Rizzi and Roberts (1989) and Suñer (1991).

Furthermore, assuming that subjects are generated VP-internally, the typical inversion effects are expected if V moves to INFL over the Specifier of VP:

(18) $[_{IP}$ Wh-phrase $[_{INFL}$ V+INFL $[_{VP}$ Subject V' . . .]]]

The overt subject would remain in the Specifier of VP at S-structure, as discussed in Chapter 5 (Section 5.2).

A third alternative as to the derived position of Wh-phrases is that they occupy the Specifier of a category between CP and IP:

(19)   . . . $[_{CP}$ $[_{C}{}^{\circ}$ que] $[_{XP}$ para quién X° $[_{IP}$ (Subject) [V+INFL] . . .]]]
             that   for   whom

The possibility that such a category is present, and is a potential landing site for Wh-phrases has been mentioned in several studies, primarily in relation to the analysis of Focus Phrases, to which we turn in 6.3. Goodall (1991, 1999) argues that, even if Wh-phrases move to the Specifier of IP, as in (18), there is also evidence for movement to a higher position. Motivation for this phrase will be discussed below in 6.3.

6.2.4   Summary

We saw in 6.2.1 that Wh-questions have two "core" properties: obligatory movement of a Wh-phrase and, in certain cases, the non-occurrence of a pre-verbal subject. These properties have been analyzed as following from the Wh-Criterion of Rizzi (1996). In 6.2.2, we saw that the possibility for pre-verbal subjects is related to the status of the Wh-phrase: only Wh-phrases that correspond to arguments of the verb are incompatible with a pre-verbal subject. Suñer (1994) proposes that this generalization follows from a licensing relation (Argumental Agreement Licensing) between the verb and its Wh-argument. This relation is blocked by the occurrence of an intervening pre-verbal subject. In 6.2.3, the co-occurrence of a complementizer and a following Wh-phrase was discussed. The issue raised by this phenomenon is the landing site of the Wh-phrase. Possibilities that have been discussed in the literature include movement: (a) to the specifier of a second CP, (b) to the Specifier of IP, and (c) to the specifier of a category between CP and IP.

6.3   (Contrastive) Focus

In this section we will examine clauses with an initial emphatic constituent, as illustrated in (21), based on the declarative (20):

(20)   María compró los tomates en el mercado.
        "Maria bought the tomatoes at the market."

(21)   a. MARÍA compró los tomates en el mercado.
           "It was Maria who bought the tomatoes at the market."
        b. En el MERCADO compró María los tomates.
           "It was at the market that Maria bought the tomatoes."

In (21), the initial phrase has an emphatic stress, shown by capitals. In Section 6.3.1, the properties of emphatic constituents – called Focus constituents – will be summarized. Section 6.3.2 will show that Focus constituents share certain basic properties with Wh-phrases, a fact which has led to an analysis of Focus phrases as derived by A'-movement. Section 6.3.3 considers the landing site for Focus phrases and Wh-phrases.

6.3.1 Properties of Focus phrases

The Focus constituents in sentences like (21) above have several characteristics that distinguish them from non-emphatic pre-verbal constituents. These are summarized in (22) (Howard 1993):

(22)   Focus Phrases:
        a. contain the intonational peak of the clause;
        b. license contrastive extensions;
        c. produce paraphrases of cleft sentences.

Let us look first at intonation. In non-emphatic sentences, the intonational peak of the sentence is normally within the predicate (the rightmost phrasal stress), as illustrated in (23):

(23)   María compró los tomates en el merCAdo.
        "Maria bought the tomatoes at the MARket."

In emphatic sentences such as (21), the constituent to the left of the verb contains the intonational peak. This shift in intonation is associated with a cleft interpretation, and with the possibility for contrastive extensions:

(24)   MARÍA compró esos tomates en el mercado, no José.
        "It was Maria who bought the tomatoes at the market, not José."

Zubizarreta (1998) describes the emphatic stress rule of sentences like (24) as giving rise to an interpretation in which (part of) the presupposition is reasserted or denied. For example in (24), the listener's presupposition (that it was José who bought the tomatoes) is denied by the speaker.[4] In the literature on

---

[4] This interpretation corresponds to the Contrastive Focus discourse role in Comrie (1989).

Spanish, this construction has been referred to under various names, such as "Topicalization," "Rhematization," "Informational Focus," "Focus Fronting" and "Focus Movement." We will refer to it as *Focus Movement*.

6.3.2   Movement properties

We turn now to properties of emphatic sentences which provide evidence as to the structure and derivation of the Focus constituent. As shown in Hernanz and Brucart (1987), Focus phrases pattern with Wh-phrases in crucial respects. This implies that Focus phrases, like Wh-phrases, are derived by A′-movement (movement to a "non-argument" position).

Like Wh-movement, Focus movement triggers subject–verb inversion, as shown by the contrast in (25):

(25)   a. ESE capítulo leyó por completo Josefina.
           that chapter read for complete J.
           "It was that chapter that Josefina read completely."
       b. *ESE capítulo Josefina leyó por completo.=(25a)
           that chapter J.   read for complete

Recall from Section 6.2 that inversion effects have been analyzed as due to the requirements of licensing criteria: the Wh-Criterion and Argumental Agreement Licensing.[5] If Focus phrases were base-generated in initial position as clausal adjuncts, they would not be expected to trigger inversion.

Focus constituents also show other properties characteristic of A′-movement. Like Wh-phrases, a Focus constituent cannot be linked to a position within an "island" such as a relative clause:

(26)   a. *ESE poema conozco a la mujer que escribió.
           "It is that poem that I know the woman who wrote."
       b. *¿Qué poema conoces a la mujer que escribió?
           "Which poem do you know the woman who wrote?"

In (26a), the phrase *ESE poema* "that poem" is the object of the verb *escribió*. The ungrammaticality of (26a) can be ascribed to the impossibility of moving any constituent out of the relative clause, which acts like an "island" for movement, as is shown in (26b) for a Wh-constituent.

Another parallel is the absence of clitic doubling for Focus phrases and for Wh-phrases:

---

[5] Within the Minimalist Program, these licensing requirements are subsumed under the feature-checking requirements of functional categories, as was discussed in Chapter 5 (Section 5.2).

(27)   a. ESOS tomates (*los) compró María.
             "It was those tomatoes that Maria bought (*them)."
         b. ¿Cuáles tomates (*los) compró María.
             "Which tomatoes did Maria buy (*them)?"

Neither movement admits two fronted constituents in a clause:

(28)   a. *¿Cuándo qué compró Juan?
             "When what did Juan buy?"
         b. *AYER los TOMATES compró Juan.
             "It was yesterday the tomatoes that Juan bought."

Furthermore, a Wh-phrase and a Focus phrase cannot be fronted in the same clause, regardless of order:

(29)   a. *¿Cuándo las MANZANAS compraron?
             "When was it the apples that they bought?"
         b. *¿Las MANZANAS cuándo compraron?
             "It was the apples when that they bought?"

Both Wh-phrases and Focus phrases can be preceded by a dislocated Topic constituent in a main clause:

(30)   a. En octubre, POCAS manzanas compraron.
             "In October, few apples they bought."
         b. En octubre, ¿qué compraron?
             "In October, what did they buy?"

Finally, both Wh-movement and Focus movement can appear in initial position of complement clauses only if the fronted constituent is compatible with the semantic selection of the matrix predicate. Wh-movement is only possible in clauses that can s-select indirect questions, as shown by the contrast in (31):

(31)   a. María se pregunta [qué compraron en agosto].
             "Maria wonders [what they bought in August]."
         b. *María anunció [qué compraron en agosto].
             "Maria announced [what they bought in August]."

Sentence (31a) is grammatical as an indirect question; (31b) is not.[6] Example (31a) admits a question interpretation because the verb *preguntarse* "wonder" semantically selects as a complement a clause that contains an interrogative ([+wh]) feature. The verb *anunciar* "announce," on the other hand, does not. In complement clauses then, interrogatives are only possible if they are consistent with lexical properties of the selecting predicate. Focus movement is

_____
[6] Example (31b) is grammatical as a declarative with a "free relative" complement, i.e., "Maria announced what they bought in August."

also restricted, although it is not restricted by the same feature, as noted in Howard (1993). Focus movement is restricted according to whether the embedded clause is assertive or presupposed (examples from Contreras (1978)):

(32)   a. Dice que MAÑANA lo operan.
           "He says that it's tomorrow that they're operating on him."
        b. *Siento que MAÑANA lo operen.
           "I regret that it's tomorrow that they're operating on him."

The verb *decir* "say" of the main clause in (32a) is an "assertive" verb in the sense that it asserts the propositional content of its complement clause. The factive verb *sentir* "regret" in (32b) is non-assertive. It presupposes the content of its complement, rather than asserting it. In the latter context, Focus movement is ungrammatical. Although it is not clear precisely what feature is present in assertive contexts that is absent in (32b), the contrast in (32) implies that semantic selection pertains for Focus phrases, as it does for interrogatives.

Summarizing, we have seen that Focus movement has properties quite close to those of Wh-movement. The only difference between the two concerns s-selection in embedded clauses. Wh-movement is s-selected by a [+wH] feature, and Focus movement is not, although it does show evidence of s-selection by some feature, whatever that may turn out to be.

6.3.3   Landing site

Based on similarities between Wh-movement and Focus constructions, it has been assumed that Focus constituents are derived by movement (rather than by base-generation as pre-clausal adjuncts, for example). Some authors (Hernanz and Brucart 1987; Campos and Zampini 1990) have analyzed both Wh-movement and Focus movement as A'-movement to the Specifier of CP, which triggers verb fronting from INFL to the Complementizer:

(33) $[_{CP}$ Las MANZANAS$_j$ $[_{C'}$ compró$_k$ $[_{IP}$ María$_i$ $[_{I'}$ t$_k$ $[_{VP}$ t$_i$ t$_k$ t$_j$]]]]]

On this analysis, all constituents lower in the structure than CP, including the subject and any IP adjuncts, follow the verb, which has moved to COMP. The only constituents that could precede the verb are the Focus constituent in the Specifier of CP and any CP adjuncts. Dislocated Topics, for example, precede the Focus constituent:

(34) $[_{CP}$ En agosto, $[_{CP}$ Las MANZANAS$_j$ $[_{C'}$ compró$_k$ $[_{IP}$ María$_i$ $[_{I'}$ t$_k$ $[_{VP}$ t$_i$ t$_k$ t$_j$]]]]]]
        "In August, it was the apples that Maria bought."

As with Wh-movement, recent studies have argued that the S-structure landing site for Focus movement is lower in clause structure than CP. One argument in support of this analysis is that in embedded clauses, the fronted constituent – a Focus constituent or a Wh-phrase – appears to the right of the complementizer:

(35)   a. Dice [$_{CP}$ que [MAÑANA lo operan]].
         "He says that it's tomorrow that they're operating on him."
         b. Me preguntaron [(que)[a quién invitas]].
         "They asked me (that) whom you're inviting."

The structure assigned to sequences like those in (35) varies according to a number of other assumptions: in particular, the articulation of the VP-related functional projections in IP. In Chapter 4, the projections discussed included Aspect Phrase, with associated Agr-o; Tense, with associated Agr-s (=IP); and Neg Phrase:[7]

(36)   NegP – IP – (Aux) – AspP – VP

The landing site of Focus movement must be at least as high as NegP, since the fronted constituent precedes *no*:

(37)   Dice que MAÑANA no lo operan.
         "He says that it's not tomorrow that they're operating on him."

Notice as well that a fronted Focus constituent must precede an *n*-word in the Specifier of NegP:

(38)   a. Dice que nunca lo operaron.
         "He says that never did they operate on him."
         b. Dice que en ese HOSPITAL (no) lo operaron.
         "He says that it's (not) in that hospital that they operated on him."
         c. *Dice que nunca en ese HOSPITAL lo operaron.
         "He says that never is it in that hospital that they operated on him."
         d. (?)Dice que en ese HOSPITAL nunca lo operaron.
         "He says that it's in that hospital that they never operated on him."

The ungrammaticality of (38c) shows that the Focus constituent is not adjoined to Neg' – between the head and a constituent in the Specifier. The grammaticality of (38d) shows that the Focus constituent is higher than NegP, either adjoined to it, or in the specifier of a higher functional category between NegP and CP. Between these alternatives, the evidence seems to point to the latter: if the Focus constituent were adjoined, it would be expected that several Focus constituents should be possible, since adjunction is generally not restricted to

---

[7] Recall from Chapter 4 (Section 4.5) that, since pre-verbal subjects precede Negation, Agr-s may be higher than Neg. This issue is left open here.

a single constituent. Furthermore, if the Focus constituent were adjoined, it would not be expected that movement should be restricted to clauses with particular features s-selected by the matrix predicate. Finally, the adjunction analysis does not capture the similarities between Wh-movement and Focus movement, since Wh-movement is uncontroversially movement to a Specifier position. These factors lead to the conclusion that there is a phrase between NegP and Comp, whose functional features are related to Focus constituents:

(39)   COMP – **Foc** – Neg – INFL – (Aux) – Aspect – VP

Focus movement is therefore movement to the specifier of "FocP."[8] This hypothesis is consistent with the properties observed: only one constituent can be fronted in a clause (like Wh-phrases and *n*-words – Chapter 4, Section 4.5) and fronting is possible in complement clauses only if s-selected. As for the impossibility of both Wh-movement and Focus movement in the same clause, the fact that WH-constituents appear to the right of Comp in certain embedded clauses suggests that Wh-phrases can appear at S-structure in the Specifier of FP if FP is specified for [+F] features.

6.3.4   Summary

It was shown above that Focus movement shares properties with Wh-movement, which suggests that it is derived by movement rather than base-generation. Like Wh-movement, Focus movement has been analyzed in recent studies as movement to a position lower than the Specifier of CP, since Focus phrases can appear to the right of a complementizer. There is some evidence which suggests that the Focus phrase is above the IP. Since Focus constituents can (at least marginally) precede preposed *n*-phrases, they must be either adjoined to NegP or in the Specifier of a higher functional category, "FP" between Comp and NegP. The adjunction analysis does not capture straightforwardly the uniqueness of the Focus constituent, its similarities to Wh-movement, or the fact that it is s-selected by some feature related to the "assertive" value of the clause. The FP hypothesis accounts for these properties straightforwardly.

6.4   Other A′-movements

This section will briefly introduce four additional constructions that have been analyzed as involving A′-movements.

---

[8] Uriagereka (1995) argues for the existence of a Focus Phrase based on the occurrence of a Focus particle in Western Romance.

6.4.1   Scrambling

Recall from Chapter 5 (Section 5.6) that VP-final subjects ("free subject inversion") in Italian and Spanish are analyzed in Rizzi (1982) as deriving from rightward movement of the subject to a VP-adjoined position:

(40)   a. Compró el   diccionario Juan.
              bought the dictionary   J.
              "Juan bought the dictionary."
         b. $[_{IP}\ t_i\ INFL\ [_{VP}\ [_{VP}\ compró\ el\ diccionario]\ Juan_i\ ]]$

In subsequent years, several theoretical developments have occurred which call this analysis into question. Among these is Kayne's (1994) hypothesis that excludes rightward movements altogether. If correct, this hypothesis implies that V-O-S order must be derived from S-V-O order by leftward movement:

(41)   [V   Obj$_i$ [S [t$_v$ t$_i$]]]

Ordóñez (1997) argues that this reordering in Spanish is a form of movement referred to as "Scrambling." On this analysis, (40a) would be derived as shown in (42):

(42)   [compró$_i$ [el diccionario$_j$ t$_i$ [$_{VP}$ Juan t$_i$ t$_j$]]]

In (42), the verb has moved from its base position through Agr-o, and then to Tense (V-to-INFL movement). The object, *el diccionario*, has also moved, to a position outside VP, so that its surface position is left of the subject. (This position might be either an adjoined position or the Specifier of a functional category below Tense.) The subject remains in its base position in the Specifier of VP (see Chapter 5, Section 5.2).

Ordóñez presents several types of evidence in favor of the analysis illustrated above. One piece of evidence concerns the hierarchical relationship between the moved object and the subject. The Scrambling analysis, unlike the rightward movement analysis, claims that the complement c-commands the subject after movement. Another type of evidence concerns the relationship between Scrambling and Wh-movement. He shows that there are restrictions on the order of complements in multiple questions. As shown in (43b) and (44b), a post-verbal WH-subject must precede a WH-complement in VP (examples from Ordóñez 1997:52):

(43)   a. ¿Qué le   compró quién a   quién?
              what CL-bought who   for whom
              "What did who buy for whom?"

b. *¿Qué le compró a quién quién?
what CL-bought for whom who
"What did for whom buy who?"

(44)   a. ¿Qué dijo quién de quién?
what said who of whom
"What did who say of whom?"
b. *¿Qué dijo de quién quién?
what said of whom who
"What did of whom say who?"

The judgments shown above reflect multiple question readings, rather than echo-questions. In the ungrammatical (b) examples, a Wh-phrase may be analyzed as having moved leftward via Scrambling. Ordóñez notes that Wh-phrases have been shown to resist Scrambling in certain languages (e.g., German). The word order patterns in (43) and (44) may therefore have a natural explanation under a Scrambling analysis. This suggestion is supported by the fact that the (b) examples cannot be excluded in terms of a more general ban on movement of WH-complements across other Wh-phrases. If the movement is Wh-movement, rather than Scrambling, no violation ensues. Ordóñez cites cases from Jaeggli (1982):

(45)   a. ¿Quién dijo qué?
"Who said what?"
b. ¿Qué dijo quién?
"What did who say?"

In (45b), the complement Wh-phrase, *qué* "what," has moved over the subject. In this instance, the object has moved to a clause-initial position. The grammaticality of (45b) compared with (43b) and (44b), suggests that the latter are excluded by some condition that is specific to Scrambling.[9]

Summarizing, it has been proposed that the order V-O-S is derived via (leftward) A'-movement of the object. This analysis claims that the object is structurally higher than the subject, which remains in its initial VP-internal position. Ordóñez (1997) argues that this analysis may account for restrictions on the order of non-clause-initial WH-phrases in multiple questions.

[9] The English equivalent of (45b) is ungrammatical:

(i)   *What did who say?

This sentence involves movement of the object across the WH-subject, and then, after S-structure, the subject WH-phrase would move across the object. It is the second, covert movement that produces a violation (compare: *What did she say?*). This type of violation is referred to descriptively as a "Superiority" violation. As Ordóñez notes, the grammaticality of (45) in the text shows that (43b) and (44b) cannot be attributed directly to "Superiority."

6.4.2   Parasitic gaps

It has been observed that A'-movement can under certain circumstances allow a second gap to appear. Consider the contrast between (46a) and (46b, c):

(46)   a. ¿Qué   libro   archivaste [sin   leer –]?
             which book   filed   without read-inf.
             "Which book did (you) file without reading?"
         b. *Archivaste ese   libro [sin   leer –].
             filed   that book without read-inf.
             "(You) filed that book without reading."
         c. *Ese libro parece haber   sido archivado [sin   leer –].
             that book seems have-inf. been filed   without read-inf.
             "That book seems to have been filed without reading."

In each of these sentences, the adjunct clause is missing the object of the verb *leer* "read." The "gap" in the adjunct clause has been referred to as a "parasitic gap," because its presence is dependent on the occurrence of an A'-chain in the main clause. That is, the parasitic gap in (46a) is in some way legitimated by the presence of the (Wh-phrase-trace) chain in the main clause. This is supported by the interpretation of (46a), where the gap takes its reference from the Wh-phrase, as well as by the ungrammaticality of (46b), where the main clause does not contain an A'-chain. In (46c), the object of the participle *archivado* "filed" has undergone movement, but in this case the movement is A-movement – that is, movement to an argument position: the matrix subject position. The ungrammaticality of (46c) shows that A-chains do not license parasitic gaps.

Chomsky (1982) argues that parasitic gaps are traces left by the movement of a phonetically null operator:

(47)   ¿Qué libro_i   archivaste t_i [sin [Op_i [PRO   leer e_i]]]?

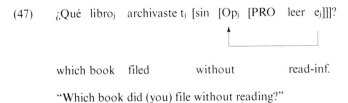

         which book   filed   without   read-inf.

"Which book did (you) file without reading?"

Evidence that supports an analysis of null operator movement for the parasitic gap is based on the relationship between the trace (the parasitic gap) and the CP that, by hypothesis, contains the null operator. As in other cases of A'-movement, the parasitic gap cannot be contained within a syntactic "island":

(48)   *¿Qué   libro$_i$ archivaste t$_i$ sin [Op$_j$ preguntarte cuándo leer e$_j$]?
        which book filed   without wonder   when   read-inf.
        "Which book did you file without wondering when to read?"

In (48), the trace of the null operator is contained within a "Wh-island": a CP whose specifier is occupied by a WH-constituent. Since this position is already occupied, the null operator cannot have moved through it. The null operator must have moved in one step across the occupied CP:

(49)   *¿Qué libro$_j$ archivaste t$_j$ sin [Op$_j$ PRO preguntarte [cuándo leer e$_j$]]?

The preceding observations imply that a null operator should be able to appear in a higher CP such as in (49) only if the operator has moved successively through lower CPs ("successive cyclically"). It has been noted, however, that Spanish parasitic gaps disallow even this type of successive movement, as is illustrated by the contrast between (50a) and (50b) (examples from García Mayo and Kempchinsky (1994)):

(50)   a. Which articles did you put on reserve without convincing the students
           to read?
        b. *¿Qué   artículos pusiste en reserva sin   convencer   a   los
           estudiantes de leer?   (=50a)
           which articles   put   on reserve without convince-inf. PA the
           students   of read-inf.

In descriptive terms, null operator movement appears to be restricted to the CP of the clause containing the parasitic gap. This relation is more local than is generally the case for A'-movements. Wh-phrases, for example, can move successive-cyclically:

(51)   ¿Qué artículo dijiste que creyó María que insistió Pedro en que leyera
        Susana?
        "Which article did you say that Maria believed that Pedro insisted that
        Susana read?"

In (51) the Wh-phrase, *qué artículo* "which article," has moved from its base position as the complement of *leyera* "read," in the most deeply embedded clause, through the specifier of CPs of intermediate clauses, to its derived position in the matrix clause. Null operator movement is thus more restricted than Wh-movement, although the two share properties of chains produced by movement.[10]

---

[10] There are a number of additional constraints on parasitic gap constructions, and a number of aspects of the analysis of null operators that have been omitted here. For further discussion, see Bordelois (1986) and García Mayo and Kempchinsky (1994), and references cited.

Summarizing, parasitic gaps have been argued to be derived by movement of a null operator, creating an A'-chain that is interpreted in relation to another A'-chain, such as that produced by Wh-movement. The null operator chain exhibits the properties typical of A'-movement, but is more restricted still: the operator and its trace are restricted to the same clause.

6.4.3   Complex adjectivals

A second construction that has been analyzed as involving null operator movement is illustrated by the pairs in (52)–(54) (examples from Aissen and Perlmutter (1976:14)):

(52)   a. Será difícil componer estas radios.
         "It will be difficult to fix these radios."
         b. Estas radios serán difíciles de componer.
         "These radios will be difficult to fix."

(53)   a. Es fácil entender los resultados.
         "It is easy to understand the results."
         b. Los resultados son fáciles de entender.
         "The results are easy to understand."

(54)   a. Fue imposible comer el postre.
         "It was impossible to eat the dessert."
         b. El postre fue imposible de comer.
         "The dessert was impossible to eat."

In the (b) sentences above, the logical object of the infinitive appears in position of the matrix subject. Aissen and Perlmutter (1976) show that the preposed NP is a clausal subject, not a topic or other adjunct. Their conclusion is based on its subject-like behavior: the fact that it can be a "null subject"; that it triggers subject–verb agreement in the matrix clause; and that it can undergo further NP movement in raising contexts:

(55)   Estas radios$_i$ parecen [t$_i$ ser difíciles de componer].
         "These radios seem to be difficult to fix."

These facts indicate that the initial NP in sentences like (52b)–(54b) is the subject of the main clause. This NP is also interpreted as the complement of the verb of the embedded clause, which implies that an empty category in that position is assigned a Theta-role by the verb:

(56)   Estas radios serán difíciles [de componer e].

A central issue raised by this construction is that the preposed NP could not have moved from the embedded object position directly to the matrix subject position without violating principles that constrain such movement. In particular, the trace left by this movement would violate Binding Principle A, which requires that certain traces (such as the trace of a moved NP) be bound by an antecedent within a local environment – not in the next higher clause. The empty category in (56) does not have an antecedent that is structurally close enough to satisfy Principle A. Furthermore, there is no way in which the movement could have occurred in a sequence of steps so that the Binding requirement could be satisfied. A movement such as that shown in (57) is not consistent with the interpretation:

(57)   Estas radios$_i$ serán difíciles [de t$_i$ componer ti].

In (57), the NP *estas radios* has moved from object position of the embedded clause to subject position, then raised to subject position of the matrix clause. Each step in this derivation would be an admissible movement. However, this derivation cannot be correct, since the subject of the embedded clause is not interpreted as *estas radios*, but as an arbitrary person or persons, i.e., a null PRO:

(58)   Estas radios$_i$ serán difíciles [de PRO componer ti].
        "These radios will be difficult (for one) to fix."

The question which remains, then, is how the preposed NP is associated with the position in which its Theta-role is assigned.

Chomsky (1981) proposes that the solution to this problem lies in the nature of the movement. Rather than NP movement to the matrix subject position, it appears that the embedded clause object is a null pronominal that undergoes movement to the specifier of the embedded CP:

(59)   Estas radios$_i$ serán difíciles [$_{CP}$ PRO$_i$ de [PRO componer ti]].

In (59), the null pronoun (which has an index different from that of the infinitival subject), moves to the specifier of CP, and is coindexed with the NP *estas radios*. This proposal is problematic with respect to the NP *estas radios*, which must be inserted in a position that is not assigned a Theta-role. Since it is not related by movement to the null pronoun or its trace in the embedded clause, the derivation should fail the Theta-Criterion already at D-Structure. To avoid this violation, Chomsky suggests that the NP is not present at D-structure, but is inserted in the course of the derivation to S-structure.

The hypothesis that complex adjectivals involve A'-movement, and not simple Raising (or A-movement) is supported by similarities between the chain formed by movement of PRO to CP, and chains formed by other A'-movements. One similarity is that both of these chains license "parasitic gaps." Recall from Section 6.4.2 that parasitic gaps are possible only if the null operator can be interpreted in relation to an overt operator. This is shown by the contrast between (46a) and (46c), repeated below:

(46)   a. ¿Qué   libro archivaste [sin   leer –]?
         which book filed   without read-inf.
         "Which book did (you) file without reading?"
         c. *Ese libro parece haber   sido archivado [sin   leer –].
         that book seems have-inf. been filed   without read-inf.
         "That book seems to have been filed without reading."

In (46c), A-movement of the complement *ese libro* to the matrix subject position does not license a parasitic gap, unlike Wh-movement in (46a). Returning to complex adjectivals, the movement shown in (59) is supported by its ability to license a parasitic gap. Compare the complex adjectival in (60a) with A-movement in (60b):

(60)   a. Este problema es fácil de resolver   sin   examinar
         detenidamente.
         this problem is easy of resolve-inf. without examine-inf.
         carefully
         "This problem is easy to solve without examining carefully."
         b. *Este problema parece haber   sido resuelto sin   examinar
         detenidamente.
         this problem seems have-inf. been solved   without examine-inf.
         carefully
         "This problem seems to have been solved without examining carefully."

In (60a), the complement of *examinar* is a well-formed parasitic gap. If it is correct that parasitic gaps are generally licensed by an A'-antecedent, then (60a) must have a null operator in the specifier of the intermediate clause. By contrast, (60b) shows that the occurrence of movement is not sufficient to license a parasitic gap, if the chain produced by movement occupies an A-position, rather than an A'-position.

A second argument supporting the analysis of complex adjectivals as involving A'-movement is that, like parasitic gap constructions, Spanish complex adjectivals allow only clause-bounded A'-movement:

(61)   *Ese libro es difícil   de convencer   a   los estudiantes de leer.
         that book is difficult of convince-inf. PA the students   of read-inf.
         "That book is difficult to convince the students to read."

Whatever the explanation for this stricter form of locality, the fact that both constructions involving A'-movement of a null operator are restricted in the same way supports a unified treatment.

Summarizing, complex adjectivals show evidence of A'- movement of a null constituent, one which takes an antecedent in a higher clause. The antecedent is, in these cases, the subject of the matrix clause. Support for a movement analysis derives from (a) the fact that the construction licenses parasitic gaps, and (b) that the null operator movement shows the same highly local character as is displayed by null operator movement in parasitic gap constructions.

6.4.4 Indefinite null objects

Null objects are not generally grammatical in Spanish, as the following examples (from Campos (1986)) illustrate:

(62)   a. Compré un/el libro.
        "I bought a/the book."
        b. Lo compré.
        CL(DO) bought
        "I bought it."
        c. *Compré.
        "I bought."

In a context such as (63), a null object is grammatical, if it is interpreted as indefinite:

(63)   a. ¿Compraste café?
        "You bought coffee?"
        b. Sí, compré.
        "Yes, I bought (some)."

As Campos (1986) notes, (63b) is not possible in Romance languages that have overt partitive clitics, including French, Catalan and Italian. Portuguese and Spanish, however, do not have partitive clitics, and allow null objects. Following Raposo (1984), Campos argues that sentences like (63) involve movement of a null operator.

Evidence for the null operator analysis derives from the fact that the construction observes the constraints that typically apply to movement. Examples such as (64) illustrate that where the null object is contained within an island, it is ungrammatical:

(64)   a. ¿Juan traerá cerveza a la fiesta?
        "Will Juan bring beer to the party?"
        b. Su novia me dijo que traería.
        "His girlfriend told me that he would bring (some)."
        c. *Existe el rumor de que traerá.
        "There is the rumor that he will bring (some)."

Example (64a) sets the discourse context for the null object. In (64b), the null object is contained in a complement clause. If the derivation involves movement through CP, (64b) is grammatical because the specifier of the embedded CP is available as an intermediate landing site for the operator:

(65) $[_{CP} Op_i [_{IP} pro\ dijo [_{CP} t_i\ que [_{IP} pro\ traería\ t_i]]]$

From this position, the operator undergoes further movement to the Specifier of the matrix CP. Note that this movement (unlike the null operator of parasitic gap and complex adjectival constructions) is not clause-bounded. Movement to the higher CP is possible. This step in the derivation is supported by the contrast between (64b) and (64c). In the latter example, the complex NP makes further movement to the matrix CP impossible:

(66)   *$[CP\ \ Op_i [_{IP} pro\ existe [_{DP} el\ rumor\ de [_{CP} t_i\ que\ traerá\ t_i]]]]$.

The observance of constraints on movement leads Campos to conclude that null objects are derived by A'-movement of a null operator. The question remains as to why this null operator construction is not clause-bound, as are parasitic gaps and complex adjectivals.

6.4.5   Summary

In this section, we have reviewed certain constructions that have been analyzed as involving A'-movement. These include Scrambling, which moves an object to the left of a subject; and those constructions which have been argued to be derived by movement of a null operator: parasitic gaps, complex adjectivals, and null objects. Although we have only sampled the evidence underlying these analyses, we nevertheless have seen similarities in their properties. In particular, all these constructions have been argued to involve movement, based in part on the observation that general constraints on movement are apparent.

6.5   Head movement to (and through) COMP

In this section, we return to the topic of head movement. It has been noted previously that, while V-to-INFL movement is characteristic of declaratives (Chapter 4, Sections 4.2 and 4.3) the evidence of non-declaratives indicates that I-to-C movement does not take place in overt syntax (Section 6.2.2). There are, however, several clause types that have been argued to involve overt movement of heads to (or through) COMP. These include several types of non-finite clauses where V-to-C movement is in evidence (6.5.1) and clauses in which clitics "climb" to a higher clause, moving through COMP (6.5.2).

6.5.1   V-to-INFL-to-C movement

It has been argued (Rivero 1994; Rooryck 1992; Belletti 1995) that certain imperative clauses are derived via movement of V-to-INFL and then I-to-C. This argument has been made for what Rivero (1994) terms *true* imperatives. Rivero distinguishes between *true* imperative constructions and *surrogate* imperative constructions. True imperatives are constructions with verb forms identifiable by a morphology not shared by the same person in any other tense in the system. True imperatives are usually only 2nd person. Surrogate imperatives are morphologically identical to the same person of an existing tense, usually a present or an infinitive, and are not restricted as to person. For example, compare the true imperative *canta* sing-I-2nd.sg. "Sing!" and *No cantes* not sing-pr-subj.-2nd.sg. "Do not sing." The latter is a surrogate imperative, as it uses the morphology of an existing tense, the present subjunctive.

Several properties of true imperatives are accounted for naturally if the derivation involves overt I-to-C movement. Cross-linguistically, it is quite common for clitics to be positioned after the verb. Compare the true imperative in (67) with the surrogate imperative in (68):[11]

(67)   a. ¡Hazlo!
        do-I.2nd.sg.+CL(DO)
        "Do it!"
        b. *¡Lohaz!

(68)   a. *¡No hágaslo!
        not do-pr.subj.2nd.sg.
        "Don't do it!"
        b. ¡No lo hagas!

Clitic order might be accounted for in several ways, depending on assumptions as to how clitics are generated and moved (see Chapter 4, Section 4.4). On the assumption that clitics occupy Agr° (either by being generated there or by movement), the order in (67) is derived by moving the verb first to Tense and then to C:

(69)   COMP   Agr   TENSE   Agr-o (CL)   [$_{VP}$ V]

In (69), the verb moves first to TENSE, bypassing Agr-o, which is occupied by object clitics. Tense then moves to COMP. Rivero (1994) assumes that

---

[11] Rooryck (1992) notes that encliticization occurs with imperatives even in languages which otherwise lack encliticization, such as French.

imperatives are non-finite, so that Agr-s is inert. She assumes also that what triggers movement of I-to-C is a feature in COMP that is associated with an imperative operator.

A second property of true imperatives is that they are incompatible with negation:

(70)   a. ¡Hazlo!
             do-I.2nd.sg.+CL(DO)
             "Do it!"
         b. *¡No hazlo!
             not do-I.2nd.sg.+CL(DO)
             "Don't do it!"
         c. ¡No lo   hagas!
             not CL(DO) do-pr.subj.2nd.sg.
             "Don't do it!"

Rivero argues that the negative head *no* blocks movement of the imperative form. This "blocking" effect can be attributed to the operator-like status of negative *no*. Neg acts like a closer antecedent for the trace of the moved verb:

(71)   [$_{C°}$ [TNS+V]$_i$ + C$_{OP}$][Neg$_{OP}$ t$_i$ ...]

The Neg head therefore blocks the antecedent–trace relationship between the verb in COMP and its trace.

Summarizing to this point, true imperative constructions have two properties which appear to be consistent with head movement to COMP. One is the broad cross-linguistic phenomenon of imperative encliticization, which is suggestive of V-movement. Second, the incompatibility of true imperatives with negation is accounted for on the assumption that I-to-C movement is necessary, since Neg blocks further movement.

Other types of non-finite clauses have been suggested to be derived via I-to-C movement. As noted in Chapter 1 (Sections 1.6.4–1.6.5), various classes of non-finite adjunct clauses disallow pre-verbal subjects:

(72)   a. habiendo terminado   la   reunión
             have-prt. finish-pprt. the meeting
             "having finished the meeting"
         b. *la reunión habiendo terminado

(73)   a. de venir María
             of come-inf. M.
             "if Maria comes"
         b. *de María venir

(74)   a. terminada   la   reunión
         finish-pprt.f.sg.   the   meeting
         "the meeting finished"
         b. *la reunión terminada

Under the assumption that movement is purely optional, this constituent order generalization would be suggestive of I-to-C movement, since nothing would block the occurrence of the subject in the Specifier of IP. Under more recent assumptions that were discussed in Chapters 4 and 5, however, the impossibility of a pre-verbal subject is not necessarily indicative of I-to-C movement, since the subject cannot always appear pre-verbally, as discussed above in 6.2.2.

The diagnostics mentioned above can shed light on the position of the verb in these clauses: if I-to-C applies, they are expected (a) to show encliticization, and (b) to disallow negation. Gerundive and infinitival clauses, like non-finite verbs in general, have enclitics rather than pro-clitics:

(75)   a. habiéndolo   terminado
         have-prt.+CL(DO)   finish-pprt.
         "having finished it"
         b. *lo habiendo terminado

(76)   a. de leerlo   Juan
         of read-inf.+CL(DO)   J.
         "if Juan reads it"
         b. *de lo leer Juan

These clauses do, however, admit negation:

(77)   a. No habiendo terminado la reunión, me quedé en la oficina.
         "Not having finished the meeting, I stayed at the office."
         b. No estando tú en la sala, hablé con Susana.
         "You not being in the room, I talked with Susana."
(78)   a. Al no encontrar el artículo, me desesperé.
         "On not finding the article, I panicked."
         b. De no venir María, no hay fiesta.
         "If Maria doesn't come, there won't be a party."

It appears that in these clauses, the INFL containing V does not move overtly to COMP, since this movement would be blocked by an intervening negative head, as in (71) above.

Absolute (participial) clauses, however, disallow both object clitics, as in (79), and negation, as in (80):[12]

---

[12] As noted in Belletti (1990:94 ff.), the Italian counterparts of these participial clauses allow object clitics, but disallow negation.

(79)   a. publicado   el   artículo
         publish-pprt. the article
         "published the article"
         b. *publicádolo
         publish-pprt.+CL(DO)
         "it published"

(80)   a. *No terminada   la   reunión,   me quedé   en la   oficina.
         not finish-pprt.f. the meeting.f. CL remained at the office
         "With the meeting not finished, I remained at the office."
         b. *No vendido   el   coche, tenía poco dinero.
         not sell-pprt. the car   had   little money
         "With the car not sold, I had little money."

The ungrammaticality of object clitics – whatever its source might be – does not provide evidence for the verb's position. Recall that encliticization is suggestive that the verb has moved to I and then I has moved to C. Evidence from order of the verb and clitics is thus unavailable in this case. Negation, however, does provide evidence. As shown in (80), participial clauses do not accept negation. In this respect, these clauses differ from participles used as adjectives, which do allow negation (e.g. *un problema no resuelto* "a problem not resolved"). Participial clauses thus pattern with true imperatives, and may be derived via I-to-C movement.

Summarizing, it has been proposed that clitic order and the impossibility of negation provide evidence for the position of V in a clause. Based on these diagnostics, there are two types of clauses that appear to be derived via V-to-INFL and subsequent I-to-C movement: true imperatives and participial clauses. A broader class of clauses (including gerundives and infinitival adjuncts) disallow pre-verbal subjects. Assuming that movement is impossible unless it is triggered by the presence of a strong feature, the subject may remain within VP unless some strong feature requires that it move. If the subject is within VP in these non-finite clauses, these cases provide no evidence as to whether I-to-C movement has applied.

6.5.2   Clitic "Climbing"

It was noted in Chapter 4 (Section 4.4) that clitics can sometimes occur in construction with the verb of a higher clause, as in (81):

(81)   María lo   quiere comprar.
         M.   CL(DO) wants buy-inf.
         "Maria wants to buy it."

In (81), *lo* "it" is understood as the complement of the infinitive *comprar* "buy." However, the clitic precedes the verb *quiere* "wants" in the matrix clause. This phenomenon is referred to informally as "Clitic Climbing," because the clitics "climb" out of the clause in which they are interpreted. Because Romance clitics generally do not behave like full phrases, they are not expected to undergo the types of movement that phrases undergo. In fact, Clitic Climbing is fairly restricted. It occurs if the clitic originates in a clause that is the complement of a particular class of "trigger verbs." Other, non-trigger verbs do not allow clitic climbing.[13] The verb *parecer* "seem," for example, is a raising verb, but is not a Clitic-Climbing trigger:

(82)   a. María parece saber**lo**.
         M.   seems know-inf.+CL(DO)
         "Maria seems to know it."
         b. *María lo parece saber.

The unusual properties of Clitic Climbing as a movement process have led to various proposals.[14] Kayne (1989) argues that Clitic Climbing is derived via movement of clitics through COMP. That is, under certain conditions, clitics can undergo head movement independently of a verb. The crucial steps in the derivation involve movement of the clitic to INFL, and I-to-C movement. The derivation of (81) would begin as shown in (83):

(83)   a. María quiere $[_{CP}$ C° $[_{IP}$ PRO INFL $[_{VP}$ comprar **lo**]]].
         b. María quiere $[_{CP}$ C° $[_{IP}$ PRO **lo** +INFL $[_{VP}$ comprar t]]].
         c. María quiere $[_{CP}$ **lo** +INFL+C° $[_{IP}$ PRO t $[_{VP}$ comprar t]]]

In (83a), the clitic is shown in the position corresponding to the complement of *comprar*. In (83b), *lo* moves to INFL, while the infinitive remains within VP. In (83c), I-to-C movement carries the clitic to COMP. Once the clitic occupies this clause-initial position, it can cliticize to the matrix verb.

Kayne (1989) presents evidence supporting the steps shown in (83b) and (83c). With regard to movement of the clitic to INFL – even in the absence of V-to-INFL movement – Kayne notes that, although Romance clitics generally attach to V, they do not always do so, as is illustrated by examples like (84):

---

[13] For discussion of the class of trigger verbs, see Aissen and Perlmutter (1976).
[14] Several studies have pursued the notion that Clitic Climbing is possible only if the complement clause has undergone structural reanalysis, so that the matrix and complement clauses are "merged" into a single clause. Other studies have argued that the trigger verbs are "light" verbs or auxiliary verbs, which select a VP complement rather than a true clause. For discussion of these approaches, see Aissen and Perlmutter (1976), Rizzi (1982), Kayne (1989), Moore (1991) and references cited.

(84)   (*) Jean a   promis   de   les bien faire.   (Kayne 1989:240)
         J.   has promised for/to CL well do
         "Jean has promised to do them well."

In (84), the clitic *les* "them" is separated from the following infinitive by an adverb. He notes that while (84) is ungrammatical in Modern French, it existed in earlier stages of French and is attested in other dialects. In such cases, the clitic can be analyzed as having "climbed" to the INFL node of the infinitive. A further point with regard to movement of clitics to INFL concerns the range of languages in which Clitic Climbing is found. Kayne proposes that there is a correlation between the admissibility of Clitic Climbing and of null subjects. Stated informally, the idea is that, in NS languages, INFL is strong enough as a governor of VP for clitics to escape VP, moving to INFL, independently.[15] This accounts for why Clitic Climbing is common to the many Romance languages which allow null subjects, including earlier stages of French, but is impossible in Modern French.

Turning to the second step in the derivation, shown in (83c) above, Kayne argues that this step is also necessary. He notes that Clitic Climbing is impossible if the complement clause is finite. This is shown in (85), where the complement is a subjunctive clause rather than an infinitive:

---

[15] Kayne's account of the correlation between null subjects and Clitic Climbing calls for revision, under assumptions of the Minimalist Program, where government is eliminated as a theoretical construct. Treviño (1990), discussing Clitic Climbing in causative constructions, argues that the relationship is indirect: null subject languages are also free-inversion languages (i.e., allow VP-final subjects), and Clitic Climbing may be blocked unless the clitic can move through the Specifier of IP. On Treviño's analysis, Clitic Climbing displays "inversion effects," as suggested by the contrast in (i):

(i)   a. **La**   hizo   construir t   por Leonardo
            CL(DO) made construct-inf. by   Leonardo
            "(S)he had it built by Leonardo."
         b. *La   hizo a Leonardo construir t
            CL(DO) made to L.   construct-inf.
            "(S)he made Leonardo build it."
         c. (?)La hizo construir t a Leonardo. (=(ib))

In (ia), the embedded clause has no argumental subject, but rather an Agent represented in a *by*-phrase. This contrasts with (ib), where the embedded clause has an argument subject occupying a canonical pre-verbal (Specifier of IP) position. In (Ic), the embedded clause has an argument subject, but it has undergone "free inversion." This implies that the Specifier of IP is empty, and is available as a landing site for the moved clitic.

(85)   a. María quiere [$_{CP}$ que [Juan **lo**   compre]].
       M.   wants   that J.   CL(DO) buy.pr.subj.
       "Maria wants that Juan buy it."
       b. *María **lo** quiere [$_{CP}$ que [Juan t compre]].

If clitics could move directly from a lower INFL to a higher one, attaching to the matrix verb, it would be unexpected that this movement should be restricted to infinitives. If clitics must move through COMP, the ungrammaticality of Clitic Climbing in (85b) can be attributed to the fact that COMP is not empty, but is occupied by the complementizer *que*. Further evidence supporting movement of clitics through COMP concerns the interaction of Clitic Climbing and Wh-movement. Citing Italian data discussed in Rizzi (1982), Kayne notes that Clitic Climbing is marginally possible where a Wh-phrase occupies the complement CP:

(86)   Non ti saprei che dire.   (Kayne 1989:243)
       (I) NEG CL(DAT.2nd.sg) would-know what to-say
       "I won't know what to say to you."

In (86), clitic *ti* "you" has moved through a [+WH] CP, whose Specifier is occupied by the Wh-phrase *che* "what." By contrast, if the Wh-expression is a head, as in (87b), Clitic Climbing is impossible:

(87)   a. Non so se farli.   (Kayne 1989:245–246)
       (I) NEG know if to-do-CL(DO-3rd.pl)
       "I don't know whether to do them."
       b. *No li so se fare. (=87a)

In (87), the COMP position is filled by the [+WH] complementizer *se* "if." The occurrence of this element makes Clitic Climbing impossible, as in (87b). A similar contrast may be apparent in Spanish:

(88)   a. ?* No lo   sé   cómo arreglar.
          (I) Neg CL(DO.3rd.sg.) know how   fix-inf.
          "I don't know how to fix it."
       b.   *No lo   sé   si   arreglar.
          (I) Neg CL(DO.3rd.sg.) know whether fix-inf.
          "I don't know whether to fix it."

Example (88a) seems to be a degree better than (88b), where COMP is filled by a [+WH] complementizer.

Summarizing, we have seen here that the phenomenon of Clitic Climbing may involve head movement through the COMP of infinitival clauses. Kayne (1989) argues that clitics can move as heads to INFL without an accompanying verb, and that this movement is possible only in NS languages. He further argues that clitics move through COMP in the process of raising to a higher verb. If this movement can only be to an empty COMP, several restrictions on Clitic Climbing are accounted for, including the restriction to infinitival complements, and the limited interaction of Clitic Climbing with Wh-movement.

6.6   Summary

This chapter has explored basic characteristics of constructions whose derivation involves the upper portions of clause structure, which has been assumed standardly to be the Complementizer Phrase. As the discussion of 6.2 showed, the standard cases of movement to CP have been analyzed as necessary to satisfy the Wh-Criterion of Rizzi (1996). However, in Spanish, the descriptive generalization is more complex, since it appears that only argument Wh-phrases are incompatible with a pre-verbal subject. Another phenomenon discussed above concerns the co-occurrence of a complementizer and a following Wh-phrase. The issue raised by this phenomenon is the landing site of the Wh-phrase. Possibilities that have been discussed in the literature include movement: (a) to the specifier of a second CP, (b) to the Specifier of IP, and (c) to the specifier of a category between CP and IP.

The hypothesis that there is a functional category between CP and IP was shown in 6.3 to be useful in accounting for the distribution of Focus phrases. Since Focus constituents can follow a complementizer and can (at least marginally) precede preposed n-phrases, they may be analyzed as moving to the Specifier of a functional category "FP" between Comp and NegP. This analysis captures the uniqueness of the Focus constituent, its relationship to the "assertive" value of the clause, and similarities between Focus movement and Wh-movement.

Sections 6.4 and 6.5 summarized additional constructions that have been analyzed as involving A'-movement. Section 6.4 discussed phrasal movements, including Scrambling, which moves an object to the left of a subject; and several constructions which have been argued to be derived by movement of a null operator: parasitic gaps, complex adjectivals, and null objects. Section 6.5 discussed head movement to COMP. As the discussion showed, these movements occur only in non-finite clauses. In 6.5.1, verb-initial clauses were examined. These included (true) imperatives and participial clauses, both of which are incompatible with negation. This fact is explained on the hypothesis that I-to-C movement is blocked by an intervening Neg°. Clauses which require I-to-C movement are expected to disallow an (active) Neg Phrase between INFL and COMP. Finally, Section 6.5.2 discussed Clitic Climbing, a phenomenon that has been analyzed also as involving movement to COMP.

In this case, the movement in question is of clitics, while the verb remains VP-internal. As argued in Kayne (1989), this accounts for the cross-linguistic correlation between Clitic Climbing and null subjects, and for restrictions on Clitic Climbing in those languages in which it is found.

References

Abney, Steven P. 1987. "The English Noun Phrase in its Sentential Aspect." Ph.D. dissertation. Cambridge, Mass.: MIT.

Aissen, Judith, and David Perlmutter. 1976. "Clause Reduction in Spanish" in *Proceedings of the Second Annual Meeting of the Berkeley Linguistics Society*, ed. Henry Thompson and Kenneth Whistler, Vicki Edge, Jeri J. Jaeger, Ronya Javkin, Miriam Petruck, Christopher Smeall, Robert D. Van Valin Jr. 1–30.

Alatorre, Antonio. 1989. *Los 1,001 años de la lengua española*. Mexico City: Tezontle. (2nd edn.)

Alvar, Manuel (ed.). 1996. *Manual de dialectología hispánica: El español de España*. Barcelona: Editorial Ariel, S. A.

Arnaiz, Alfredo. 1996. "N-words and Wh-in-situ: Nature and Interactions." Unpublished Ph.D. dissertation. Los Angeles: University of Southern California.

Belletti, Adriana. 1988. "The Case of Unaccusatives" *Linguistic Inquiry* 19, 1–34.

1990. *Generalized Verb Movement: Aspects of Verb Syntax*. Turin: Rosenberg & Sellier.

1995. "Italian/Romance Clitics: Structure and Derivation." Paper presented at the 25th Linguistic Symposium on Romance Languages (Seattle, March).

Bello, Andrés. (1847, 1971). *Gramática de la lengua castellana*. Mexico: Editora Nacional.

Bethell, Leslie (ed.). 1984. *The Cambridge History of Latin America*. Vol. II. Cambridge: Cambridge University Press.

Bonet, Eulalia. 1991. "Morphology after Syntax: Pronominal Clitics in Romance." Unpublished doctoral dissertation. Cambridge, Mass: MIT.

1995. "Feature Structure of Romance Clitics" *Natural Language and Linguistic Theory* 13, 607–647.

Bordelois, Ivonne. 1986. "Parasitic Gaps: Extensions of Restructuring" in Bordelois (1986), 1–24.

Bordelois, Ivonne, Heles Contreras and Karen Zagona (eds.). 1986. *Generative Studies in Spanish Syntax*. Dordrecht: Foris Publications.

Borer, Hagit. 1984. *Parametric Syntax*. Dordrecht: Foris Publications.

Bosque, Ignacio. 1980. *Sobre la negación*. Madrid: Ediciones Cátedra, S. A.

(ed.). 1996. *El sustantivo sin determinación: La ausencia de determinante en la lengua española*. Madrid: Visor Libros.

Bright, William (ed.). 1992. *International Encyclopedia of Linguistics*. New York: Oxford University Press.

Brucart, José María. 1994. "Sobre una incompatibilidad entre posesivos y relativas especificativas" in Demonte (1994b), 51–86.

Burzio, Luigi. 1986. *Italian Syntax: A Government–Binding Approach.* Dordrecht: Reidel.

Camacho, José, Liliana Paredes and Liliana Sánchez. 1995. "The Genitive Clitic and the Genitive Construction in Andean Spanish" *Probus* 7.2, 133–146.

Campos, Héctor. 1986. "Indefinite Object Drop" *Linguistic Inquiry* 17, 354–359.

1993. *De la oración simple a la oración compuesta: Curso superior de sintaxis española.* Washington, D. C.: Georgetown University Press.

Campos, Hector, and Mary Zampini. 1990. "Focalization Strategies in Spanish" *Probus* 2, 47–64.

Chomsky, Noam. 1965. *Aspects of the Theory of Syntax.* Cambridge, Mass.: The MIT Press.

1977. "On Wh-Movement" in Culicover *et. al.*, (1977), 71–132.

1981. *Lectures on Government and Binding.* Dordrecht: Foris Publications.

1982. *Some Concepts and Consequences of the Theory of Government and Binding.* Cambridge, Mass.: The MIT Press.

1986. *Knowledge of Language.* New York: Praeger.

1993. "A Minimalist Program for Linguistic Theory" in Hale and Keyser (1993), 1–52.

1995. *The Minimalist Program.* Cambridge, Mass.: The MIT Press.

Cinque, Guglielmo. 1990. *Types of A' Dependencies.* Cambridge, Mass.: The MIT Press.

1992. "Functional Projections and N-movement within the DP" *GLOW Newsletter*, 28, 12–13. (Abstract of paper presented at the 1992 GLOW Conference.)

Clements, J. Clancy. 1994. "Notes on Topicalization and Object Drop in Spanish" in Mazzola (1994), 219–237.

Comrie, Bernard. 1989. *Language Universals and Linguistic Typology.* Chicago: The University of Chicago Press.

Contreras, Heles. 1978. *El orden de palabras en español.* Madrid: Cátedra.

1989. "Closed Domains" *Probus* 1, 163–180.

1991. "On the Position of Subjects" in *Perspectives on Phrase Structure: Heads and Licensing,* (Syntax and Semantics; 25) ed. Susan Rothstein. New York: Academic Press, 63–79.

1996. "Sobre la distribución de los sintagmas nominales no predicativos sin determinante" in Bosque (1996), 141–168.

Culicover, Peter W., Thomas Wasow and Adrian Akmajian. 1977. *Formal Syntax.* New York: Academic Press.

Décsy, Gyula (ed.). 1986. *Statistical Report on the Languages of the World as of 1985.* Bloomington, Ind.: Eurolingua.

Demonte, Violeta. 1986. "C-Command, Prepositions, and Predication" *Linguistic Inquiry* 17, 147–157.

1994a. "La ditransitividad en español: léxico y sintaxis" in Demonte (1994b), 431–470.

(ed.). 1994b. *Gramática del español.* Mexico: El Colegio de México, Centro de Estudios Lingüísticos y Literarios (Publicaciones de la Nueva revista de filología hispánica; 6).

1995. "Dative Alternation in Spanish" *Probus* 7, 5–30.

Ritter, Elizabeth. 1991. "Two Functional Categories of Noun Phrases: Evidence from Modern Hebrew" in *Perspectives on Phrase Structure: Heads and Licensing*, ed. Susan D. Rothstein. New York: Academic Press (Syntax and Semantics 25), 37–62.

Rivas, Alberto. 1977. "A Theory of Clitics." Unpublished Ph.D. dissertation. Cambridge, Mass.: MIT.

Rivero, María-Luisa. 1978. "Topicalization and WH-Movement in Spanish" *Linguistic Inquiry* 9, 513–517.

——. 1980. "On Left-dislocation and Topicalization in Spanish" *Linguistic Inquiry* 11, 363–393.

——. 1986. "Parameters in the Typology of Clitics in Romance and Old Spanish" *Language* 64, 774–807.

——. 1990. "Especificidad y existencia" in *Indicativo y subjuntivo*, ed. Ignacio Bosque. Madrid: Taurus Universitaria, 261–279.

——. 1991. "Clitic and NP Climbing in Old Spanish" in *Current Studies in Spanish Linguistics*, ed. Héctor Campos and Fernando Martínez-Gil. Washington, D.C.: Georgetown University Press, 241–284.

——. 1993. "Long Head Movement vs. V2 and Null Subjects in Old Romance" *Lingua* 89, 217–245.

——. 1994. "Clause Structure and V-movement in the Languages of the Balkans" *Natural Language and Linguistic Theory* 12, 63–120.

Rizzi, Luigi. 1982. *Issues in Italian Syntax*. Dordrecht: Foris Publications.

——. 1996. "Residual Verb Second and the Wh-Criterion" in *Parameters and Functional Heads: Essays in Comparative Syntax*, ed. Adriana Belletti and Luigi Rizzi. New York and Oxford: Oxford University Press, 63–90.

Rizzi, Luigi, and Ian Roberts. 1989. "Complex Inversion in French" *Probus* 1, 1–30.

Roberts, Ian. 1990. "L'accord et les auxiliaires dans l'histoire de l'anglais." Talk given at the Séminaire de Recherche, University of Geneva (cited in Belletti (1990)).

Rooryck, Johan. 1992. "Romance Enclitic Ordering and Universal Grammar" *Linguistic Review* 9, 219–250.

Rothstein, Susan. 1983. "The Syntactic Forms of Predication." Unpublished Ph.D. dissertation. Cambridge, Mass: MIT. (Circulated by Indiana University Linguistics Club, Bloomington, 1985.)

Saltarelli, Mario. 1994. "Voice in Latin and Romance: On the Representation of Lexical Subjects" in *Issues and Theory in Romance Linguistics: Selected Papers from the Linguistic Symposium on Romance Languages XXIII*, ed. Michael L. Mazzola. Washington, D.C.: Georgetown University Press, 445–478.

Sánchez, Liliana, and José Camacho. 1995. "Equative *ser* in Spanish." Unpublished MS. Los Angeles: The University of Southern California.

Sánchez-Albornoz, Nicolás. 1984. "The Population of Colonial Spanish America" in Bethell (1984) 3–36.

Sportiche, Dominique. 1988. "A Theory of Floating Quantifiers and Its Corollaries for Constituent Structure" *Linguistic Inquiry* 19, 425–449.

Stalnaker, Robert C. 1978. "Assertion" in *Pragmatics*, ed. Peter Cole. New York: Academic Press (Syntax and Semantics; 9), 315–332.

Emonds, Joseph. 1975. "A Transformational Analysis of French Clitics Without Positive Output Constraints" *Linguistic Analysis* 1, 1–32.

——. 1976. *A Transformational Approach to English Syntax: Root, Structure-Preserving, and Local Transformations*. New York: Academic Press.

——. 1978. "The Verbal Complex V'–V in French" *Linguistic Inquiry* 9, 151–175.

Fontana, Josep M. 1993. "Phrase Structure and the Syntax of Clitics in the History of Spanish." Unpublished Ph.D. dissertation. The University of Pennsylvania.

Franco, Jon. 1993. "On Object Agreement in Spanish." Unpublished Ph.D. dissertation. Los Angeles: The University of Southern California.

Galmés de Fuentes, Álvaro. 1996. "Mozarabe" in Alvar (1996), 97–110.

García Mayo, Pilar, and Paula Kempchinsky. 1994. "Finiteness in Romance vs. English Parasitic Gap Constructions" in Mazzola (1994), 303–316.

Giusti, Giuliana. 1991. "The Categorial Status of Quantified Nominals" *Linguistische Berichte* 136, 438–454.

Goodall, Grant. 1991. "Spec of IP and Spec of CP in Spanish Wh-questions." Paper read at the 21st Linguistic Symposium on Romance Languages (University of California, Santa Barbara, February).

——. 1999. "On Preverbal Subjects in Spanish." Paper presented at the 29th Linguistic Symposium on Romance Languages (Michigan State University).

Green, John. 1992. "Spanish" in Bright (1992), IV, 58–64.

Grimes, Ruth (ed.). 1988. *Ethnologue: Languages of the World*. Dallas, Tex.: Summer Institute of Linguistics.

Grimshaw, Jane. 1991. "Extended Projection." Unpublished MS. Brandeis University, Waltham, Mass.

Haegeman, Liliane, and Raffaella Zanuttini. 1991. "Negative Heads and the NEG Criterion" *Linguistic Review* 8, 233–251.

Hale, Kenneth, and Samuel J. Keyser (eds.). 1993. *The View from Building 20*. Cambridge, Mass.: The MIT Press.

Hanssen, Federico. 1945. *Gramática histórica de la lengua castellana*. Buenos Aires: Librería y Editorial "El Ateneo."

Hatcher, Anna Granville. 1956. "Theme and Underlying Question. Two Studies of Spanish Word Order" *Word* 12, Supplement 3.

Hernanz, Maria Luisa, and José María Brucart. 1987. *La sintaxis*. Barcelona: Editorial Crítica.

Higginbotham, James. 1985. "On Semantics" *Linguistic Inquiry* 16, 547–593.

Howard, Harry. 1993. "ΣP, Affective Inversion, and Topicalization in English and Spanish." Unpublished Ph.D. dissertation. Cornell University, Ithaca, NY.

Hurtado, Alfredo. 1989a. "El control mediante clíticos" *Revista Argentina de Lingüística* 5, 13–56.

——. 1989b. "Las cadenas clíticas" *Revista Argentina de Lingüística* 5, 77–133.

Iatridou, Sabine. 2000. "The Grammatical Ingredients of Counterfactuality" *Linguistic Inquiry* 31, 231–270.

Jackendoff, Ray. 1972. *Semantic Interpretation in Generative Grammar*. Cambridge, Mass.: The MIT Press.

——. 1977. *X-Bar Syntax: A Study of Phrase Structure*. Cambridge, Mass.: The MIT Press.

Jaeggli, Osvaldo. 1982. *Topics in Romance Syntax*. Dordrecht: Foris Publications.

Kaisse, Ellen. 1983. "The Syntax of Auxiliary Reduction in English" *Language* 59, 93–102.

Kany, Charles. 1951. *American Spanish Syntax*. Chicago: University of Chicago Press.

Kayne, Richard. 1975. *French Syntax: The Transformational Cycle*. Cambridge, Mass.: The MIT Press.

1981. "Unambiguous Paths" in *Levels of Syntactic Representation*, ed. Robert May and Jan Koster. Dordrecht: Foris Publications, 143–183.

1989. "Null Subjects and Clitic Climbing" in *The Null Subject Parameter*, ed. Osvaldo Jaeggli and Kenneth Safir. Dordrecht: Klewer Academic Publishers, 239–261.

1994. *The Antisymmetry of Syntax*. Cambridge, Mass.: The MIT Press.

Koopman, Hilda, and Dominique Sportiche. 1991. "The Position of Subjects" *Lingua* 85, 211–258.

Kurian, George (ed.). 1992. *Encyclopedia of the Third World*. New York: Facts on File.

Laka, Itziar. 1990. "Negation in Syntax: On the Nature of Functional Categories and Projections." Unpublished Ph.D. dissertation. Cambridge, Mass.: MIT.

Lapesa, Rafael. 1968. "Sobre los orígenes y evolución del leísmo, laísmo y loísmo" in *Festschrift Walther von Wartburg*, 2 vols. Tübingen: Max Niemeyer, 1, 523–551.

1981. *Historia de la lengua española*. Madrid: Editorial Gredos. (8th edn.)

Larson, Richard K. 1985. "Bare-NP Adverbs" *Linguistic Inquiry* 16, 595–621.

1988. "On the Double Object Construction". *Linguistic Inquiry* 19, 335–391.

Lema, José. 1991. "Licensing Conditions on Head Movement." Unpublished Ph.D. dissertation. University of Ottawa.

Levin, Beth. 1993. *English Verb Classes and Alternations: A Preliminary Investigation*. Chicago: University of Chicago Press.

Levin, Beth, and M. Rappaport-Hovav. 1994. *Unaccusativity: At the Syntax – Lexical Semantics Interface*. Cambridge, Mass.: The MIT Press.

Lipski, John M. 1977. "Preposed Subjects in Questions: Some Considerations" *Hispania* 60, 61–67.

1994. *Latin American Spanish*. London and New York: Longman.

Lloyd, Paul M. 1987. *From Latin to Spanish*, vol. I: *Historical Phonology and Morphology of the Spanish Language*. Philadelphia: American Philosophical Society (Memoirs of the American Philosophical Society; 173).

Lois, Ximena. 1982. "Sur L'Accusatif Prépositionnel." Master's essay. Université de Paris VIII.

1986. "Les groups nominaux sans déterminant en espagnol" *Recherches linguistiques de Vincennes*.

Longobardi, Giuseppe. 1994. "Reference and Proper Names" *Linguistic Inquiry* 25, 609–665.

Luján, Marta. 1976. "The Analysis of Reflexive Inchoatives" in *Current Studies in Romance Linguistics*, ed. Marta Luján and Fritz Hensey. Washington, D.C.: Georgetown University Press, 377–387.

1987. "Clitic-doubling in Andean Spanish and the Theory of Case Absorption" in *Language and Language Use: Studies in Spanish*, ed. T. Morgan, J. Lee and B. Vanpatten. Washington: University Press of America, 109–121.

Mallén, Enrique. 1989. "The Internal Structure of Determiner Phrases." Unpublished Ph.D. dissertation. Cornell University, Ithaca, NY.

1992. "Subject Topicalization and Inflection in Spanish" *Theoretical Linguistics* 18, 179–208.

Masullo, Pascual José. 1992. "Incorporation and Case Theory in Spanish: A Crosslinguistic Perspective." Unpublished Ph.D. dissertation. University of Washington, Seattle, Wash.

Mazzola, Michael (ed.). 1994. *Issues and Theory in Romance Linguistics: Selected Papers from the Linguistic Symposium on Romance Languages XXIII*. Washington, D.C.: Georgetown University Press.

Montalbetti, Mario. 1986. "How Pro is it?" in *Studies in Romance Linguistics*, ed. Osvaldo Jaeggli and Carmen Silva-Corvalán. Dordrecht: Foris, 137–152.

Moore, John. 1991. "Reduced Constructions in Spanish." Unpublished doctoral dissertation. The University of California, Santa Cruz.

Olarrea, Antxon. 1996. "Pre- and Postverbal Subject Positions in Spanish: A Minimalist Account." Unpublished Ph.D. dissertation. University of Washington, Seattle, Wash.

Ordóñez, Francisco. 1997. "Word Order and Clause Structure in Spanish and Other Romance Languages." Unpublished Ph.D. dissertation. New York: The City University of New York.

Otero, Carlos P. 1971. *Evolución y revolución en romance*, 2 vols. Barcelona: Seis Barral.

1975. "The Development of the Clitics in Hispano-Romance" in *Diachronic Studies in Romance Linguistics*, ed. Mario Saltarelli and Dieter Wanner. The Hague: Mouton, 153–175.

Palmer, L. R. 1954. *The Latin Language*. London: Faber and Faber Limited.

Parodi, Claudia. 1994. "On Case and Agreement in Spanish and English DPs" in Mazzola (1994), 403–416.

Perlmutter, David. 1971. *Deep and Surface Structure Constraints in Syntax*. New York: Holt, Rinehart and Winston.

1978. "Impersonal Passives and the Unaccusative Hypothesis" *Proceedings of the Fourth Annual Meeting of the Berkeley Linguistics Society*, ed. Jen J. Jaeger, Anthony C. Woodbury, Farrell Ackerman *et al.* Berkeley: Berkeley Linguistic Society, 157–189.

Plann, Susan. 1980. *Relative Clauses in Spanish Without Overt Antecedents and Related Constructions*. Berkeley: University of California Press.

1982. "Indirect Questions in Spanish" *Linguistic Inquiry* 13, 297–312.

Pollock, Jean-Yves. 1989. "Verb Movement, Universal Grammar and the Structure of IP" *Linguistic Inquiry* 20, 365–424.

Quicoli, Carlos. 1976. "Conditions on Clitic Movement in Portuguese" *Linguistic Analysis* 2, 199–223.

Raposo, Eduardo. 1984. "The Null Object in Portuguese." Paper presented at the 14th Linguistic Symposium on Romance Languages (University of Southern California, Los Angeles).

Reichenbach, Hans. 1947. *Elements of Symbolic Logic*. New York: Macmillan.

Reinhart, Tanya. 1982. "Pragmatics and Linguistics: An Analysis of Sentence Topics" distributed by the Indiana University Linguistics Club, Bloomington.

Rigau, Gemma. 1992. "Propiedades de FLEX en las construcciones temporales de infinitivo: la legitimación del sujeto." Paper presented at the Second Colloquium on Generative Grammar (Vitoria, Basque Country).

Stowell, Tim. 1981. "Origins of Phrase Structure." Unpublished Ph.D. dissertation. Cambridge, Mass: MIT.

Strozer, Judith. 1976. "Clitics in Spanish." Unpublished Ph.D. dissertation. Los Angeles: The University of California.

Suñer, Margarita. 1982. *Syntax and Semantics of Presentational Sentence-Types.* Washington, D.C.: Georgetown University Press.

1984. "Free Relatives and the Matching Parameter" *Linguistic Review*, 363–387.

1986. "Lexical Subjects of Infinitives in Caribbean Spanish" *Studies in Romance Linguistics*, ed. Osvaldo Jaeggli and Carmen Silva-Corvalán. Dordrecht: Foris, 189–203.

1987. "*Haber* + Past Participle" *Linguistic Inquiry* 18, 683–690.

1988. "The Role of Agreement in Clitic-doubled Constructions" *Natural Language and Linguistic Theory* 6, 391–434.

1991. "Indirect Questions and the Structure of CP: Some Consequences" in *Current Studies in Spanish Linguistics*, ed. Héctor Campos and Fernando Martínez-Gil. Washington, D.C.: Georgetown University Press, 283–312.

1994. "V-Movement and the Licensing of Argumental Wh-Phrases in Spanish" *Natural Language and Linguistic Theory* 12, 335–372.

1995. "Negative Elements, Island Effects and Resumptive *no*" *Linguistic Review* 12, 233–273.

Toribio, Almeida Jacqueline. 1993. "Parametric Variation in the Licensing of Nominals." Unpublished Ph.D. dissertation. Ithaca, NY: Cornell University.

1996. "Dialectal Variation in the Licensing of Null Referential and Expletive Subjects" in *Aspects of Romance Linguistics: Selected Papers from the Linguistic Symposium on Romance Languages XXIV*, ed. Claudia Parodi, Carlos Quicoli, Mario Saltarelli and María Luisa Zubizarreta. Washington, D.C.: Georgetown University Press, 409–432.

Torrego, Esther. 1984. "On Inversion in Spanish and Some of its Effects" *Linguistic Inquiry* 15, 103–129.

1989. "Unergative–Unaccusative Alternations in Spanish" *MIT Working Papers in Linguistics* 10, 253–272.

1998. *The Dependencies of Objects.* Cambridge, Mass.: The MIT Press (Linguistic Inquiry Monograph: 34).

Tortora, Christina M. 1997. "The Syntax and Semantics of the Weak Locative." Unpublished Ph.D. dissertation. University of Delaware.

Tovena, L. M. 1996. "An Expletive Negation Which Is Not So Redundant" in Zagona (1996), 263–274.

Treviño, Esthela. 1990. "Non-Canonical Subjects in Spanish: Evidence from Causatives and Psych Verbs." Unpublished MS. University of Ottawa.

Uriagereka, Juan. 1992. "Extraction Parameters: A Case Study on Underspecification." Unpublished MS. University of Maryland.

1995. "A Focus Position in Western Romance" in *Discourse Configurational Languages*, ed. Katalin E. Kiss. Oxford: Oxford University Press, 153–175.

Uribe-Etxebarría, Miriam. 1994. "Interface Licensing Conditions on Negative Polarity Items: A Theory of Polarity and Tense Interactions." Unpublished Ph.D. dissertation. Storrs: The University of Connecticut.

Vendler, Zeno. 1967. "Verbs and Times" in *Linguistics and Philosophy*. Ithaca, N.Y.: Cornell University Press, 97–121.

Vincent, Nigel. 1982. "The Development of the Auxiliaries HABERE and ESSE in Romance" in *Studies in the Romance Verb*, ed. Nigel Vincent and Martin Harris. London and Canberra: Croom Helm, 71–96.

Wanner, Dieter. 1987. *The Development of Romance Clitic Pronouns: From Latin to Old Romance*. Berlin: Mouton de Gruyter.

Williams, Edwin. 1982. "The NP Cycle" *Linguistic Inquiry* 13, 277–295.

Wright, Roger (ed.). 1991. *Latin and the Romance Languages in the Early Middle Ages*. London and New York: Routledge.

Zagona, Karen. 1988. *Verb Phrase Syntax: A Parametric Study of English and Spanish*. Dordrecht: Kluwer Academic Publishers.

(ed.). 1996. *Grammatical Theory and Romance Languages*. Amsterdam/Philadelphia: John Benjamins Publishing Company.

Zanuttini, Rafaella. 1990. "Two Types of Negative Markers" in *Proceedings of NELS 20*, ed. Juli Carter, Rose-Marie D'Echaine, Bill Philip and Tom Sherer. Amherst: Graduate Linguistic Student Association of the University of Massachusetts, II, 517–530.

Zubizarreta, María Luisa. 1987. *Levels of Representation in the Lexicon and in the Syntax*. Dordrecht: Foris Publications.

1994. "El orden de palabras en español y el caso nominativo" in Demonte (1994), 21–49.

1998. *Prosody, Focus, and Word Order*. Cambridge, Mass.: The MIT Press (Linguistic Inquiry Monograph; 33).

Zwicky, Arnold. 1977. "On Clitics". Bloomington: Indiana University Linguistics Club.

Index

Emonds, Joseph. 1975. "A Transformational Analysis of French Clitics Without Positive Output Constraints" *Linguistic Analysis* 1, 1–32.

1976. *A Transformational Approach to English Syntax: Root, Structure-Preserving, and Local Transformations.* New York: Academic Press.

1978. "The Verbal Complex V'–V in French" *Linguistic Inquiry* 9, 151–175.

Fontana, Josep M. 1993. "Phrase Structure and the Syntax of Clitics in the History of Spanish." Unpublished Ph.D. dissertation. The University of Pennsylvania.

Franco, Jon. 1993. "On Object Agreement in Spanish." Unpublished Ph.D. dissertation. Los Angeles: The University of Southern California.

Galmés de Fuentes, Álvaro. 1996. "Mozarabe" in Alvar (1996), 97–110.

García Mayo, Pilar, and Paula Kempchinsky. 1994. "Finiteness in Romance vs. English Parasitic Gap Constructions" in Mazzola (1994), 303–316.

Giusti, Giuliana. 1991. "The Categorial Status of Quantified Nominals" *Linguistische Berichte* 136, 438–454.

Goodall, Grant. 1991. "Spec of IP and Spec of CP in Spanish Wh-questions." Paper read at the 21st Linguistic Symposium on Romance Languages (University of California, Santa Barbara, February).

1999. "On Preverbal Subjects in Spanish." Paper presented at the 29th Linguistic Symposium on Romance Languages (Michigan State University).

Green, John. 1992. "Spanish" in Bright (1992), IV, 58–64.

Grimes, Ruth (ed.). 1988. *Ethnologue: Languages of the World.* Dallas, Tex.: Summer Institute of Linguistics.

Grimshaw, Jane. 1991. "Extended Projection." Unpublished MS. Brandeis University, Waltham, Mass.

Haegeman, Liliane, and Raffaella Zanuttini. 1991. "Negative Heads and the NEG Criterion" *Linguistic Review* 8, 233–251.

Hale, Kenneth, and Samuel J. Keyser (eds.). 1993. *The View from Building 20,* Cambridge, Mass.: The MIT Press.

Hanssen, Federico. 1945. *Gramática histórica de la lengua castellana.* Buenos Aires: Librería y Editorial "El Ateneo."

Hatcher, Anna Granville. 1956. "Theme and Underlying Question. Two Studies of Spanish Word Order" *Word* 12, Supplement 3.

Hernanz, Maria Luisa, and José María Brucart. 1987. *La sintaxis.* Barcelona: Editorial Crítica.

Higginbotham, James. 1985. "On Semantics" *Linguistic Inquiry* 16, 547–593.

Howard, Harry. 1993. "ΣP, Affective Inversion, and Topicalization in English and Spanish." Unpublished Ph.D. dissertation. Cornell University, Ithaca, NY.

Hurtado, Alfredo. 1989a. "El control mediante clíticos" *Revista Argentina de Lingüística* 5, 13–56.

1989b. "Las cadenas clíticas" *Revista Argentina de Lingüística* 5, 77–133.

Iatridou, Sabine. 2000. "The Grammatical Ingredients of Counterfactuality" *Linguistic Inquiry* 31, 231–270.

Jackendoff, Ray. 1972. *Semantic Interpretation in Generative Grammar.* Cambridge, Mass.: The MIT Press.

1977. *X-Bar Syntax: A Study of Phrase Structure.* Cambridge, Mass.: The MIT Press.

Jaeggli, Osvaldo. 1982. *Topics in Romance Syntax.* Dordrecht: Foris Publications.

Kaisse, Ellen. 1983. "The Syntax of Auxiliary Reduction in English" *Language* 59, 93–102.

Kany, Charles. 1951. *American Spanish Syntax*. Chicago: University of Chicago Press.

Kayne, Richard. 1975. *French Syntax: The Transformational Cycle*. Cambridge, Mass.: The MIT Press.

1981. "Unambiguous Paths" in *Levels of Syntactic Representation*, ed. Robert May and Jan Koster. Dordrecht: Foris Publications, 143–183.

1989. "Null Subjects and Clitic Climbing" in *The Null Subject Parameter*, ed. Osvaldo Jaeggli and Kenneth Safir. Dordrecht: Klewer Academic Publishers, 239–261.

1994. *The Antisymmetry of Syntax*. Cambridge, Mass.: The MIT Press.

Koopman, Hilda, and Dominique Sportiche. 1991. "The Position of Subjects" *Lingua* 85, 211–258.

Kurian, George (ed.). 1992. *Encyclopedia of the Third World*. New York: Facts on File.

Laka, Itziar. 1990. "Negation in Syntax: On the Nature of Functional Categories and Projections." Unpublished Ph.D. dissertation. Cambridge, Mass.: MIT.

Lapesa, Rafael. 1968. "Sobre los orígenes y evolución del leísmo, laísmo y loísmo" in *Festschrift Walther von Wartburg*, 2 vols. Tübingen: Max Niemeyer, 1, 523–551.

1981. *Historia de la lengua española*. Madrid: Editorial Gredos. (8th edn.)

Larson, Richard K. 1985. "Bare-NP Adverbs" *Linguistic Inquiry* 16, 595–621.

1988. "On the Double Object Construction". *Linguistic Inquiry* 19, 335–391.

Lema, José. 1991. "Licensing Conditions on Head Movement." Unpublished Ph.D. dissertation. University of Ottawa.

Levin, Beth. 1993. *English Verb Classes and Alternations: A Preliminary Investigation*. Chicago: University of Chicago Press.

Levin, Beth, and M. Rappaport-Hovav. 1994. *Unaccusativity: At the Syntax – Lexical Semantics Interface*. Cambridge, Mass.: The MIT Press.

Lipski, John M. 1977. "Preposed Subjects in Questions: Some Considerations" *Hispania* 60, 61–67.

1994. *Latin American Spanish*. London and New York: Longman.

Lloyd, Paul M. 1987. *From Latin to Spanish*, vol. I: *Historical Phonology and Morphology of the Spanish Language*. Philadelphia: American Philosophical Society (Memoirs of the American Philosophical Society; 173).

Lois, Ximena. 1982. "Sur L'Accusatif Prépositionnel." Master's essay. Université de Paris VIII.

1986. "Les groups nominaux sans déterminant en espagnol" *Recherches linguistiques de Vincennes*.

Longobardi, Giuseppe. 1994. "Reference and Proper Names" *Linguistic Inquiry* 25, 609–665.

Luján, Marta. 1976. "The Analysis of Reflexive Inchoatives" in *Current Studies in Romance Linguistics*, ed. Marta Luján and Fritz Hensey. Washington, D.C.: Georgetown University Press, 377–387.

1987. "Clitic-doubling in Andean Spanish and the Theory of Case Absorption" in *Language and Language Use: Studies in Spanish*, ed. T. Morgan, J. Lee and B. Vanpatten. Washington: University Press of America, 109–121.

Mallén, Enrique. 1989. "The Internal Structure of Determiner Phrases." Unpublished Ph.D. dissertation. Cornell University, Ithaca, NY.

1992. "Subject Topicalization and Inflection in Spanish" *Theoretical Linguistics* 18, 179–208.

Masullo, Pascual José. 1992. "Incorporation and Case Theory in Spanish: A Crosslinguistic Perspective." Unpublished Ph.D. dissertation. University of Washington, Seattle, Wash.

Mazzola, Michael (ed.). 1994. *Issues and Theory in Romance Linguistics: Selected Papers from the Linguistic Symposium on Romance Languages XXIII.* Washington, D.C.: Georgetown University Press.

Montalbetti, Mario. 1986. "How Pro is it?" in *Studies in Romance Linguistics*, ed. Osvaldo Jaeggli and Carmen Silva-Corvalán. Dordrecht: Foris, 137–152.

Moore, John. 1991. "Reduced Constructions in Spanish." Unpublished doctoral dissertation. The University of California, Santa Cruz.

Olarrea, Antxon. 1996. "Pre- and Postverbal Subject Positions in Spanish: A Minimalist Account." Unpublished Ph.D. dissertation. University of Washington, Seattle, Wash.

Ordóñez, Francisco. 1997. "Word Order and Clause Structure in Spanish and Other Romance Languages." Unpublished Ph.D. dissertation. New York: The City University of New York.

Otero, Carlos P. 1971. *Evolución y revolución en romance*, 2 vols. Barcelona: Seis Barral.

1975. "The Development of the Clitics in Hispano-Romance" in *Diachronic Studies in Romance Linguistics*, ed. Mario Saltarelli and Dieter Wanner. The Hague: Mouton, 153–175.

Palmer, L. R. 1954. *The Latin Language.* London: Faber and Faber Limited.

Parodi, Claudia. 1994. "On Case and Agreement in Spanish and English DPs" in Mazzola (1994), 403–416.

Perlmutter, David. 1971. *Deep and Surface Structure Constraints in Syntax.* New York: Holt, Rinehart and Winston.

1978. "Impersonal Passives and the Unaccusative Hypothesis" *Proceedings of the Fourth Annual Meeting of the Berkeley Linguistics Society*, ed. Jen J. Jaeger, Anthony C. Woodbury, Farrell Ackerman et al. Berkeley: Berkeley Linguistic Society, 157–189.

Plann, Susan. 1980. *Relative Clauses in Spanish Without Overt Antecedents and Related Constructions.* Berkeley: University of California Press.

1982. "Indirect Questions in Spanish" *Linguistic Inquiry* 13, 297–312.

Pollock, Jean-Yves. 1989. "Verb Movement, Universal Grammar and the Structure of IP" *Linguistic Inquiry* 20, 365–424.

Quicoli, Carlos. 1976. "Conditions on Clitic Movement in Portuguese" *Linguistic Analysis* 2, 199–223.

Raposo, Eduardo. 1984. "The Null Object in Portuguese." Paper presented at the 14th Linguistic Symposium on Romance Languages (University of Southern California, Los Angeles).

Reichenbach, Hans. 1947. *Elements of Symbolic Logic.* New York: Macmillan.

Reinhart, Tanya. 1982. "Pragmatics and Linguistics: An Analysis of Sentence Topics" distributed by the Indiana University Linguistics Club, Bloomington.

Rigau, Gemma. 1992. "Propiedades de FLEX en las construcciones temporales de infinitivo: la legitimación del sujeto." Paper presented at the Second Colloquium on Generative Grammar (Vitoria, Basque Country).

Ritter, Elizabeth. 1991. "Two Functional Categories of Noun Phrases: Evidence from Modern Hebrew" in *Perspectives on Phrase Structure: Heads and Licensing*, ed. Susan D. Rothstein. New York: Academic Press (Syntax and Semantics 25), 37–62.

Rivas, Alberto. 1977. "A Theory of Clitics." Unpublished Ph.D. dissertation. Cambridge, Mass.: MIT.

Rivero, María-Luisa. 1978. "Topicalization and WH-Movement in Spanish" *Linguistic Inquiry* 9, 513–517.

  1980. "On Left-dislocation and Topicalization in Spanish" *Linguistic Inquiry* 11, 363–393.

  1986. "Parameters in the Typology of Clitics in Romance and Old Spanish" *Language* 64, 774–807.

  1990. "Especificidad y existencia" in *Indicativo y subjuntivo*, ed. Ignacio Bosque. Madrid: Taurus Universitaria, 261–279.

  1991. "Clitic and NP Climbing in Old Spanish" in *Current Studies in Spanish Linguistics*, ed. Héctor Campos and Fernando Martínez-Gil. Washington, D.C.: Georgetown University Press, 241–284.

  1993. "Long Head Movement vs. V2 and Null Subjects in Old Romance" *Lingua* 89, 217–245.

  1994. "Clause Structure and V-movement in the Languages of the Balkans" *Natural Language and Linguistic Theory* 12, 63–120.

Rizzi, Luigi. 1982. *Issues in Italian Syntax*. Dordrecht: Foris Publications.

  1996. "Residual Verb Second and the Wh-Criterion" in *Parameters and Functional Heads: Essays in Comparative Syntax*, ed. Adriana Belletti and Luigi Rizzi. New York and Oxford: Oxford University Press, 63–90.

Rizzi, Luigi, and Ian Roberts. 1989. "Complex Inversion in French" *Probus* 1, 1–30.

Roberts, Ian. 1990. "L'accord et les auxiliaires dans l'histoire de l'anglais." Talk given at the Séminaire de Recherche, University of Geneva (cited in Belletti (1990)).

Rooryck, Johan. 1992. "Romance Enclitic Ordering and Universal Grammar" *Linguistic Review* 9, 219–250.

Rothstein, Susan. 1983. "The Syntactic Forms of Predication." Unpublished Ph.D. dissertation. Cambridge, Mass: MIT. (Circulated by Indiana University Linguistics Club, Bloomington, 1985.)

Saltarelli, Mario. 1994. "Voice in Latin and Romance: On the Representation of Lexical Subjects" in *Issues and Theory in Romance Linguistics: Selected Papers from the Linguistic Symposium on Romance Languages XXIII*, ed. Michael L. Mazzola. Washington, D.C.: Georgetown University Press, 445–478.

Sánchez, Liliana, and José Camacho. 1995. "Equative *ser* in Spanish." Unpublished MS. Los Angeles: The University of Southern California.

Sánchez-Albornoz, Nicolás. 1984. "The Population of Colonial Spanish America" in Bethell (1984) 3–36.

Sportiche, Dominique. 1988. "A Theory of Floating Quantifiers and Its Corollaries for Constituent Structure" *Linguistic Inquiry* 19, 425–449.

Stalnaker, Robert C. 1978. "Assertion" in *Pragmatics*, ed. Peter Cole. New York: Academic Press (Syntax and Semantics; 9), 315–332.